THESAURUS

of Information Science, Technology, and Librarianship

THIRD EDITION

Edited by
**Alice Redmond-Neal and
Marjorie M. K. Hlava**

ASIST Monograph Series

Published on behalf of the
American Society for Information Science and Technology
by Information Today, Inc.

Information Today, Inc.

Medford, New Jersey

First Printing, August 2005

ASIST Thesaurus of Information Science, Technology, and Librarianship, Third Edition

Copyright © 2005 by American Society for Information Science and Technology

Library of Congress Cataloging-in-Publication Data

ASIS&T thesaurus of information science, technology, and librarianship.--
3rd ed. / edited by Alice Redmond-Neal and Marjorie M.K. Hlava.
    p. cm. -- (ASIST monograph series)
  Rev. ed. of: ASIS thesaurus of information science and librarianship /
Jessica L. Milstead, editor. 2nd ed. 1998.
   ISBN 1-57387-243-1
  1. Subject headings--Information science. 2. Subject headings--Information technology. 3. Subject headings--Library science. I. Title: Thesaurus of information science, technology, and librarianship. II. Redmond-Neal, Alice. III. Hlava, Marjorie M. K. IV. Milstead, Jessica L. ASIS thesaurus of information science and librarianship. V. American Society for Information Science and Technology. VI. Series.
  Z695.1.I56M54 2005
  025.4'902--dc22

                                                       2005017842

Printed and bound in the United States of America

President and CEO: Thomas H. Hogan, Sr.
Editor-in-Chief and Publisher: John B. Bryans
Managing Editor: Amy M. Holmes
VP Graphics and Production: M. Heide Dengler
Cover Designer: Shelley Szajner

Table of Contents

About the ASIS&T Thesaurus

As any field of inquiry develops, establishing a recognized and consistent vocabulary is a landmark along the way to recognition, understanding and acceptance.

The field of information science and technology is still relatively young but growing rapidly and pushing tentative borders in every direction. Standardizing, defining, and clarifying the language of the field is critical to meaningful communication. Delineating the scope of coverage for information science and technology is an ongoing challenge as every year brings new discoveries, new concepts, and new perspectives.

Since information organization and retrieval are fundamental components of information science and technology, and a thesaurus is the starting point for those activities, it is only appropriate that ASIS&T should take the lead in establishing a thesaurus describing the field.

History of the ASIS&T Thesaurus

In 1994, Jessica Milstead and Harold Borko chronicled in "Shoes for the Cobbler's Children: The ASIS Thesaurus" (*BASIS* Oct-Nov 1994) the early history of standardizing terminology for the field of information science and technology. They noted the long time elapsed since the 1968 publication of Claire Schultz's *Thesaurus of Information Science* and the opinion of ASIS (as it was known at the time) that there was a clear need for an updated thesaurus to reflect the burgeoning field and facilitate information retrieval. Milstead edited the first version of the ASIS Thesaurus, published in 1994, and, in recognition of the rapid changes in the field, updated the Thesaurus in 1996. However, the Thesaurus was not implemented for indexing, its primary purpose. The four publications of the Society—*The Journal of the American Society for Information Science and Technology* (*JASIST*), *Bulletin of the American Society for Information Science and Technology* (*BASIS*), *Annual Review of Information Science and Technology* (*ARIST*), and *Conference Proceedings of the American Society for Information Science and Technology*—were not indexed using a consistent descriptive vocabulary for the domain. *Information Science Abstracts* (now known as *Information Science & Technology Abstracts*), under the editorial direction of Donald Hawkins, started using the ASIS Thesaurus in 2002, adding many candidate terms.

In 2004, we undertook the challenge of revising Milstead's work, to update it to reflect the current state of the field and to implement it for indexing the Society's publications for the ASIS&T Digital Library. The expanded Thesaurus would also serve as a descriptive outline of information science and technology, available for use by those active in the field as well as others. A comprehensive review of the publications revealed a wealth of new terms representing developments in the field. The Thesaurus expanded from 1,312 terms to 1,970 (as of January 2005) with nine hierarchical levels, and was further enhanced by numerous links between terms and notes on usage of individual terms. A number of term placements and hierarchical relationships were revised.

We used the resulting work to index the materials for the ASIS&T Digital Library. The documents covered included 19 years of *JASIST* from 1986 through 2004, the *Bulletin* from October 1995 through December 2004, *ARIST* from 2001 through 2004, and the *Proceedings* from 2001 through 2004. These legacy files provided a firm basis in the usage of the terminology and concepts represented in this revision of the Thesaurus.

Numerous prominent leaders in the field reviewed the draft Thesaurus. They submitted their observations, questions, and suggestions for the work in progress, and were instrumental in fine-tuning the product (see *Acknowledgements*).

What is a thesaurus?

A thesaurus is a controlled vocabulary used for descriptive indexing. The terms of the vocabulary are divided into broad topical areas and then arranged in a hierarchical structure that reflects their relative generality or specificity. Terms having a hierarchical relationship are known as *Broader Terms* and *Narrower Terms*. Terms that are conceptually associated but are neither more general nor more specific examples of a topic are considered *Related Terms*. Words that are not part of the thesaurus but may be considered by the user community to be synonyms, quasi-synonyms, or functional equivalents to thesaurus terms are considered as *Nonpreferred Terms*. These words have an equivalence relationship to specified thesaurus terms. Each *Nonpreferred Term* directs a user to *Use* the appropriate equivalent thesaurus term. The thesaurus term indicates that it is *Used for* the *Nonpreferred Term*.

Purpose of a thesaurus

The primary purpose of a thesaurus is for descriptive indexing to assist information management. Terms of the thesaurus are used as tags or labels to represent the information and then facilitate storage and retrieval of that information. For ASIS&T, the information consists mainly of articles from its four publications. Tagging an article with a thesaurus term goes beyond spotting a particular word in a free-text search. Simple word match is easily undermined by homographs, i.e., words having the same spelling but different meanings, such as *organization* (process or state of being organized) and *organization* (group of people working together). Word-match is also circumvented by alternative spellings for the same concept, e.g. *organization* and *organisation*. Application of thesaurus descriptors involves interpretation and analysis of the text to match the author's idea to the appropriate thesaurus term(s). The result is consistent retrieval of materials on the basis of concepts rather than specific words or character strings.

Scope of the ASIS&T Thesaurus

The ASIS&T Thesaurus covers the following broad areas pertaining to information science and technology, with their associated thesaurus headings:

- people and organizations
  - *(organizations)*
  - *(persons and informal groups)*
  - *(product and service providers)*
- actions, events, and processes
  - *(activities and operations)*
  - *(natural processes and events)*
- physical objects
  - *(buildings and facilities)*
  - *(communications networks)*
  - *(hardware, software, and equipment)*
  - *(physical media)*
- theoretical concepts and influences on information
  - *(attributes)*
  - *(fields and disciplines)*
  - *(language)*
  - *(sociocultural aspects)*
- information, information delivery formats and channels
  - *(communications media)*
  - *(document types)*
  - *(knowledge and information)*
- methods of study
  - *(research and analytic methods)*
- geographic information
  - *(countries and regions)*

Structure of the ASIS&T Thesaurus

Each of the 18 headings under the seven areas outlined above represents a Top Term or broad grouping of concepts and is presented as a facet in the ASIS&T Thesaurus. The titles are node labels (also known as "facet indicators"), entirely enclosed within parentheses, e.g. *(attributes)*, and not available for indexing. Under each of these node labels, additional concepts are presented in a hierarchical structure. Hierarchies branch out further, proceeding directly to Narrower Terms, or term groups may be subdivided by additional facets, followed by Narrower Terms.

For example, the broad topic "Knowledge and information" is marked by the node label *(knowledge and information)* and branches out to the more specific topics *information content*, *information representations*, and *knowledge organization systems*. Each of these terms is a valid thesaurus term available for use in indexing. On the other hand, the broad area of "Attributes," marked by the node label *(attributes)* expands to further facets *(attributes of information)*, *(attributes of systems)*, *(general attributes)*, and *(human attributes)*. These node labels are not available as indexing terms, but they open to further terms, such as *aboutness*, *bandwidth*, *obsolescence*, and *user attributes*, which are valid terms for indexing.

A term may be used both as a node label for a group of concepts, and then repeated as a valid term for indexing. An example is *(language)*, followed by the Narrower Terms *language*, *language types*, and *linguistic elements*. In this case, *language types* and *linguistic elements* are logical aspects of the Broader Term *(language)*. Since the concept "language" is critical for the field but the node label *(language)* is not available for indexing, the term is repeated, minus the parentheses, as a valid indexing term.

This faceted style of thesaurus construction maintains the format designed by Milstead for the first two editions of the ASIS&T Thesaurus.

Thesaurus construction standards and tools

The ASIS&T Thesaurus, Third Edition, was constructed following existing standards for thesaurus construction, ANSI/NISO Z39.19 1993, with an eye toward the 2005 revision of that standard (in draft form). ISO 2788 standards were followed in two instances: 1) the use of Preferred/Nonpreferred nomenclature, which we find clearer than Use/Used For, and 2) the use of multiple Broader Terms.

The product was developed as a thesaurus, not a taxonomy, and as such focuses on topical concepts and subjects, excluding proper names for the most part. Following standards, terms are presented in lower case except where conventions on proper names dictate otherwise.

Data Harmony's MAIstro package Version 3.2, consisting of Thesaurus Master and M.A.I., was used for the development of the ASIS&T Thesaurus, for ongoing thesaurus management, and for application of thesaurus descriptors to index ASIS&T documents.

Guide to Using the ASIS&T Thesaurus

How to use the ASIS&T Thesaurus

The most common usages of the ASIS&T Thesaurus are anticipated to be for indexing the literature of the field and for developing familiarity with the coverage of the domain. Effective use of the Thesaurus starts with selecting a topic to browse or search. A glance at the main topic groupings indicates the scope of the thesaurus (see page vii).

Indexing of the ASIS&T publications follows accepted standard indexing practices:
- ✓ Focus on the key topics of the article. Minor references, assumptions, implications, and background topics are not generally indexed.
- ✓ Index to the degree of specificity reflected in the article. Certain very broad terms, e.g. *information science*, are reserved for the most general articles.

Indexing terms may be combined post-coordinately to represent a complex concept. For example, the terms *transborder data flow, data security, Mexico, Canada,* and *United States* can be combined to reflect the concept of maintaining security of data crossing between the three countries. Similarly, the concept of user-centered design may be captured by a combination of *interfaces, systems design,* and *end users*. A limited number of concepts have pre-coordinated terms, e.g. *information science history*, due to their frequent occurrence in the literature.

How the Thesaurus is displayed

The ASIS&T Thesaurus is presented in three parts:

1. Alphabetical listing of term records

    The first section of the Thesaurus is an alphabetical listing of all term records, for both main or "preferred" terms and cross-reference terms. Terms starting with numerals (e.g., *3-D representation*) are sorted at the beginning, followed by all other terms, regardless of case. Terms enclosed within parentheses (node labels in the ASIS&T Thesaurus) are sorted alphabetically without regard to the parentheses.

    Entries for preferred terms are in **bold type**; the cross-references are in regular type. Entries for Nonpreferred terms are in *Italic type*. Scope notes (SN) are in *Italic type* and explain a term's coverage, specialized usage, or rules for assigning the term.

    The relationships between terms in a term record can be either hierarchical or associative.

Hierarchical relationships

TT	Top term (broadest or most general descriptor)
BT	Broader term (more general than the displayed term)
NT	Narrower term (subordinate to the displayed term)

Associative relationships

RT	Related term (conceptually associated but not linked hierarchically)
USE	Use term, which links a Nonpreferred or "Used for" term to the Preferred thesaurus term
UF	Used For term, which links a Preferred thesaurus term, i.e., the Use term, with a Nonpreferred term
NP	Nonpreferred term, a synonym that is not part of the thesaurus but links back to a Preferred thesaurus term

A term record can also include notes on the term's usage.

SN	Scope note

Here is a typical term record for a Preferred term:

locators

SN	*Devices, which indicate the position of information items within files.*
UF	page references
	reference locators
BT	knowledge organization systems
NT	URL
RT	URI
	call numbers

The term record for a Nonpreferred term looks like this:

NP	*page references*
USE	locators

2. Hierarchical display of terms

This display presents all the terms in their hierarchical structure under the top terms (TT) of the hierarchy. Only Preferred terms and node labels appear in the hierarchical display.

Here is a sample of the hierarchical display of terms:

(physical media)
. artifacts
. electronic ink
. electronic paper
. magnetic media
. . magnetic disks
. . . floppy disks
. . . hard disks
. . . magneto-optical disks
. . magnetic tapes
. . . audiotapes
. . . . audiocassettes
. . . . digital audio
. . smart cards

Node labels serve to subgroup terms, although the labels themselves are not valid terms available for indexing. In the ASIS&T Thesaurus, node labels are entirely enclosed by parentheses, e.g. *(attributes)* and *(document types)*.

3. Permuted display of terms

Often called a KWIC list (KeyWord In Context), the permuted display presents both Preferred and cross-reference terms according to an alphabetic listing based on each of the component words in terms. The term *information science* is listed as *information science* along with other terms starting with the letter *"I"*. The term is also presented in its permuted form as *science, information* along with other terms having a component word starting with *"S"* such as *staff development* and *speech, human*. The permuted list displays together all terms that share a common word, such as *analysis, cost*; *analysis, domain*; *analysis, qualitative*; and *analysis, semantic*. It also provides an additional way to access terms when you are uncertain what the first word of the term might be, but you know one of the words in the term.

A sample of a permuted display follows, with Nonpreferred terms shown in *Italic type*:

	thesauri
bilingual	*thesauri (Nonpreferred)*
graphical	thesauri
multilingual	thesauri
displays	*(thesauri) (Nonpreferred)*
	thesaurofacet
	thesaurus construction (Nonpreferred)
	thesaurus displays
automatic	*thesaurus generation (Nonpreferred)*
	thesaurus management

Electronic access to the ASIS&T Thesaurus

The Thesaurus is also available online through the ASIS&T Digital Library and on CD-ROM. The electronic versions allow searching and sorting, and provide facility to submit candidate terms for editorial review and consideration for future editions of the Thesaurus.

Acknowledgements

We wish to acknowledge the leadership of Richard Hill, Executive Director of ASIS&T, who recognized the need to update and maintain the Thesaurus for indexing Society publications. We recognize and applaud Jessica Milstead for creating and nurturing the ASIS&T Thesaurus through its first two versions.

Our sincere appreciation is passed to the review board and additional contributors: David Batty, Bert Boyce, Donald Hawkins, Gail Hodge, Don Kraft, Katherine McCain, Jessica Milstead, Candy Schwartz, Debora Shaw, and Leonard Will.

We also extend our thanks to Samantha Hastings for her support as ASIS&T President.

We thank the members of the Access Innovations, Inc. staff including Jay Ven Eman, Tao Liu, Gina Woodhouse, Scott Denning, Scott Roberts, and Alex Yamauchi for their technical support and availability for discussion of concepts.

Our appreciation also goes to Amy Holmes, managing editor at Information Today, for her meticulous attention to the myriad details in preparing this publication.

Finally, we thank in advance all the information scientists who use this thesaurus in their scholarly pursuits and their academic instruction and learning. Since a thesaurus is never complete but must grow along with the field it represents, we welcome your comments, suggestions, and contributions.

Alice Redmond-Neal
Marjorie M.K. Hlava

Alphabetic Listing of Term Records

(activities and operations)
NT communications activities
    computer operations
    educational activities
    general activities
    information operations
    library operations
    management operations
    socioeconomic activities
    technical and manufacturing
        operations

(attributes of information and data)
SN *Including properties and rights.*
BT (attributes)
NT aboutness
    accuracy
    ambiguity
    attribute inheritance
    bibliometric scatter
    citation order
    credibility
    error rates
    fallout
    file integrity
    frequency of use
    indexing depth
    indexing discrimination
    indexing exhaustivity
    indexing specificity
    information retrieval noise
    interdisciplinarity
    legibility
    overlap
    pertinence
    precision
    recall
    relevance
    similarity
    temporal currency
    uncertainty
    validity
    warrant

(attributes of systems and equipment)
BT (attributes)
NT bandwidth
    connectivity
    fault tolerance
    interoperability
    maintainability
    modularity

(attributes of systems and equipment) (cont.)
    response time
    scalability
    search time
    transmission speed

(attributes)
UF attributes
NT (attributes of information and data)
    (attributes of systems and equipment)
    (general attributes)
    (human attributes)

(buildings and facilities)
NT buildings
    computer centers
    computer laboratories

(communications media)
NT information channels
    mass media
    satellite communications

(communications networks)
NT intranets
    library networks
    nodes
    telecommunications networks

(countries and regions)
NT Africa
    Asia
    Australia
    Central America
    developing countries
    Europe
    New Zealand
    North America
    regions
    South America
RT international aspects
    national aspects
    regional aspects

(document types)
SN *Document in the broad sense, to include any*
    physical or electronic carrier of information.
NT (documents by availability, access,
        organization)
    (documents by information content, purpose)
    (documents by medium, physical form)
BT (document types)

(documents by availability, access, organization)
NT banned materials
   collections
   grey literature
   hypertext
   library materials
   non English language materials
   preprints
   public domain
   publications
   rare materials
   source materials
   technical reports

(documents by information content, purpose)
BT (document types)
NT authority files
   bibliographies
   catalogs (bibliographic)
   children's literature
   contracts
   core literature
   correspondence
   courseware
   curricula
   dissertations
   document surrogates
   ephemera
   erotic materials
   information resources
   information retrieval indexes
   inverted files
   licenses
   marginalia
   obscene materials
   patents
   personal files
   popular materials
   primary literature
   questionnaires
   records
   reviews
   spreadsheets
   standards
   stoplists
   surveys
   user aids
   young adult literature

(documents by medium, physical form)
BT (document types)
NT books
   digital objects
   graphics

(documents by medium, physical form)
(cont.)
   manuscripts
   media
   multimedia
   nonprint media
   physical objects
   vertical files

(fields and disciplines)
NT aerospace
   agriculture
   architecture
   area studies
   behavioral sciences
   cartography
   computer science
   engineering
   finance
   fine arts
   human factors
   humanities
   information science
   law
   lexicography
   librarianship
   linguistics
   mathematics
   natural sciences
   physical sciences
   semiotics
   social sciences

(general attributes)
BT (attributes)
NT bias
   compatibility
   complexity
   costs
   design
   durability
   effectiveness
   efficiency
   obsolescence
   performance
   permanence
   physical attributes
   probability
   proximity
   quality
   randomness
   redundancy
   reliability
   usability
   utility
   value added

(general processes)
BT (natural processes and events)
NT aging of materials
    change
    disasters
    growth
    stochastic processes

(hardware, software, and equipment)
NT adaptive technologies
    audiovisual equipment
    cameras
    computer architecture
    computer equipment
    computer software
    computer systems
    control systems
    display devices
    educational technology
    information technology
    instrumentation
    integrated systems
    kiosks
    lasers
    library equipment
    library supplies
    optical equipment
    photocopiers
    robots
    telecommunications equipment

(human attributes)
BT (attributes)
NT human productivity
    indexer consistency
    information needs
    skills
    user attributes

(human processes)
BT (natural processes and events)
NT human speech
    injury
    mental processes
    sensory processes

(indexing by feature indexed)
BT indexing
NT image indexing
    name indexing
    subject indexing

(indexing by item indexed)
BT indexing
NT book indexing
    database indexing

(indexing by item indexed) (cont.)
    periodical indexing

(indexing by method used)
BT indexing
NT automatic indexing
    content based indexing
    description based indexing
    machine aided indexing
    manual indexing

(information and data processes)
BT (natural processes and events)
NT data corruption
    errors
    information entropy
    information explosion
    information flow
    information life cycle

(knowledge and information)
NT information content
    information representations
    knowledge organization
      systems

(language)
NT language
    language types
    linguistic elements

(natural processes and events)
SN *Includes information functions.*
NT (general processes)
    (human processes)
    (information and data processes)

(organizations)
SN *Professional societies, forms of*
    organization, affinity groups. For
    organizations whose primary function is to
    provide a specific group of products or
    services, see "product and service
    providers."
NT armed forces
    colleges and universities
    consortia
    friends of libraries
    labor unions
    professional associations
    schools
    standards developing organizations
RT organization theory
    organizational communication
    organizational culture
    organizational environment

(persons and informal groups)
NT authors
    communities
    customers
    early adopters
    employees
    entrepreneurs
    focus groups
    human information resources
    information workers
    managers
    medical personnel
    men
    minorities and ethnic groups
    scientists
    stakeholders
    users
    volunteers
    women
    youth

(physical media)
NT artifacts
    electronic ink
    electronic paper
    magnetic media
    microforms
    optical media
    paper
    photographic films

(product and service providers)
NT archives
    bibliographic utilities
    binderies
    computer industry
    consultants
    government agencies
    information analysis centers
    information brokers
    information industry
    information utilities
    libraries
    museums
    publishers
    service bureaus
    software industry
    telecommunications industry
    vendors

(research and analytic methods)
NT analytic models
    comparison
    cost analysis
    data analysis
    data collection

(research and analytic methods) (cont.)
    data distribution
    data segmentation
    decision making
    environmental scanning
    forecasting
    needs assessment
    optimization
    practical methods
    problem solving
    qualitative analysis
    quantitative analysis
    remote sensing
    research and development
    research methods
    simulation
    task analysis
    testing

(sociocultural aspects)
NT cultural aspects
    geopolitical aspects
    legal aspects
    political aspects
    psychological aspects
    social aspects
    socioeconomic aspects

3-D representation
USE electronic visualization

80/20 rule
USE Pareto principle

A & I services
USE abstracting and indexing service bureaus

AACR
USE Anglo American Cataloguing Rules

abbreviations
BT information representations
RT acronyms

aboutness
BT (attributes of information and data)
RT information storage and retrieval systems
    subject indexing
    topics

abstract data types
SN *Data structures with associated*
    axioms defining the semantics of
    the operations.
BT data structures
NT data objects

abstracting and indexing service bureaus
UF A & I services
    indexing services
BT service bureaus
RT abstracting
    abstracts
    bibliographic databases
    current awareness services
    database indexing
    database producers
    databases
    indexing
    information infrastructure
    information retrieval indexes
    information services
    overlap
    periodical indexes
    secondary publishers
    value added

abstracting
BT summarization
NT automatic abstracting
RT abstracting and indexing service bureaus
    abstracts

abstraction
BT mental processes
RT classification
    generalization

abstracts
UF overviews
BT document surrogates
NT author abstracts
RT abstracting
    abstracting and indexing service bureaus
    annotations
    digests

academic communities
BT communities
NT faculty
    invisible colleges
    scholars
    students

academic freedom
BT intellectual freedom
RT colleges and universities

academic institutions
USE colleges and universities

academic libraries
UF college libraries

academic libraries (cont.)
    university libraries
BT libraries
NT community college libraries
RT colleges and universities
    library networks
    research libraries

academic publishing
USE scholarly publishing

access control (computer systems)
USE computer access control

access points
SN *The terms by means of which*
    access may be gained to the
    information in a file; in
    controlled vocabularies, both
    preferred and nonpreferred terms.
BT knowledge organization systems
NT entries
    entry vocabularies
    headings
    hypermedia links
RT citation order

access to resources
SN *Access to information and document*
    resources.
BT library operations
NT bibliographic access
    document access
    information access
    library access
    library reserves
    remote access
    universal access

access vocabularies
USE entry vocabularies

accessions
BT materials acquisitions

accounting
BT management operations
NT auditing
RT financial management
    funding
    inventory

accreditation
BT educational activities
RT colleges and universities
    education

accreditation (cont.)
    evaluation
    schools

accuracy
BT (attributes of information and data)
RT data corruption
    error correction
    error detection
    error rates
    errors
    temporal currency
    usability

acid free paper
USE permanent paper

acoustic data
UF acoustics
    auditory information
    sound
BT data
RT audio retrieval
    hearing
    physical attributes
    spoken communication

acoustics
USE acoustic data

acquisitions (of materials)
USE materials acquisitions

acronyms
UF initialisms
BT information representations
RT abbreviations

adaptive technologies
SN *Modifications designed to facilitate use by*
    persons with physical impairments.
BT (hardware, software, and equipment)
RT disabled persons

adjacency searching
USE proximity searching

adjectives
BT linguistic elements

administration
USE management

administrative records
BT records
RT management

administrators
USE managers

admissibility of records
SN *Admissibility in the legal process.*
BT legal aspects
RT records

adolescent literature
USE young adult literature

adolescents
BT youth
RT young adult literature

adult education
BT education
RT basic education
    continuing education
    lifelong learning
    off campus education

adult literacy
USE literacy

adult programs
USE library programs

adverbs
BT linguistic elements

advertising
BT marketing

aerospace
BT (fields and disciplines)
RT armed forces
    astronomy
    engineering
    satellite communications

affect
UF emotion
BT mental processes

affirmative action
BT socioeconomic activities
RT civil rights
    cultural diversity
    employment
    minorities and ethnic groups
    social discrimination

affixes
UF infixes
    prefixes

affixes (cont.)
   suffixes
BT morphemes
RT stemming
   syntactics
   truncation

Africa
BT (countries and regions)
NT Algeria
   Kenya
   Nigeria
   South Africa

African Americans
UF blacks
BT minorities and ethnic groups

aggregators
USE search services

aging of literatures
USE obsolescence

aging of materials
SN *Physical aging.*
BT (general processes)
RT information life cycle
   materials conservation
   materials preservation

agriculture
BT (fields and disciplines)
RT botany

air force
USE armed forces

algebra
BT mathematics

Algeria
BT Africa

algorithms
BT information content
NT decision trees
   extension matrices
   genetic algorithms
RT computer software
   information retrieval models
   self organizing maps

alkaline paper
USE permanent paper

almanacs
BT reference materials

alphabetic characters
USE alphabetic letters

alphabetic letters
UF alphabetic characters
BT alphabets

alphabetical arrangement
UF alphabetical order
   alphabetization
BT arrangement
NT letter by letter arrangement
   word by word arrangement
RT sort sequences

alphabetical order
USE alphabetical arrangement

alphabetico classed indexes
BT information retrieval indexes

alphabetization
USE alphabetical arrangement

alphabets
BT writing systems
NT alphabetic letters
RT transliteration

alternative materials
USE alternative publications

alternative publications
UF alternative materials
   fugitive materials
   underground publications
BT publications
RT grey literature
   small presses

ambiguity
BT (attributes of information and data)
RT disambiguation
   uncertainty

American Indians
USE Native Americans

analog data
BT data
RT digitization

7

analog systems
BT computer systems

analog to digital conversion
USE digitization

analogies
USE metaphors

analysis of variance
UF ANOVA
BT statistical methods

analytic models
UF modeling
   theoretical models
BT (research and analytic methods)
NT connectionist models
   database models
   hierarchical models
   information models
   information retrieval models
   mathematical models
   predictive models
   user models
RT operations research
   simulation

analytical bibliography
SN *Analysis of the processes of making books,*
   especially the material modes of production
   and the effect of processes of material
   production on the nature and state of the text
   preserved in the book. For a list of works on a
   subject or by a particular author, use
   "bibliographies."
UF descriptive bibliography
   historical bibliography
BT bibliography construction

anaphora
BT information representations
RT syntactics

Anglo American Cataloguing Rules
UF AACR
BT cataloging rules
RT bibliographic cataloging

animation
BT computer graphics

annotations
BT document surrogates
RT abstracts
   digests

annotations (cont.)
   marginalia

anonymous ftp
USE ftp

ANOVA
USE analysis of variance

ANSI
USE standards developing
   organizations

answer passage retrieval
UF question answering retrieval
BT information retrieval
RT fact retrieval systems

anthropology
BT behavioral sciences
   social sciences
NT ethnography

antiquarian materials
USE rare materials

antonymy
BT semantic relationships

approval ordering
USE approval plans

approval plans
UF approval ordering
BT materials acquisitions

architecture
SN *Pertains to structures, not to computers, for*
   which see "computer architectures."
BT (fields and disciplines)
RT buildings
   engineering
   visual arts

architectures, computer
USE computer architecture

archival cataloging
BT cataloging
RT archives

archival science
SN *Subfield of information science*
   focused on identification, acquisition, and
   preservation of significant records that
   document the history of an organization.

archival science (cont.)
UF archivistics
BT information science
RT archives
   archivists
   history
   library and archival services

archival storage
USE data storage devices

archives
UF archival storage
   historical records
BT (product and service providers)
NT national archives
RT archival cataloging
   archival science
   archivists
   genealogy
   libraries
   library and archival services
   manuscripts
   rare materials
   records management

archivistics
USE archival science

archivists
BT information professionals
RT archival science
   archives
   library and archival services

area studies
BT (fields and disciplines)
RT geography
   social sciences

Argentina
BT South America

armed forces
UF air force
   army
   military services
   navy
BT (organizations)
RT aerospace
   military intelligence

army
USE armed forces

arrangement
UF filing
BT knowledge organization systems
NT alphabetical arrangement
   systematic arrangement
   temporal arrangement
RT classification
   sort sequences
   sorting

art
USE fine arts

articles, periodical
USE periodical articles

artifacts
BT (physical media)
RT physical objects

artificial intelligence
UF computational intelligence
   machine intelligence
BT computer applications
NT computer vision
   expert systems
   knowledge engineering
   machine learning
   natural language processing
   neural networks
   semantic networks
RT cognitive space
   cybernetics
   intelligent agents
   intelligent interfaces
   knowledge bases
   knowledge engineering

artificial neural networks
USE neural networks

artificial speech production
USE speech synthesis

Asia
BT (countries and regions)
NT China
   India
   Japan
   Korea
   Philippines
   Southeast Asia

assessment, needs
USE needs assessment

assigned indexing
USE assignment indexing

assignment indexing
UF assigned indexing
BT subject indexing
RT vocabulary control

assisted searching
SN *Information searching in which the search
tool suggests refinements or expansion on the
initial query, e.g. "Do you mean Paris,
France, or Paris, Texas?"*
BT searching
RT query refinement

associations
USE professional associations

associative memory
BT computer memory
RT associative retrieval

associative processing
USE associative retrieval

associative relationships
UF RT relationships
nonhierarchical relationships
related term relationships
BT semantic relationships
RT cross references
thesauri

associative retrieval
UF associative processing
BT information retrieval models
RT associative memory
probabilistic indexing
probabilistic retrieval

astronomy
BT physical sciences
RT aerospace

atlases
BT reference materials
RT maps

attitudes
UF perceptions (attitudes)
BT psychological aspects

attribute breadcrumbs
SN *Display of alternative navigational paths to
a site.*

attribute breadcrumbs (cont.)
BT breadcrumbs

attribute inheritance
BT (attributes of information and data)
RT genus species relationships

audio cassettes
USE audiocassettes

audio communications
UF audio streaming
BT telecommunications
NT telephony
voice communications
RT digital audio files

audio interfaces
UF vocal interfaces
voice input
BT interfaces
RT speech recognition
speech synthesis

audio recorders
UF sound recorders
tape recorders
BT recording equipment

audio recordings
UF audiodisk recordings
recordings, sound
sound recordings
BT nonprint media
NT audiotapes
talking books
RT compact disks
ISRC

audio retrieval
BT information retrieval
RT acoustic data
digital audio files

audio streaming
USE data streaming

audio tapes
USE audiotapes

audio visual materials
USE nonprint media

audiocassettes
UF audio cassettes
audiotape cassettes

audiocassettes (cont.)
    cassettes, audiotape
BT audiotapes

audiodisk recordings
USE audio recordings

audiotape cassettes
USE audiocassettes

audiotapes
UF audio tapes
BT audio recordings
    magnetic tapes
NT audiocassettes
    digital audio tapes

audiovisual aids
USE nonprint media

audiovisual equipment
BT (hardware, software, and equipment)
NT recording equipment
RT cameras

audiovisual materials
USE nonprint media

auditing
BT accounting

auditory information
USE acoustic data

Australia
BT (countries and regions)

authentication
SN *Controlling access to computers or services
    by authorizing users.*
BT computer security

author abstracts
BT abstracts

author indexes
SN *Indexes to authors; for indexes prepared by
    authors of the works involved, use "author-
    prepared indexes."*
BT information retrieval indexes
RT name indexing

author productivity
SN *Measure of the number of articles in which
    an author is cited.*
BT citation analysis

authoring software
BT computer software applications
RT hypermedia authoring

authority files
BT (documents by information content, purpose)
RT bibliographic cataloging
    controlled vocabularies
    entries
    indexing
    personal names
    proper names

author-prepared indexes
BT information retrieval indexes

authors
UF writers
BT (persons and informal groups)
RT authorship

authorship
SN *Of linear texts. For preparation of
    hypermedia, use "hypermedia authoring."*
UF writing
BT human communications
NT corporate authorship
    hypermedia authoring
    joint authorship
    personal authorship
RT authors
    Lotka's law
    technical writing

automata
BT computer science
RT context free languages

automated language processing
USE natural language processing

automatic abstracting
BT abstracting
    computer applications
RT automatic extracting

automatic categorization
UF automatic tagging
    categorization, automatic
    tagging, automatic
BT automatic indexing
RT automatic classification
    categories

automatic classification
BT classification

automatic classification (cont.)
    computer applications
RT automatic categorization
    automatic indexing
    cluster analysis

automatic data processing
USE data processing

automatic extracting
BT computer applications
    extracting
NT content mining
    knowledge discovery
RT automatic abstracting

automatic indexing
BT (indexing by method used)
    computer applications
NT automatic categorization
RT automatic classification
    computational linguistics
    content based indexing
    information processing
    machine aided indexing
    natural language processing

automatic tagging
USE automatic categorization

automatic taxonomy generation
UF automatic thesaurus generation
BT computer applications
RT index language construction
    taxonomies

automatic thesaurus generation
USE automatic taxonomy generation

automatic translation
USE machine translation

automation
USE computer applications

availability of information
USE information access

awards
USE honors

back end processors
SN *Equipment which processes data in response*
    to a query presented at a host processor,
    before any data are actually transferred to
    the host.

back end processors (cont.)
BT computer processing units

back of book indexes
USE book indexes

back of book indexing
USE book indexing

backlogs
BT library operations
RT library technical services
    planning
    scheduling

backward compatibility
USE serial conversion

bandwidth
BT (attributes of systems and equipment)
RT data transmission
    performance
    response time

banned materials
UF censored materials
BT (documents by availability, access,
    organization)
RT censorship
    freedom to read
    intellectual freedom
    library materials

bar codes
BT information representations
RT data entry
    pattern recognition

basic education
SN *Fundamental education that is basic to later*
    learning.
BT education
RT adult education

batch processing
BT data processing

baud rate
USE transmission speed

Bayesian functions
UF Bayesian systems
    Bayesian theory
BT information retrieval models
    statistical methods
RT probability

Bayesian systems
USE Bayesian functions

Bayesian theory
USE Bayesian functions

BBS
USE bulletin board systems

behavior, human
USE human behavior

behavioral sciences
BT (fields and disciplines)
NT anthropology
  psychology
  sociology
RT social sciences

belles lettres
USE literature

benchmarks
BT standards
RT evaluation
  standardization

bestsellers
BT publications
RT books
  fiction

bias
BT (general attributes)

bibliographic access
BT access to resources
RT document access
  information access

bibliographic cataloging
BT cataloging
RT Anglo American Cataloguing Rules
  authority files
  bibliographic control
  call numbers
  cataloging rules
  catalogs (bibliographic)
  metadata

bibliographic citations
UF citations, bibliographic
BT bibliographic records
RT bibliographic coupling
  bibliographic software
  citation analysis

bibliographic citations (cont.)
  citation searching
  source materials

bibliographic control
BT library operations
RT bibliographic cataloging
  bibliographic databases
  bibliographic records
  bibliographies
  bibliography construction

bibliographic coupling
SN *Citation of two or more documents in a third
  one.*
UF citation coupling
  coupling, bibliographic
BT citation analysis
RT bibliographic citations
  citation indexes
  co-citation analysis

bibliographic data
USE bibliographic records

bibliographic databases
BT databases
NT OPACs
RT abstracting and indexing service
    bureaus
  bibliographic control
  bibliographies
  full text databases
  information retrieval indexes
  reference retrieval systems

bibliographic description
USE descriptive cataloging

bibliographic families
SN *Sets of related bibliographic works derived
  from a common progenitor.*
UF canonicity
BT citation analysis

bibliographic instruction
UF library instruction
  media instruction
  use instruction
BT training
RT information and reference skills
  information literacy
  user training
  users

13

bibliographic records
UF bibliographic data
    catalog records
BT document surrogates
    records
NT bibliographic citations
    bibliographic references
    MARC records
RT bibliographic control
    bibliographic software
    metadata

bibliographic references
BT bibliographic records
NT indirect collective references
RT reference retrieval systems

bibliographic retrieval systems
USE reference retrieval systems

bibliographic software
SN *Software used to organize bibliographic*
    references into a database, and to produce
    formatted citations.
UF reference management software
BT database management systems
RT bibliographic citations
    bibliographic records

bibliographic utilities
UF host computers
BT (product and service providers)
RT information utilities

bibliographies
BT (documents by information content, purpose)
NT national bibliographies
    webliographies
RT bibliographic control
    bibliographic databases
    bibliography construction
    information retrieval indexes

bibliography construction
SN *Manuscript studies focusing on the*
    description and identification of the editions,
    dates of issue, authorship, and typography of
    books or other written material. For a list of
    works on a subject or by a particular author,
    use "bibliographies."
BT library operations
NT analytical bibliography
RT bibliographic control
    bibliographies

bibliometric scatter
BT (attributes of information and data)
RT bibliometrics
    Bradford's law
    data distribution

bibliometrics
UF co-word analysis
BT informetrics
NT Bradford's law
    citation analysis
    journal productivity
    Lotka's law
    Zipf's law
RT bibliometric scatter
    co-occurrence analysis
    growth
    information use

bibliotherapy
BT library operations
RT reading

bilingual thesauri
USE multilingual thesauri

bilingualism
USE multilingualism

binderies
UF binders
    bookbinders
BT (product and service providers)
RT binding

binders
USE binderies

binding
UF book binding
    bookbinding
BT materials preservation
NT library binding
RT binderies
    books
    library technical services

biochemistry
BT biology
    chemistry

biography
BT nonfiction
RT oral history

bioinformatics
BT informatics
NT medical informatics
RT scientometrics

biology
UF life sciences
BT natural sciences
NT biochemistry
   biotechnology
   botany
   environmental sciences

biomedical information
UF medical information
BT scientific and technical information
NT genomic information
RT medical informatics
   medical libraries
   medical science
   MeSH

biotechnology
BT biology

bit-mapped images
BT images
RT digitized images

blacks
USE African Americans

blanket orders
BT materials orders

blind persons
USE visually impaired persons

Bliss Bibliographic Classification
BT classification schemes

blogs
USE weblogs

boards (library)
USE library boards

Bolivia
BT South America

book binding
USE binding

book collecting
UF collecting, book
BT library operations

book collecting (cont.)
RT rare materials

book collection
USE collection development

book collections
USE library collections

book detection systems
USE library security systems

book indexes
SN *Indexes to individual books, not indexes in book form.*
UF back of book indexes
BT information retrieval indexes
RT book indexing

book indexing
UF back of book indexing
BT (indexing by item indexed)
RT book indexes

book jobbers
USE jobbers

book reviews
UF literary reviews
BT reviews

book security
USE library security

book selection
USE materials selection

book stock
USE library collections

book trade
USE book vendors

book vendors
UF book trade
   booksellers
BT vendors
RT jobbers
   materials acquisitions

bookbinders
USE binderies

bookbinding
USE binding

bookmobiles
BT mobile libraries

books
BT (documents by medium, physical form)
    publications
NT paperbacks
    talking books
    textbooks
RT bestsellers
    binding
    fiction
    ISBN
    large print materials
    monographs
    nonfiction

booksellers
USE book vendors

Boolean functions
USE Boolean logic

Boolean logic
UF Boolean functions
    logical operators
BT information retrieval models
    logic
RT Boolean searching

Boolean operators
USE Boolean searching

Boolean searching
UF Boolean operators
    coordinate searching
BT searching
RT Boolean logic

borrowers
USE library users

borrowing (library materials)
USE library circulation

botany
BT biology
RT agriculture

bots
USE Internet search systems

boundary spanners
SN *Links between two or more systems whose goals and expectations are at least partially conflicting.*

boundary spanners (cont.)
BT human information resources
RT gatekeepers
    information filtering
    information flow
    interdisciplinarity
    invisible colleges
    social networking

Bradford's law
BT bibliometrics
RT bibliometric scatter
    core literature
    Zipf's law

braille
BT writing systems
RT visually impaired persons

branch libraries
BT libraries
RT public libraries

branch library closings
USE library closings

Brazil
BT South America

breadcrumbs
SN *String of navigational steps leading to a particular page within a website.*
UF crumb trails
BT information representations
NT attribute breadcrumbs
    location breadcrumbs
    path breadcrumbs
RT faceted browsing
    navigation
    search histories

bridge agents
USE gatekeepers

broadband transmission
BT data transmission

broadcasting
BT telecommunications
RT radio
    television

broader term references
USE cross references

broader term relationships
USE hierarchical relationships

browse-wrap
USE usage agreements

browsing
BT information seeking
NT faceted browsing
    serendipity

BT references
USE cross references

BT relationships
USE hierarchical relationships

budgeting
BT financial management

buildings
BT (buildings and facilities)
NT library buildings
RT architecture

bulletin board systems
UF BBS
    electronic bulletin boards
BT message systems

business information
UF business intelligence
BT domain information
RT company information

business intelligence
USE business information

business models
BT business

business
UF industry
BT management operations
NT business models
RT entrepreneurs
    entrepreneurship

cache
BT computer memory

CAD
USE computer aided design

CAE
USE computer aided engineering

CAI
USE computer assisted instruction

call numbers
BT knowledge organization systems
RT bibliographic cataloging
    locators

CAM
USE computer aided manufacturing

cameras
BT (hardware, software, and equipment)
RT audiovisual equipment
    optical equipment
    television

Canada
BT North America

candidate descriptors
SN *Terms proposed for addition to a
    controlled vocabulary.*
UF proposed descriptors
BT descriptors
RT thesauri

canonical correlation
BT statistical methods

canonicity
USE bibliographic families

capitalization
BT linguistic elements

card catalogs
UF card files
BT catalogs (bibliographic)

card files
USE card catalogs

career development
BT socioeconomic activities
RT employees
    employment
    information professionals
    mentoring

Caribbean region
BT regions

cartography
UF mapping (cartography)
BT (fields and disciplines)

cartography (cont.)
RT geography
   maps

case grammar
BT grammars

case histories
USE case studies

case studies
UF case histories
BT research methods

CASE
USE computer aided software engineering

cassettes, audiotape
USE audiocassettes

catalog entries
USE entries

catalog records
USE bibliographic records

cataloging in publication
SN *Document description provided by the*
   publisher or a bibliographic agency at time of
   publication.
UF CIP
BT cataloging

cataloging rules
BT knowledge organization systems
NT Anglo American Cataloguing Rules
RT bibliographic cataloging

cataloging
BT library technical services
   organization of information
NT archival cataloging
   bibliographic cataloging
   cataloging in publication
   computerized cataloging
   descriptive cataloging
   minimal cataloging
   retrospective cataloging
   shared cataloging
   subject cataloging

categories
BT knowledge organization systems
RT automatic categorization
   classification schemes
   hierarchies

categories (cont.)
   semantic relationships

categorization, automatic
USE automatic categorization

cathode ray tube terminals
USE video display terminals

CD (compact disks)
USE compact disks

CD recordable
USE compact disk recordable

CD-I
USE compact disk interactive

CD-ROM
BT compact disks
   electronic publications
RT CD-ROM drives
   compact disk interactive
   digital video interactive

CD-ROM drives
BT disk drives
RT CD-ROM

cellular communications
UF cellular telephones
   mobile telephones
BT mobile communications

cellular telephones
USE cellular communications

censored materials
USE banned materials

censorship
BT legal aspects
RT banned materials
   information filtering
   intellectual freedom
   policy
   universal access
census data
USE demographics

Central America
BT (countries and regions)

central libraries
UF main libraries
BT libraries

central processing units
USE computer processing units

centralization
BT management operations
RT decentralization

chain indexing
BT subject indexing
RT citation order

chalk
BT library supplies

change
SN *Also use area of change if appropriate, e.g.,*
  "social aspects" or "technology impact."
BT (general processes)
NT trends
RT growth
  innovation
  modification

chaos theory
BT mathematical models

character recognition
USE optical character recognition

character sets
BT information representations
RT diacriticals
  legibility

charges
USE pricing

charging systems
USE library circulation

chat reference services
USE electronic reference services

chat rooms
BT message systems

chemical connection tables
SN *Digital structure representation of atoms and*
  their bonds in a chemical compound.
BT chemical information
  information representations

chemical information
BT scientific and technical information
NT chemical connection tables
  chemical nomenclature

chemical information (cont.)
  chemical structure models
RT chemistry

chemical nomenclature
UF nomenclature, chemical
BT chemical information
  terminology

chemical structure models
BT chemical information
  information representations

chemistry
BT physical sciences
NT biochemistry
RT chemical information
  pharmacology

children
BT youth
RT children's literature

children's books
USE children's literature

children's librarianship
USE children's services

children's libraries
BT libraries
RT children's services

children's literature
UF children's books
BT (documents by information content, purpose)
RT children
  children's services
  young adult literature

children's services
UF children's librarianship
BT library and archival services
RT children's libraries
  children's literature
  storytelling

Chile
BT South America

China
BT Asia

Chinese language
BT non English languages

chronological order
USE temporal arrangement

CIM
USE computer integrated manufacturing

CIP
USE cataloging in publication

citation analysis
UF citation frequency
BT bibliometrics
NT author productivity
   bibliographic coupling
   bibliographic families
   co-citation analysis
   database tomography
   half life measures
   impact factor
   organization productivity
   self citation
RT bibliographic citations
   citation indexes
   citation networks

citation coupling
USE bibliographic coupling

citation frequency
USE citation analysis

citation indexes
BT information retrieval indexes
RT bibliographic coupling
   citation analysis
   citation searching

citation maps
USE citation networks

citation networks
UF citation maps
BT data maps
RT citation analysis

citation order
SN *The order in which elements are listed in an
   index entry; used particularly with regard to
   chain indexing.*
UF facet formula
   preferred order
BT (attributes of information and data)
RT access points
   chain indexing
   faceted classification
   index terms

citation order (cont.)
   PMEST facets

citation searching
SN *Searching for documents that have cited a
   known document.*
BT searching
RT bibliographic citations
   citation indexes

citations, bibliographic
USE bibliographic citations

civil rights
BT human rights
NT intellectual freedom
   privacy
RT affirmative action

classification construction
USE index language construction

classification schemes
UF taxonomies
BT index languages
NT Bliss Bibliographic Classification
   Colon Classification
   Dewey Decimal Classification
   International Patent Classification
   Library of Congress Classification
   Universal Decimal Classification
RT categories
   classification
   classifcd catalogs
   controlled vocabularies
   index language construction
   indexing
   notation
   systematic arrangement
   taxonomies
   thesaurofacet

classification
SN *Theory of classification. For particular
   schemes, use "classification schemes."*
BT organization of information
NT automatic classification
   faceted classification
   hierarchical classification
   synthetic classification
RT abstraction
   arrangement
   classification schemes
   classified catalogs
   index terms
   indexing

classification (cont.)
    knowledge representation
    notation
    systematic arrangement

classified arrangement
USE systematic arrangement

classified catalogs
BT catalogs (bibliographic)
RT classification
    classification schemes
    systematic arrangement

classified information
USE security classification

clearinghouses (community information)
USE community information services

clearinghouses (information analysis)
USE information analysis centers

clearinghouses (special libraries)
USE special libraries

clickstream analysis
USE web usage studies

click-wrap
USE usage agreements

client server software
BT computer software
NT web browsers
RT client server systems
    data transmission

client server systems
UF host computers
BT computer systems
RT client server software
    file servers

cliometrics
USE informetrics

cluster analysis
SN *Systematic grouping of variables, terms, etc.,*
    based on their similarity or co-occurrence.
BT data analysis
RT automatic classification
    co-occurrence analysis

coauthorship
USE joint authorship

coaxial cable
BT telecommunications equipment

co-citation analysis
BT citation analysis
RT bibliographic coupling

CODEN
BT knowledge organization systems
    standards
RT periodicals

cognition
UF cognitive behavior
    thinking
BT mental processes
NT external cognition
RT cognitive models
    cognitive science
    cognitive styles
    comprehension

cognitive behavior
USE cognition

cognitive controls
USE cognitive styles

cognitive filtering
USE content filtering

cognitive models
SN *Cognitive representations of a problem,*
    situation, or system.
UF conceptual models
    mental models
BT information models
NT cognitive space
RT cognition
    cognitive science
    concepts
    paradigms

cognitive perception
SN *Recognition and interpretation of data or*
    ideas, a component in the formulation of a
    concept. Distinguish from "sensory
    perception."
UF concept formation
BT mental processes
RT concepts

cognitive psychology
USE cognitive science

cognitive science
SN *Study of the processes of intelligent reasoning, involving input from a number of disciplines.*
UF cognitive psychology
BT psychology
RT cognition
    cognitive models
    cognitive styles
    computer science
    information science
    linguistics
    mental processes

cognitive space
SN *Representation of the generic concepts and relations among them stored in one's memory; a pattern imposed on reality or experience to facilitate explanation; contrast with "information space."*
UF concept space
    conceptual space
    schemata
BT cognitive models
RT artificial intelligence

cognitive styles
SN *Ways in which individuals consistently receive and respond to information.*
UF cognitive controls
BT psychological aspects
RT cognition
    cognitive science
    individual differences

collaboration
UF collaborative work
    cooperative work
    group work
BT general activities
NT resource sharing
    shared cataloging
RT communication patterns
    consortia
    group decision support systems
    groupware
    interlibrary loans
    joint authorship
    library networks

collaborative filtering
SN *Filtering information on the basis of what other individuals with similar interests have found relevant.*
UF social filtering
BT information filtering

collaborative work
USE collaboration

collecting, book
USE book collecting

collection assessment
BT collection management

collection development
UF book collection
BT collection management
NT materials acquisitions
    materials selection

collection management
BT information resources management
    library technical services
NT collection assessment
    collection development
    deselection
    subscription cancellation
RT library materials
    records management

collection reduction
USE deselection

collections
BT (documents by availability, access, organization)
NT library collections
    personal collections
    special collections
RT core literature

college libraries
USE academic libraries

colleges and universities
UF academic institutions
    higher education
    universities
BT (organizations)
NT information science schools
    library schools
RT academic freedom
    academic libraries
    accreditation
    schools

collocation analysis
USE co-occurrence analysis

Colombia
BT South America

Colon Classification
BT classification schemes
RT PMEST facets

color displays
BT display devices

color printers
BT printers

color
BT physical attributes

COM
USE computer output microforms

command driven interfaces
BT interfaces
RT command languages

command languages
BT language types
NT common command language
RT command driven interfaces
    interfaces

commerce
BT socioeconomic activities
NT electronic commerce
RT marketing

commercial publishers
BT publishers

common carrier networks
BT telecommunications networks

common carriers
USE telecommunications industry

common command language
BT command languages

common sense knowledge
UF world knowledge
BT knowledge
RT knowledge bases

communication patterns
BT human communications
RT collaboration

communication skills
BT skills
RT human communications

communications activities
BT (activities and operations)
NT human communications
    telecommunications

communications networks
USE telecommunications networks

communications protocols
UF network protocols
    protocols
BT standards
NT ftp
    http
    telnet
RT data transmission
    telecommunications

communications satellites
USE satellite communications

communications stars
USE gatekeepers

communications theory
USE information theory

communities
BT (persons and informal groups)
NT academic communities
    communities of practice
    discourse communities
    peer groups
    virtual communities
RT social aspects

communities of practice
SN *Informal groups of individuals,*
    characterized by voluntary membership, self-
    regulation and management, based on a
    largely tacit understanding of common
    interests and issues of concern.
BT communities

community based library services
USE library outreach services

community college libraries
BT academic libraries

community information services
UF I&R services
    clearinghouses (community information)
    information and referral services
    referral services
BT information services

community information services (cont.)
RT community resource files
    library outreach services

community resource files
BT nonbibliographic databases
RT community information services

compact discs
USE compact disks

compact disk interactive
SN *A software and hardware standard for*
    storing video, audio, and binary data on
    compact optical disks. Not widely accepted.
UF CD-I
BT compact disks
RT CD-ROM

compact disk recordable
UF CD recordable
BT compact disks

compact disks
UF CD (compact disks)
    compact discs
BT optical disks
NT CD-ROM
    compact disk interactive
    compact disk recordable
    DVD
    digital video interactive
    photo CD
RT audio recordings

compact shelving
USE library shelving

compact storage
UF compact shelving
BT materials storage

company information
UF corporate intelligence
    organizational intelligence
BT domain information
RT business information
    competitive intelligence

company libraries
USE corporate libraries

comparative librarianship
BT librarianship
RT international librarianship

comparison
BT (research and analytic methods)

compatibility
BT (general attributes)
RT connectivity
    data conversion

competition
BT socioeconomic activities
RT competitive intelligence
    private sector

competitive intelligence
UF competitor intelligence
BT domain information
RT company information
    competition
    environmental scanning

competitor intelligence
USE competitive intelligence

complexity
BT (general attributes)
RT reliability
    usability

comprehension
UF understanding (comprehension)
BT mental processes
RT cognition

compression
SN *Also use the type of data being*
    compressed, e.g., "data" or "images."
UF data compression
    image compression
BT data processing
RT high density data storage
    signal processing

compulsory deposit
USE legal deposit

computational intelligence
USE artificial intelligence

computational lexicography
BT lexicography
RT computational linguistics
    natural language processing

computational linguistics
BT linguistics
NT context free languages

computational linguistics (cont.)
RT automatic indexing
  computational lexicography
  natural language processing

computer access control
UF access control (computer systems)
  password control
BT computer security
RT identification

computer aided design
UF CAD
  interactive design
BT computer applications
  design

computer aided engineering
UF CAE
BT computer applications
  technical and manufacturing operations

computer aided indexing
USE machine aided indexing

computer aided instruction
USE computer assisted instruction

computer aided manufacturing
UF CAM
BT computer applications
  technical and manufacturing operations
RT computer integrated manufacturing

computer aided software engineering
SN *Use of computer-assisted methods to organize and control the development of software, especially on large, complex projects involving many software components and people.*
UF CASE
  computer assisted software engineering
BT software engineering

computer aided translation
USE machine translation

computer applications
SN *Automation or computerization as an issue; for particular applications, use the name of the application, e.g., "automatic indexing."*
UF automation
  computerized operations
BT computer operations
NT artificial intelligence
  automatic abstracting

computer applications (cont.)
  automatic classification
  automatic extracting
  automatic indexing
  automatic taxonomy generation
  computer aided design
  computer aided engineering
  computer aided manufacturing
  computer assisted instruction
  computer graphics
  computer integrated manufacturing
  computer mediated communications
  computer simulation
  cryptography
  electronic funds transfer
  library automation
  machine aided indexing
  machine translation
  office automation
  online searching
  teleshopping
  virtual reality
RT computer software applications
  robots

computer architecture
UF architectures, computer
BT (hardware, software, and equipment)
RT computers

computer assisted instruction
UF CAI
  computer aided instruction
BT computer applications
  education

computer assisted software engineering
USE computer aided software
  engineering

computer centers
SN *Facilities housing the central computer or computers for an organization.*
BT (buildings and facilities)
RT computer laboratories
  computers
  mainframe computers

computer conferencing
UF electronic meeting systems
BT computer mediated communications
NT web conferencing
RT meetings

computer crime
BT crime

computer crime (cont.)
NT hacking
RT computer security
    computer viruses
    data security
    disclosure

computer equipment
UF computer hardware
    hardware, computer
BT (hardware, software, and equipment)
NT computer peripherals
    computers
    integrated circuits
RT computer industry
    computing resource management

computer games
USE video games

computer graphics
BT computer applications
    graphics
NT animation
RT images

computer hardware
USE computer equipment

computer human interaction
USE human computer interaction

computer human interfaces
USE interfaces

computer industry
BT (product and service providers)
RT computer equipment
    computer peripherals
    computers
    software industry

computer integrated manufacturing
UF CIM
BT computer applications
    technical and manufacturing operations
RT computer aided manufacturing

computer laboratories
SN *Facilities containing multiple computers,*
    used for educational and class purposes.
BT (buildings and facilities)
RT computer centers

computer languages
USE programming languages

computer learning
USE machine learning

computer literacy
BT literacy
RT digital divide
    information literacy
    professional competencies

computer matching
USE cross matching

computer mediated communications
UF electronic communications
BT computer applications
    telecommunications
NT computer conferencing
    message systems
    multiuser Internet games
    newsgroups
RT ftp
    telnet

computer memory
BT computers
NT associative memory
    cache
    holographic memory
    random access memory
    read only memory
    virtual memory

computer multitasking
SN *Simultaneous execution of two or more*
    computer operations.
BT data processing

computer networks
USE telecommunications networks

computer operations
BT (activities and operations)
NT computer applications
    computer programming
    data processing
    distributed computing
    documentation
    electronic visualization
    human computer interaction
    information processing
    message filtering
    signal processing
    software reuse

computer output microfilm
USE computer output microforms

computer output microforms
UF COM
    computer output microfilm
BT microforms
RT microfilm

computer peripherals
UF peripherals, computer
BT computer equipment
NT data storage devices
    input equipment
    output equipment
    video display terminals
RT computer industry
    computers

computer processing units
UF central processing units
    data processors
    CPU
BT computers
NT back end processors
    microprocessors
    multiprocessors
    parallel processors

computer programmers
BT information professionals

computer programming
UF programming (computer)
BT computer operations
NT logic programming
    object oriented programming
    software engineering
RT computer software
    modularity
    programming languages
    software reuse

computer programs
USE computer software

computer resource management
USE computing resource management

computer science
BT (fields and disciplines)
NT automata
    cybernetics
    dynamic systems
    programming languages
    robotics
RT cognitive science
    computers
    cybernetics

computer science (cont.)
    information science
    software engineering

computer security
BT security
NT authentication
    computer access control
    network security
RT computer crime
    data security

computer simulation
BT computer applications
    simulation

computer software
UF computer programs
    programs, computer
    software, computer
BT (hardware, software, and equipment)
NT client server software
    computer software applications
    groupware
    malicious software
    open source
    operating systems
    shareware
RT algorithms
    computer programming
    computers
    programming languages
    software industry

computer software applications
BT computer software
NT authoring software
    database management systems
    decision support systems
    e-mail software
    grammar checkers
    information retrieval software
    spelling checkers
    text editors
    utility software
    video games
RT computer applications

computer storage
USE data storage devices

computer systems
BT (hardware, software, and equipment)
NT analog systems
    client server systems
    dedicated systems

computer systems (cont.)
    hybrid systems
    interactive systems
    interfaces
    turnkey systems
RT computers
    integrated systems

computer translation
USE machine translation

computer typesetting
USE typesetting

computer viruses
BT malicious software
RT computer crime

computer vision
UF machine vision
BT artificial intelligence
RT robotics
    robots
    vision

computer worms
BT malicious software

computerized cataloging
BT cataloging
    library automation

computerized operations
USE computer applications

computers
BT computer equipment
NT computer memory
    computer processing units
    database machines
    file servers
    mainframe computers
    microcomputers
    minicomputers
    network computers
    optical computers
    RISC
    supercomputers
    workstations
RT computer architecture
    computer centers
    computer industry
    computer peripherals
    computer science
    computer software
    computer systems

computers (cont.)
    computing resource management
    robots

computing resource management
UF computer resource management
    resource management (computing)
BT management
RT computer equipment
    computers

concept association
BT mental processes
RT concepts

concept discrimination
SN *For discrimination among persons on the*
    basis of a characteristic, use "social
    discrimination."
BT mental processes
RT disambiguation

concept formation
USE cognitive perception

concept space
USE cognitive space

concepts
BT information content
RT cognitive models
    cognitive perception
    concept association
    domain information
    index terms
    knowledge
    topic threads

conceptual models
USE cognitive models

conceptual relationships
USE semantic relationships

conceptual space
USE cognitive space

concordances
BT keyword indexes

concurrent processing
USE parallel processing

conference proceedings
UF proceedings (conference)
BT publications

conference proceedings (cont.)
RT meetings
    primary literature
    serials

conferences
USE meetings

confidential records
BT records
RT data security
    freedom of information
    medical records
    personal information
    privacy
    security classification

confidentiality
USE privacy

configuration
USE design

congruence
USE similarity

connectionist models
SN *Models for analysis and machine learning*
    based on artificial neural networks, weighted
    synapses, and threshold logic units.
BT analytic models

connectivity
BT (attributes of systems and equipment)
RT compatibility

conservation of materials
USE materials conservation

consistency, indexer
USE indexer consistency

consortia
BT (organizations)
RT collaboration

consultants
UF consulting services
BT (product and service providers)
RT vendors

consulting services
USE consultants

consumer information
BT domain information

content
USE information content

content analysis
BT text processing
RT information content

content based indexing
SN *Indexing based on processing of image and*
    associated textual information. Includes
    analysis of shape, color, texture, object
    identity, and abstract attributes; generally an
    automatic processing approach.
BT (indexing by method used)
RT automatic indexing
    image indexing

content filtering
SN *Filtering by extracting features of documents*
    to assess the relevance of the documents.
UF cognitive filtering
BT information filtering

content management
BT information resources management
NT web content management
RT information storage and retrieval systems

content management systems
USE information storage and retrieval systems

content mining
SN *Extracting content from typically*
    inaccessible formats; no analysis or
    interpretation is implied.
BT automatic extracting

content tagging
USE subject indexing

contents lists
UF table of contents lists
BT document surrogates
RT SDI services

context
USE contextual information

context free languages
BT computational linguistics
RT automata

contextual information
UF context
BT information content
RT relevance

contextual information (cont.)
    situated knowledge

continuing education
BT education
RT adult education
    lifelong learning
    workshops

contracts
BT (documents by information content, purpose)
RT law
    licenses

control systems
BT (hardware, software, and equipment)
NT remote control

controlled vocabularies
BT index languages
NT ontologies
    subject heading lists
    switching languages
    syndetic structures
    taxonomies
    thesauri
    thesaurofacet
RT authority files
    classification schemes
    entry vocabularies
    information mapping
    terminology
    vocabulary control

co-occurrence analysis
UF collocation analysis
    cooccurrence analysis
    term co-occurrence analysis
    word co-occurrence analysis
BT data analysis
RT bibliometrics
    cluster analysis

cooccurrence analysis
USE co-occurrence analysis

cooperative work
USE collaboration

coordinate indexing
USE postcoordinate indexing

coordinate searching
USE Boolean searching

copiers
USE photocopiers

copying
USE photocopying

copyright
BT intellectual property
RT copyright infringement
    copyright piracy
    fair use
    law
    legal deposit
    open access publications
    public lending right
    royalties
    trade secrets
    trademarks

copyright infringement
BT crime
NT copyright piracy
RT copyright

copyright piracy
BT copyright infringement
RT copyright
    intellectual property
    trademark infringement

core competencies
USE professional competencies

core literature
BT (documents by information content, purpose)
RT Bradford's law
    collections

corporate authorship
BT authorship
RT organization productivity

corporate culture
USE organizational culture

corporate intelligence
USE company information

corporate libraries
UF company libraries
BT special libraries

corporate name indexing
USE name indexing

corporate names
UF organization names
BT proper names
RT name indexing

correction, error
USE error correction

correctional institution libraries
USE prison libraries

correspondence
UF letters
    memoranda
BT (documents by information content, purpose)
RT records management

correspondence study
BT distance learning

cost analysis
BT (research and analytic methods)
RT cost effectiveness
    costs
    decision making
    economics of information

cost effectiveness
BT effectiveness
RT cost analysis
    costs
    decision making

cost recovery
BT financial management
RT costs

costs
SN *Also use specific topic if applicable, e.g.,*
    "data processing."
BT (general attributes)
NT overhead costs
RT cost analysis
    cost effectiveness
    cost recovery
    economics
    performance

coupling, bibliographic
USE bibliographic coupling

courseware
BT (documents by information content, purpose)
RT curricula
    educational technology

co-word analysis
USE bibliometrics

CPM
USE critical path method

CPU
USE computer processing units

crawlers
USE Internet search systems

creativity
BT psychological aspects
RT intelligence

credibility
BT (attributes of information and data)

crime
UF theft
    vandalism
BT legal aspects
NT computer crime
    copyright infringement
    fraud
    terrorism
    trademark infringement
RT law
    security

criminal justice
USE law

criteria
BT information content

critical incident method
SN *Method for systematically identifying*
    contributors to success or failure of
    individuals or organisations in specific
    situations.
UF critical incident technique
BT planning
    practical methods

critical incident technique
USE critical incident method

critical path method
SN *Analysis of the sequence of events needed to*
    perform all tasks necessary to reach a target.
UF CPM
BT planning
    practical methods

cross cultural aspects
BT cultural aspects
RT cultural diversity
    language barriers

cross disciplinary fertilization
SN *Import or export of methods, ideas, models,*
    or empirical results between disciplines.
BT information flow
RT interdisciplinarity

cross lingual retrieval
USE multilingual retrieval

cross matching
SN *Of data files.*
UF computer matching
BT data processing
RT information mapping

cross references
UF broader term references
    BT references
    narrower term references
    nonpreferred term references
    NT references
    preferred term references
    related term references
    RT references
    see also references
    see references
    UF references
    use references
    used for references
BT syndetic structures
RT associative relationships
    equivalence relationships
    hierarchical relationships
    part whole relationships

crossborder data flow
USE transborder data flow

CRT terminals
USE video display terminals

crumb trails
USE breadcrumbs

cryptography
BT computer applications
NT decryption
    encryption
RT data security

cultural aspects
BT (sociocultural aspects)
NT cross cultural aspects
    cultural diversity
    entertainment
    honors
    language barriers
    literacy
    multilingualism
    organizational culture
    organizational environment
    popular culture
    social discrimination
    social networking

cultural diversity
SN *Acceptance and encouragement of*
    individuals of various racial and ethnic
    backgrounds, sexual orientation, etc.
BT cultural aspects
RT affirmative action
    cross cultural aspects
    disabled persons
    gays and lesbians
    gender
    minorities and ethnic groups
    social discrimination

cumulative indexes
BT information retrieval indexes

current awareness services
UF current awareness systems
BT information services
NT SDI services
RT abstracting and indexing service bureaus

current awareness systems
USE current awareness services

curricula
BT (documents by information content, purpose)
RT courseware
    education

cursive script
BT writing systems

customers
BT (persons and informal groups)

customization
UF personalization
BT general activities

customized materials
USE personal files

cybercash
USE electronic cash

cybermetrics
USE webometrics

cybernetics
BT computer science
RT artificial intelligence
    computer science
    feedback
    information science
    interfaces
    stochastic processes

cyberspace
USE Internet

DAT
USE digital audio tapes

data
SN *The basis of information and, ultimately,*
    knowledge. Focus on the type or form of data,
    with preference given to the specific type of
    data, e.g., "images" or "numeric data." For
    focus on the informational content of data,
    use terms under "domain information."
UF data compression
BT information content
NT acoustic data
    analog data
    field formatted data
    machine readable data
    metadata
    numeric data
    test data
RT data corruption
    data entry
    databases
    domain information
    images
    records

data acquisition
USE data collection

data analysis
BT (research and analytic methods)
NT cluster analysis
    co-occurrence analysis
    meta analysis
    network analysis

data analysis (cont.)
RT data collection

data banks
USE databases

data capture
USE data collection

data collection
UF data acquisition
    data capture
BT (research and analytic methods)
RT data analysis
    data entry
    sensors

data communications
USE data transmission

data compression
USE data

data conversion
UF database conversion
    document conversion
BT data processing
NT retrospective conversion
RT compatibility

data corruption
BT (information and data processes)
RT accuracy
    data
    error detection
    error rates
    errors
    file integrity
    reliability

data definition languages
SN *Language which enable the structure and*
    instances of a database to be defined in a
    human- and machine-readable form.
BT language types

data dictionaries
BT databases

data distribution
BT (research and analytic methods)
NT normal distribution
    Pareto principle
    skewed distribution
RT bibliometric scatter

data dredging
USE data mining

data entry
UF keyboarding
   keying
BT data processing
RT bar codes
   data
   data collection
   repetitive stress injury

data files
USE databases

data formats
UF formats, data
BT knowledge organization systems
NT document schemas
   DSSSL
   DTDs
   interchange formats
RT electronic data interchange

data fusion
USE unified retrieval models

data interchange
USE electronic data interchange

data maps
UF topology
BT graphics
NT citation networks
   ET-maps
   Pathfinder networks
   self organizing maps
   semantic networks
   topic maps
RT electronic visualization
   vector space models

data mining
SN *Analytical stage of knowledge discovery*
   involving data cleaning, warehousing, and
   visualization.
UF data dredging
   database mining
   information extraction
BT knowledge discovery
RT data warehousing
   latent semantic analysis

data models
SN *Products of the database design process*
   which aim to identify and organize the

data models (cont.)
   required data logically and physically.
BT database models
RT normalization

data objects
SN *Self-contained entities that incorporate both*
   their properties and the operations to be
   performed on the entities.
UF information objects
BT abstract data types
RT object oriented databases
   object oriented programming

data parsing
SN *Separating data into more easily processed*
   components, e.g. for database fields.
BT data processing
RT data segmentation
   document schemas
   field formatted data
   sorting

data presentation
SN *Computer operations used to present data in*
   a visual format.
BT data processing
RT electronic visualization
   knowledge representation

data processing
UF automatic data processing
   DP
   EDP
   electronic data processing
BT computer operations
NT batch processing
   compression
   computer multitasking
   cross matching
   data conversion
   data entry
   data parsing
   data presentation
   data reduction
   decoding
   digital to analog conversion
   digitization
   encoding
   end user computing
   form filling
   formatting
   hash coding
   multiprocessing
   normalization
   parallel processing

data processing (cont.)
    pattern recognition
    real time processing
    scanning
    sorting
    validation
    verification
    word processing
RT electronic visualization
    information production
    text processing

data processors
USE computer processing units

data protection
USE data security

data reduction
SN *The transformation of a set of raw data into*
    a more useful form.
BT data processing
NT dimensionality reduction
RT hash coding

data representation
USE electronic visualization

data security
UF data protection
BT security
RT computer crime
    computer security
    confidential records
    cryptography
    encryption
    information policy
    personal information
    privacy

data segmentation
BT (research and analytic methods)
RT data parsing
    signal boundary detection

data sets
USE numeric databases

data storage
USE data storage devices

data storage devices
UF archival storage
    computer storage
    data storage
    file systems

data storage devices (cont.)
BT computer peripherals
NT disk drives
    high density data storage
RT hash coding
    magnetic media
    microforms
    optical media

data streaming
UF audio streaming
    motion video streaming
    streaming audio
    streaming media
    streaming video
    video streaming
BT data transmission
RT motion video

data structures
BT knowledge organization systems
NT abstract data types
    network structures
    tree structures
RT databases

data transmission
UF data communications
BT telecommunications
NT broadband transmission
    data streaming
    digital communications
    electronic data interchange
    electronic filing
    file transfers
    voice transmission
RT bandwidth
    client server software
    communications protocols
    OpenURL

data utilization
USE information use

data warehouses
USE databases

data warehousing
BT materials storage
RT data mining

databanks
USE databases

database conversion
USE data conversion

database design
BT design
    organization of information
RT metadata

database hosts
USE search services

database indexing
SN *Indexing of documents to be included in*
    electronic databases.
BT (indexing by item indexed)
RT abstracting and indexing service bureaus
    periodical indexing

database leasing
UF leasing, database
    tape leasing
BT library operations
RT database producers
    financial management
    search services

database machines
BT computers
RT databases

database maintenance
USE database management

database management
UF database maintenance
BT information resources management
RT databases

database management systems
UF file systems
BT computer software applications
NT bibliographic software
    electronic document management systems
    geographic information systems
    image information systems
RT databases

database mining
USE data mining

database models
BT analytic models
NT data models
    relational models
RT databases

database producers
BT publishers
RT abstracting and indexing service bureaus

database producers (cont.)
    database leasing
    information industry
    information infrastructure
    information services
    online industry
    overlap
    search services

database tomography
SN *Database analysis based on phrase*
    frequency and proximity, paired with human
    editorial analysis.
BT citation analysis

database vendors
USE search services

databases
UF data banks
    data files
    data warehouses
    databanks
    files
BT information resources
NT bibliographic databases
    data dictionaries
    distributed databases
    full text databases
    nonbibliographic databases
    object oriented databases
    online databases
    relational databases
    very large databases
RT abstracting and indexing service bureaus
    data
    data structures
    database machines
    database management
    database management systems
    database models
    knowledge bases
    metadata
    periodical indexes

DDC
USE Dewey Decimal Classification

deacidification
SN *Of paper.*
BT materials conservation

deaf persons
USE hearing impaired persons

deans
USE faculty

decentralization
BT management operations
RT centralization

decision making
BT (research and analytic methods)
RT cost analysis
    cost effectiveness
    decision support systems
    decision theory
    decision trees
    operations research
    problem solving

decision support systems
UF DSS
BT computer software applications
NT group decision support systems
RT decision making
    management
    management information systems
    problem solving

decision theory
BT statistics
RT decision making
    operations research
    problem solving

decision trees
BT algorithms
RT decision making
    problem solving

decoding
BT data processing
RT decryption

decryption
BT cryptography
RT decoding

dedicated systems
BT computer systems

deduction
USE inference

deep web
USE invisible web

default values
BT information content

definitions (of terms)
USE terminology

delivery of documents
USE document delivery

Delphi studies
SN *Studies seeking reliable consensus of opinion*
    through a series of questionnaires with
    controlled opinion feedback.
BT research methods
RT forecasting

democracy
USE political aspects

demographics
UF census data
    population
BT socioeconomic aspects
NT gender
    socioeconomic status
RT gender
    minorities and ethnic groups
    social sciences

density ranking
BT ranking

depository libraries
BT libraries
RT government publications

derivative indexing
UF free text indexing
BT subject indexing
RT stoplists

description (research method)
USE qualitative analysis

description based indexing
SN *Indexing images on the basis of keywords,*
    captions and other verbal descriptions;
    generally requires human input.
BT (indexing by method used)

descriptive bibliography
USE analytical bibliography

descriptive cataloging
UF bibliographic description
BT cataloging

descriptors
SN *Terms chosen as the preferred expression of*

descriptors (cont.)
concepts in an indexing language.
BT index terms
NT candidate descriptors
RT subject headings
thesauri

deselection
UF collection reduction
weeding
BT collection management
RT subscription cancellation

design
UF configuration
BT (general attributes)
NT computer aided design
database design
forms design
screen design
RT prototyping

desktop computers
USE personal computers

desktop metaphor
BT metaphors
RT graphical user interfaces

desktop publishing
BT publishing
RT electronic publishing

detection, error
USE error detection

developing countries
BT (countries and regions)

Dewey Decimal Classification
UF DDC
BT classification schemes

diacriticals
SN *Signs used to indicate different values,
semantic or phonetic, of alphabetic
characters.*
BT information representations
RT character sets

dictionaries
UF glossaries
BT reference materials
RT encyclopedias
lexicography
terminology

dictionaries (cont.)
thesauri

diffusion of innovation
SN *Process by which new ideas or practices are
disseminated among the members of a social
system.*
BT innovation
RT early adopters
innovation
technology transfer

digests
SN *Condensed versions of documents; for
digests of periodical articles use "abstracts."*
UF summaries
BT document surrogates
RT abstracts
annotations

digital audio files
BT digital objects
RT audio communications
audio retrieval

digital audio tapes
UF DAT
BT audiotapes

digital communications
BT data transmission
RT digital to analog conversion
digitization

digital divide
SN *Disparity that exists across certain
demographic groups in access to technology,
primarily the Internet.*
BT socioeconomic aspects
RT computer literacy
social equity
socioeconomic status

digital documents
USE electronic documents

digital ink
USE electronic ink

digital libraries
SN *Libraries whose contents are primarily in
electronic form and are accessed by means of
computers. The contents may be held locally
or accessed remotely by means of
communications networks.*
UF distributed information management system

digital libraries (cont.)
electronic libraries
BT libraries
RT electronic publications
virtual libraries

digital object identifiers
SN *Persistent identifier given to a web file or other Internet document, identifying the intellectual property entity itself rather than its location. If the Internet address of the file changes, users are redirected to its new address.*
UF DOI
BT persistent identifiers
RT digital objects
URL

digital object preservation
UF digital preservation
BT materials preservation
NT emulation
migration
serial conversion
RT digital objects
digitization

digital objects
SN *Items in digital form that require a computer to support their existence and display.*
BT (documents by medium, physical form)
NT digital audio files
digital video files
electronic documents
RT digital object identifiers
digital object preservation
digital rights management
peer to peer file sharing
uniform resource names

digital paper
USE electronic paper

digital preservation
USE digital object preservation

digital reference services
USE electronic reference services

digital rights management
UF DRM
ECMS
Electronic Copyright Management Systems
Electronic Rights Management Systems
ERMS
BT management

digital rights management (cont.)
RT digital objects
legal aspects

digital to analog conversion
BT data processing
RT digital communications
digitization

digital video disks
USE DVD

digital video files
BT digital objects
RT video communications
video recordings

digital video interactive
SN *A technology that enables a computer to store and display moving video images like those on television. Generally replaced by MPEG.*
UF DV-I
BT compact disks
RT CD-ROM

digitization
UF analog to digital conversion
BT data processing
RT analog data
digital communications
digital object preservation
digital to analog conversion
digitized images
retrospective conversion

digitized images
BT images
RT bit-mapped images
digitization

dimensionality reduction
SN *Trimming irrelevant features to focus on critical elements, facilitating analysis, comparisons and computer applications, e.g. data visualization.*
BT data reduction
RT electronic visualization
factor analysis
multidimensional scaling
self organizing maps

direct manipulation interfaces
BT interfaces

direct read after write technology
USE DRAW

directories
BT reference materials

disabled persons
UF handicapped persons
　　physically challenged persons
BT minorities and ethnic groups
NT hearing impaired persons
　　learning disabled persons
　　mobility impaired persons
　　reading disabled persons
　　visually impaired persons
RT adaptive technologies
　　cultural diversity
　　social discrimination

disambiguation
BT linguistic analysis
RT ambiguity
　　concept discrimination
　　homography

disasters
UF natural disasters
BT (general processes)
RT security

disclosure
BT human communications
RT computer crime
　　ethics
　　freedom of information
　　privacy
　　security

discourse analysis
SN *Processing of multi-sentence texts.*
BT natural language processing
RT discourse generation

discourse communities
SN *Group of people who share certain
　　language- using practices conventionalized
　　by social interactions within the group and in
　　its dealings with outsiders.*
BT communities

discourse generation
SN *Generation of multi-sentence texts.*
BT natural language processing
RT discourse analysis

discs
USE optical disks

discussion groups
USE newsgroups

disk drives
BT data storage devices
NT CD-ROM drives
　　DVD drives
　　multidisk drives

disks
USE optical disks

display devices
BT (hardware, software, and equipment)
NT color displays
　　flat panel displays
　　high resolution displays
　　video display terminals
RT instrumentation

displays (library)
USE library exhibits and displays

displays (thesauri)
USE thesaurus displays

dissemination, information
USE information dissemination

dissertations
UF theses
BT (documents by information content, purpose)

distance education
USE distance learning

distance learning
UF distance education
BT education
　　learning
NT correspondence study
RT lifelong learning
　　off campus education

distributed communities
USE virtual communities

distributed computing
UF distributed processing
BT computer operations
RT distributed databases

distributed databases
BT databases
RT distributed computing

distributed information management system
USE digital libraries

distributed processing
USE distributed computing

DNS
USE domain naming system

document access
BT access to resources
RT bibliographic access

document as query
USE query by example

document conversion
USE data conversion

document delivery
UF delivery of documents
BT library operations
NT facsimile transmission
    interlibrary loans
RT document retrieval
    virtual libraries

document handling
BT library operations
RT document management

document management
BT information resources management
RT document handling
    electronic document management systems

document representations
USE document surrogates

document retention
BT records management

document retrieval
BT information retrieval
    library operations
RT document delivery
    information retrieval
    information retrieval software

document schemas
SN *Specifications for documents, including their
    contents, fields, and attributes.*

document schemas (cont.)
BT data formats
RT data parsing
    field formatted data

document storage
USE materials storage

document style semantics and specification
    language
USE DSSSL

document surrogates
UF document representations
    passages
BT (documents by information content, purpose)
NT abstracts
    annotations
    bibliographic records
    contents lists
    digests
    ISBN
    ISFN
    ISMN
    ISRC
    ISSN
    thumbnail views

document titles
BT information representations
RT KWIC indexes
    KWOC indexes

document type descriptions
USE DTDs

document use
USE information use

documentation
SN *Of software, hardware, and systems. For the
    theoretical meaning, use "information
    science."*
BT computer operations
    library operations
RT help systems
    user aids

DOI
USE digital object identifiers

domain analysis
BT organization of information
RT domain information
    domain knowledge
    knowledge representation

domain information
SN *Very broad term; prefer specific type or aspect, e.g., "consumer information" or "information access." Or also use the subject, e.g., "finance."*
BT information content
NT business information
    company information
    competitive intelligence
    consumer information
    financial information
    government information
    legal information
    military intelligence
    multidisciplinary information
    personal information
    public domain information
    scientific and technical information
    spatial information
    temporal information
RT concepts
    data
    domain analysis
    domain knowledge
    knowledge

domain knowledge
UF subject expertise
BT knowledge
RT domain analysis
    domain information
    knowledge bases
    knowledge modeling
    task knowledge

domain naming system
SN *Global naming system which converts TCP/IP network numbers into human-readable Internet address, e.g. asist.org*
UF DNS
BT information science
RT URL
    online industry

downloading
BT file transfers
RT online searching
    output reformatting

DP
USE data processing

DRAM
UF dynamic random access memory
BT random access memory

DRAW
UF direct read after write technology
BT WORM disks

drawings, engineering
USE engineering drawings

DRM
USE digital rights management

drugs
USE pharmacology

DSS
USE decision support systems

DSSSL
UF document style semantics and specification language
BT data formats
RT SDQL
    SGML

DTDs
UF document type descriptions
BT data formats

Dublin Core
USE metadata standards

duplicate detection
BT quality control
RT duplicate records
    error detection

duplicate records
BT records
RT duplicate detection

durability
BT (general attributes)
RT maintainability
    performance
    permanence
    reliability

DVD
UF digital video disks
BT compact disks

DV-I
USE digital video interactive

DVD drives
BT disk drives

dynamic random access memory
USE DRAM

dynamic systems
BT computer science

dyslexia
USE reading disabled persons

early adopters
BT (persons and informal groups)
RT diffusion of innovation
   gatekeepers
   innovation

early books
USE incunabula

earth sciences
UF geology
BT physical sciences
RT geographic information systems
   geography

ease of use
USE usability

e-books
USE electronic books

e-cash
USE electronic cash

ECMS
USE digital rights management

e-commerce
USE electronic commerce

econometrics
BT economics
   measurement

economic indicators
USE indicators

economic sectors
BT socioeconomic aspects
NT information sector
   nonprofit sector
   private sector
   public sector
RT economics

economics
BT social sciences

economics (cont.)
NT econometrics
   economics of information
   socioeconomics
RT costs
   economic sectors
   finance
   indicators

economics of information
UF information economics
   value of information
BT economics
   information science
RT cost analysis
   information society

Ecuador
BT South America

EDI
USE electronic data interchange

editing
BT human communications
NT proofreading
RT editors
   markup languages
   publishing

editorial policy
BT policy

editors
SN *Persons; for software use "text editors."*
BT information professionals
RT editing

EDMS
USE electronic document management systems

EDP
USE data processing

education
UF instruction
   teaching
BT social sciences
NT adult education
   basic education
   computer assisted instruction
   continuing education
   distance learning
   home education
   information science education
   library education

education (cont.)
    off campus education
RT accreditation
    curricula
    educational technology
    reading
    students
    training

educational activities
BT (activities and operations)
NT accreditation
    learning
    mentoring
    staff development
    training

educational technology
SN *Limit to general information. For specific*
    technologies, use the name of the technology,
    e.g. "telecommunications networks."
UF instructional technology
BT (hardware, software, and equipment)
RT courseware
    education

effectiveness
BT (general attributes)
NT cost effectiveness
    retrieval effectiveness
RT efficiency
    evaluation
    indexer consistency
    performance
    usability
    utility

efficiency
BT (general attributes)
RT effectiveness

EFTS
USE electronic funds transfer

e-government
USE electronic government

e-ink
USE electronic ink

EIS
USE management information systems

e-journals
USE electronic journals

electronic books
UF e-books
BT electronic publications
RT electronic publications
    full text databases
    machine readable data

electronic bulletin boards
USE bulletin board systems

electronic cash
UF cybercash
    e-cash
    payments, electronic
BT electronic funds transfer
RT smart cards

electronic commerce
SN *As it relates to information services and*
    products.
UF e-commerce
BT commerce
RT teleshopping

electronic communications
USE computer mediated
    communications

electronic conferencing
BT teleconferencing
RT meetings

Electronic Copyright Management Systems
USE digital rights management

electronic data interchange
UF EDI
    data interchange
BT data transmission
RT data formats
    electronic funds transfer
    interchange formats

electronic data processing
USE data processing

electronic document interchange formats
USE interchange formats

electronic document management systems
UF EDMS
BT database management systems
RT document management
    image information systems

electronic documents
UF digital documents
BT digital objects
NT electronic publications
    weblogs

electronic filing
SN *Submission of data in electronic form rather
    than on paper, especially of required
    government forms.*
BT data transmission

electronic funds transfer
UF EFTS
BT computer applications
NT electronic cash
RT electronic data interchange

electronic government
SN *Online source of governmental information
    and services.*
UF e-government
BT government agencies
RT government
    government information

electronic imaging
USE imaging

electronic information dissemination
USE information dissemination

electronic information products
USE electronic publications

electronic information systems
USE information storage and retrieval systems

electronic ink
SN *Electrically charged particles that, when
    imprinted on paper or plastic, reveal or
    conceal dye, enabling change in the
    appearance of text and images.*
UF digital ink
    e-ink
BT (physical media)
RT electronic paper

electronic journals
UF e-journals
BT electronic publications
    journals

electronic libraries
USE library automation

electronic mail
USE e-mail

electronic meeting systems
USE computer conferencing

electronic offices
USE office automation

electronic paper
SN *Thin sheets embedded with microscopic
    beads that rotate when electrically charged,
    displaying a white or black surface similar to
    a pixel in text or graphics.*
UF digital paper
    e-paper
    flexible electronic displays
    smart paper
BT (physical media)
RT electronic ink

electronic publications
UF electronic information products
BT electronic documents
    publications
NT CD-ROM
    electronic books
    electronic journals
RT digital libraries
    electronic books
    electronic publishing

electronic publishing
BT publishing
RT desktop publishing
    electronic publications

electronic reference services
UF chat reference services
    digital reference services
    live reference services
    virtual reference services
BT reference services

electronic reserves
UF e-reserves
BT library reserves

Electronic Rights Management Systems
USE digital rights management

electronic visualization
SN *Representation of electronic data in the form
    of images, e.g., on a video display.*
UF 3-D representation
    data representation

electronic visualization (cont.)
    information visualization
BT computer operations
RT data maps
    data presentation
    data processing
    dimensionality reduction
    mental visualization

elementary schools
BT schools

e-mail
UF electronic mail
    email
BT message systems
NT unsolicited e-mail
RT e-mail list servers
    e-mail software
    message filtering

e-mail list servers
SN *Services to which subscribers may send*
    communications for distribution to all other
    subscribers to the listserv.
UF listservs
BT message systems
RT e-mail
    Internet
    SDI services
    topic threads

e-mail software
BT computer software applications
RT e-mail

email
USE e-mail

emotion
USE affect

empirical studies
BT research methods
RT quantitative analysis

employees
UF personnel
BT (persons and informal groups)
RT career development
    employment
    human resources management
    labor unions
    mentoring
    staff development

employment
BT socioeconomic activities
NT telecommuting
    working at home
RT affirmative action
    career development
    employees
    human productivity
    information workers
    labor unions
    social discrimination

emulation
SN *Production of facsimile hardware to preserve*
    access to stored digital object.
BT digital object preservation

encoding
BT data processing
NT superimposed coding
RT encryption

encryption
SN *Modification of stored data using a*
    transformation algorithm, in order to render
    the data incomprehensible to unauthorized
    examiners.
BT cryptography
RT data security
    encoding
    privacy

encyclopedias
BT reference materials
RT dictionaries

end user computing
BT data processing
RT end user searching
    end users

end user searching
BT searching
RT end user computing
    end users
    search behavior

end users
BT users
NT experienced users
    novice users
RT end user computing
    end user searching
    information society

engineering
BT (fields and disciplines)
NT ergonomics
    software engineering
RT aerospace
    architecture
    engineering drawings

engineering drawings
UF drawings, engineering
BT graphics
RT engineering

England
BT Great Britain

English language
BT human language

entertainment
UF recreation
BT cultural aspects

entrepreneurs
BT (persons and informal groups)
RT business
    entrepreneurship

entrepreneurship
BT socioeconomic activities
RT business
    entrepreneurs
    innovation

entries
SN *Records of items contained in files; normally used with regard to library catalogs and indexes.*
UF catalog entries
    index entries
BT access points
RT authority files

entry vocabularies
SN *The nonpreferred terms in a controlled vocabulary, leading to the preferred terms which are used in indexing.*
UF access vocabularies
BT access points
RT controlled vocabularies

environmental information
SN *Used for climate, ecology, etc. For business or social environments, use "organizational environment" or "social aspects."*
BT scientific and technical information

environmental information (cont.)
RT environmental sciences

environmental scanning
BT (research and analytic methods)
RT competitive intelligence
    forecasting
    planning

environmental sciences
BT biology
RT environmental information

e-paper
USE electronic paper

ephemera
BT (documents by information content, purpose)
RT grey literature
    pamphlets
    vertical files

epistemology
SN *Study of the nature and theories of knowledge and ways of knowing.*
BT philosophy
RT information theory

equivalence relationships
UF UF relationships
    use relationships
    used for relationships
BT semantic relationships
NT quasi-synonymous relationships
RT cross references
    synonyms
    thesauri

erasable optical disks
UF rewritable optical disks
BT optical disks

e-reserves
USE electronic reserves

ergonomics
SN *The science of refining the design of products to optimize them for human use.*
UF human factors engineering
BT engineering
    human factors
RT repetitive stress injury

ERMS
USE digital rights management

erotic materials
BT (documents by information content, purpose)
RT pornographic materials

error correction
UF correction, error
BT quality control
RT accuracy
    error detection
    error rates
    errors
    evaluation
    fault tolerance
    reliability
    validation
    verification

error detection
UF detection, error
BT quality control
RT accuracy
    data corruption
    duplicate detection
    error correction
    error messages
    error rates
    errors
    evaluation
    fault tolerance
    reliability
    validation
    verification

error messages
BT interfaces
RT error detection
    errors
    help systems
    validation

error rates
BT (attributes of information and data)
RT accuracy
    data corruption
    error correction
    error detection
    errors
    evaluation
    reliability
    validation
    verification

errors
BT (information and data processes)
NT typographical errors
RT accuracy

errors (cont.)
    data corruption
    error correction
    error detection
    error messages
    error rates
    evaluation
    failure analysis
    false information
    fault tolerance
    fraud
    reliability
    validation
    verification

ethics
UF morals
BT psychological aspects
RT disclosure
    social equity

ethnic groups
USE minorities and ethnic groups

ethnography
BT anthropology

etiquette
UF netiquette
BT social aspects
RT human behavior

ET-maps
SN *Category maps that group documents that share many noun phrase terms together in a neighborhood on a 2-D map.*
BT data maps

etymology
BT linguistics
RT words

Europe
BT (countries and regions)
NT France
    Germany
    Hungary
    Ireland
    Italy
    Netherlands
    Poland
    Russia
    Spain
    United Kingdom
RT European Union

European Union
BT regions
RT Europe

evaluation
BT general activities
NT failure analysis
    refereeing
    reviewing
RT accreditation
    benchmarks
    effectiveness
    error correction
    error detection
    error rates
    errors
    feedback
    indexer consistency
    information retrieval noise
    monitoring
    pertinence
    precision
    quality
    quality control
    recall
    relevance
    research and development
    retrieval effectiveness
    standardization
    testing

evolution based algorithms
USE genetic algorithms

exchange formats
USE interchange formats

exchanges (of materials)
USE gifts and exchanges

executive information systems
USE management information systems

exhibits and displays (library)
USE library exhibits and displays

experienced users
BT end users
RT user expertise

experiments
BT research methods
RT research design
    testing

expert services
USE information services

expert systems
UF knowledge based systems
BT artificial intelligence
RT knowledge acquisition
    knowledge bases
    knowledge engineering

experts, subject
USE subject experts

explanation
BT human communications

extension campuses
USE off campus education

extension matrices
BT algorithms

external cognition
SN *Knowledge or perception based on the interplay between internal and external representations.*
BT cognition
RT interfaces

extracting
UF extraction
BT summarization
NT automatic extracting

extraction
USE extracting

face to face communication
BT spoken communication

facet analysis
BT organization of information
RT faceted browsing
    faceted classification
    index language construction
    indexing

facet formula
USE citation order

facet indicators
USE node labels

faceted browsing
SN *Using a sequence of content filters to progressively narrow a selection set and*

faceted browsing (cont.)
   locate desired content.
UF faceted navigation
   winnowing
BT browsing
RT breadcrumbs
   facet analysis
   faceted classification
   facets

faceted classification
SN *Classification in which concepts are*
   arranged in a series of facets, and the
   notation for subjects is derived by combining
   the notations of its individual facets.
BT classification
RT citation order
   facet analysis
   faceted browsing
   node labels
   PMEST facets
   thesaurofacet

faceted navigation
USE faceted browsing

facets
SN *Subclasses based on a single characteristic*
   of a class, e.g., age or composition.
BT knowledge organization systems
NT PMEST facets
RT faceted browsing
   node labels

facsimile transmission
UF fax
   telefacsimile
BT document delivery
   telecommunications
RT image processing

fact databases
UF factual databases
BT nonbibliographic databases
RT fact retrieval systems
   factual information

fact retrieval systems
UF question answering systems
BT information storage and retrieval systems
RT answer passage retrieval
   fact databases
   factual information

factor analysis
BT mathematical methods

factor analysis (cont.)
RT dimensionality reduction
   statistical methods

factual databases
USE fact databases

factual information
BT information content
RT fact databases
   fact retrieval systems
   false information

faculty
UF deans
   professors
   teachers
BT academic communities
RT scholars

failure analysis
BT evaluation
RT errors
   information retrieval noise

fair use
UF private copying
BT intellectual property
RT copyright

fallout
SN *A measure of retrieval effectiveness; the*
   ratio of nonrelevant items retrieved by a
   query to the total number of nonrelevant
   items in the database.
BT (attributes of information and data)
RT information retrieval noise
   precision
   recall
   relevance
   retrieval effectiveness

false drops
USE information retrieval noise

false information
UF misinformation
BT information content
RT errors
   factual information

fault tolerance
BT (attributes of systems and equipment)
RT error correction
   error detection
   errors

fault tolerance (cont.)
    reliability

fax
USE facsimile transmission

feature extraction
BT optical character recognition
RT font learning

federated searching
BT searching

feedback
SN *Communications; not electronic feedback;*
    for relevance feedback, use "query by
    example."
UF user feedback
BT human communications
RT cybernetics
    evaluation
    query by example
    similarity

fees for service
BT pricing

fiber optics
UF optical fibers
BT telecommunications equipment
RT optical equipment

fiction
UF novels
BT literature
RT bestsellers
    books
    popular materials

field formatted data
UF fielded data
BT data
RT data parsing
    document schemas

fielded data
USE field formatted data

figurative language
USE idioms

figures of speech
USE idioms

file integrity
BT (attributes of information and data)

file integrity (cont.)
RT data corruption
    reliability

file servers
UF network servers
BT computers
NT image servers
RT client server systems
    local area networks

file structures
BT knowledge organization systems
NT hierarchical file structures

file systems
USE information storage and retrieval systems

file transfer protocol
USE ftp

file transfers
BT data transmission
NT downloading
    uploading
RT ftp

files
USE databases

filing
USE arrangement

filmstrips
BT images
RT motion picture films

filtering, information
USE information filtering

finance
BT (fields and disciplines)
RT economics
    financial management
    funding

financial information
BT domain information

financial management
BT management
NT budgeting
    cost recovery
    pricing
RT accounting
    database leasing

financial management (cont.)
    finance
    funding
    grants

fine arts
UF art
BT (fields and disciplines)
NT music
    performing arts
    visual arts

finite element analysis
BT mathematical methods

flat panel displays
BT display devices
NT LCD panels

flexible disks
USE floppy disks

flexible electronic displays
USE electronic paper

flexible manufacturing systems
BT technical and manufacturing operations

floppy disks
UF flexible disks
BT magnetic disks

floptical disks
BT optical disks

flow charting
UF workflow
BT systems analysis
RT systems design

focus groups
BT (persons and informal groups)
RT marketing
    user studies

folklore
USE social aspects

font learning
BT machine learning
    optical character recognition
RT feature extraction

forecasting
UF future
    prediction

forecasting (cont.)
BT (research and analytic methods)
RT Delphi studies
    environmental scanning
    planning
    predictive models
    strategic planning

foreign language materials
USE non English language materials

foreign languages
USE non English languages

forenames
USE personal names

form filling
BT data processing

formats, data
USE data formats

formatting
BT data processing

forms design
BT design

Fourier analysis
UF Fourier transforms
BT mathematical methods

Fourier transforms
USE Fourier analysis

frame based systems
USE knowledge bases

frames
BT web sites
RT hypermedia links

France
BT Europe

fraud
BT crime
NT plagiarism
RT errors

free text indexing
USE derivative indexing

free text searching
USE full text searching

freedom of information
BT intellectual freedom
RT confidential records
   disclosure
   information access
   public records

freedom of speech
SN *As it relates to information issues.*
BT intellectual freedom

freedom to read
BT intellectual freedom
RT banned materials

freeware
USE shareware

frequency of use
UF usage frequency
BT (attributes of information and data)
NT web site traffic
   word frequency
RT information use
   journal productivity

friends of libraries
UF friends of the library organizations
BT (organizations)
RT libraries

friends of the library organizations
USE friends of libraries

front ends
BT interfaces

ftp
UF anonymous ftp
   file transfer protocol
BT communications protocols
RT Internet
   computer mediated communications
   file transfers
   remote access

fugitive materials
USE grey literature

full motion video
USE motion video

full text databases
UF full text information systems
   full text systems
   text databases

full text databases (cont.)
   textbases
   textual databases
BT databases
RT bibliographic databases
   electronic books
   full text searching
   keywords

full text information systems
USE full text databases

full text retrieval
USE full text searching

full text searching
SN *Searching of text of full documents.*
UF free text searching
   full text retrieval
   natural language searching
   text retrieval
BT searching
RT full text databases
   keyword searching
   natural language processing
   online searching
   search engines
   stoplists
   subject searching

full text systems
USE full text databases

functional literacy
USE literacy

funding
BT management operations
NT library fines
   subsidies
RT accounting
   finance
   financial management

fusion
USE integration

future
USE forecasting

fuzzy logic
UF fuzzy set theory
BT set theory
RT rough set theory

53

fuzzy retrieval systems
UF fuzzy search
   partial match retrieval systems
BT information storage and retrieval systems
RT relevance ranking
   searching

fuzzy search
USE fuzzy retrieval systems

fuzzy set theory
USE fuzzy logic

game theory
BT mathematical models
RT mathematics

gatekeepers
UF bridge agents
   communications stars
   liaison agents
   technological gatekeepers
BT human information resources
RT boundary spanners
   early adopters
   information filtering
   information flow
   invisible colleges
   social networking

gateways
USE portals

gays and lesbians
UF lesbians
BT minorities and ethnic groups
RT cultural diversity

gender
UF sex
   sex discrimination
BT demographics
RT cultural diversity
   demographics
   men
   social discrimination
   women

genealogy
BT history
RT archives

general activities
BT (activities and operations)
NT collaboration
   customization

general activities (cont.)
   evaluation
   identification
   imaging
   integration
   maintenance
   modification
   monitoring
   selection
   standardization
   user multitasking

generalization
BT mental processes
RT abstraction

generic posting
SN *Posting of items under both specific and
   more general headings.*
BT subject indexing

generic relationships
USE genus species relationships

genetic algorithms
SN *Models of machine learning based on the
   concept of natural evolutionary processes.*
UF evolution based algorithms
BT algorithms

genomic information
BT biomedical information

genus species relationships
UF generic relationships
BT hierarchical relationships
RT attribute inheritance

geographic information systems
UF GIS
BT database management systems
RT earth sciences
   geography
   image information systems

geography
BT natural sciences
RT area studies
   cartography
   earth sciences
   geographic information systems
   regional aspects

geology
USE earth sciences

geopolitical aspects
BT (sociocultural aspects)
NT international aspects
  national aspects
  regional aspects

geospatial information
BT spatial information

Germany
BT Europe

gifts and exchanges
UF exchanges (of materials)
BT materials acquisitions

GIS
USE geographic information systems

gist
USE summarization

global aspects
USE international aspects

global village
USE information society

glossaries
USE dictionaries

goals
UF objectives
BT psychological aspects
RT planning

Google
USE search engines

gophers
BT information retrieval software
RT Internet
  remote access

government
BT political aspects
RT electronic government
  · government agencies
  government information
  public policy

government agencies
UF public agencies
  state agencies
BT (product and service providers)
NT electronic government

government agencies (cont.)
  state library agencies
RT government
  government information
  government libraries
  government publications
  public sector

government documents
USE government publications

government information
BT domain information
RT electronic government
  government
  government agencies

government libraries
BT libraries
NT national libraries
  state library agencies
RT government agencies
  state library agencies

government policy
USE public policy

government publications
UF government documents
  government records
BT publications
RT depository libraries
  government agencies
  technical reports

government records
USE government publications

grammar checkers
BT computer software applications

grammars
BT linguistics
NT case grammar
  large scale grammars

grants
BT subsidies
RT financial management
  refereeing

graph processing
BT information processing
RT graph theory
  graphs

graph theory
BT mathematical models
RT graph processing
    graphs
    mathematics

graphic images
USE graphics

graphical representations
USE graphics

graphical thesauri
BT thesauri

graphical user interfaces
UF GUI
    windows interfaces
BT interfaces
NT zoomable user interfaces
RT desktop metaphor
    icons
    menu based interfaces
    mice
    pointing devices
    trackballs

graphics
UF graphic images
    graphical representations
BT (documents by medium, physical form)
NT computer graphics
    data maps
    engineering drawings
    illustrations
    organization charts
RT illustrations
    images

graphics terminals
USE video display terminals

graphs
BT information representations
NT sociograms
RT graph processing
    graph theory

gray literature
USE grey literature

Great Britain
BT United Kingdom
NT England
    Scotland
    Wales

grey literature
SN *Fugitive literature; documents which are*
    difficult to locate or acquire because of such
    factors as unavailability, poor distribution
    or non-publication.
UF fugitive materials
    gray literature
    near-published literature
BT (documents by availability, access,
    organization)
RT alternative publications
    ephemera
    preprints
    technical reports

group decision support systems
BT decision support systems
RT collaboration
    groupware

group work
USE collaboration

groupware
SN *Computer software designed to support*
    collaborative work.
UF workgroup computing
BT computer software
RT collaboration
    group decision support systems
    teleconferencing

growth
BT (general processes)
RT bibliometrics
    change

GUI
USE graphical user interfaces

guide terms
USE node labels

guidelines
USE standards

Guyana
BT South America

hacking
BT computer crime

half life measures
SN *Half the period of time over which a journal*
    is used, either by citation or in circulation; a
    reflection of longevity of influence.

half life measures (cont.)
BT citation analysis
RT journal productivity
    obsolescence

hand held computers
USE personal digital assistants

handbooks
UF manuals
BT reference materials
RT user aids

Handheld Device Markup Language
USE HDML

handicapped persons
USE disabled persons

handwritten input
USE pen based computers

hard disks
BT magnetic disks

hardware, computer
USE computer equipment

hash coding
SN *Hashing is the transformation of a string of*
    characters into a usually shorter fixed-length
    value or key that represents the original
    string.
UF hashing
BT data processing
RT data reduction
    data storage devices

hashing
USE hash coding

HCI
USE human computer interaction

HDML
UF Handheld Device Markup Language
BT markup languages

headings
SN *Terms under which entries are made in*
    indexes or catalogs; usually used in the print
    context.
BT access points
RT index terms

health informatics
USE medical informatics

health sciences
USE medical science

hearing
BT sensory processes
RT acoustic data

hearing impaired persons
UF deaf persons
BT disabled persons

help systems
BT interfaces
    user aids
RT documentation
    error messages

heuristics
SN *Problem solving technique in which the most*
    appropriate solution found by alternative
    methods is selected at successive stages of a
    program for use in the next step of the
    program. Increases in efficiency may be
    traded off against finding a good solution
    which may not be the best possible solution.
BT problem solving

hidden web
USE invisible web

hierarchical classification
BT classification

hierarchical file structures
BT file structures

hierarchical models
BT analytic models
NT ranking

hierarchical relationships
UF broader term relationships
    narrower term relationships
      BT relationships
      NT relationships
BT semantic relationships
NT genus species relationships
    part whole relationships
RT cross references
    hierarchies
    thesauri

hierarchies
BT knowledge organization systems
RT categories
    hierarchical relationships

high density data storage
BT data storage devices
RT compression

high level languages
BT programming languages

high performance computing
USE supercomputers

high resolution displays
BT display devices

high schools
BT schools

higher education
USE colleges and universities

Hispanics
UF Latinos
BT minorities and ethnic groups

historical bibliography
USE analytical bibliography

historical records
USE archives

history
BT humanities
NT gcnealogy
    information science history
    oral history
RT archival science
    oral history

holdings (library)
USE library collections

holographic memory
BT computer memory
RT holography

holography
SN *Producing a three-dimensional image of an object with the use of a split laser beam.*
UF thrcc dimensional imagery
BT imaging
RT holographic memory

home education
UF home schooling
BT education

home information services
BT information services

home schooling
USE home education

home work
USE working at home

homebound patrons
BT library users

homography
UF polysemy
BT semantic relationships
RT disambiguation
    orthography
    qualifiers

honors
UF awards
BT cultural aspects

host computers
USE search services

host services
USE search services

HTML
SN *A markup language which permits linking of documents or parts of documents.*
UF hypertext markup language
BT markup languages
RT hypertext
    World Wide Web

http
UF hypertext transfer protocol
BT communications protocols

human behavior
UF behavior, human
BT psychological aspects
RT etiquette
    psychology
    social aspects
    social networking

human communications
BT communications activities
NT authorship

human communications (cont.)
    communication patterns
    disclosure
    editing
    explanation
    feedback
    informal communication
    negotiation
    nonverbal communication
    organizational communication
    public relations
    publishing
    reading
    scholarly communication
    spoken communication
    technical writing
RT communication skills
    human language
    social networking

human computer interaction
UF computer human interaction
    HCI
BT computer operations
NT ubiquitous computing
RT interfaces
    screen design

human computer interfaces
USE interfaces

human engineering
USE human factors

human factors engineering
USE ergonomics

human factors
SN *Study of how humans perform in a task-
    oriented environment interacting physically
    and psychologically with equipment, other
    people, or both.*
UF human engineering
BT (fields and disciplines)
NT ergonomics
    user expectations
RT repetitive stress injury
    usability

human indexing
USE manual indexing

human information resources
BT (persons and informal groups)
    information resources
NT boundary spanners

human information resources (cont.)
    gatekeepers
    subject experts
RT invisible colleges
    social networking

human language
BT language types
NT English language
    idioms
    jargon
    non English languages
RT human communications
    multilingualism

human memory
BT mental processes
NT long term memory
    short term memory
    visual memory

human productivity
BT (human attributes)
RT employment
    Lotka's law

human resource files
UF skills databases
BT nonbibliographic databases
RT human resources management

human resources management
BT management
RT employees
    human resource files
    information workers

human rights
BT legal aspects
NT civil rights

human speech
BT (human processes)
RT speech recognition
    speech synthesis
    spoken communication

humanities
BT (fields and disciplines)
NT history
    literature
    logic
    philosophy
    religion

Hungary
BT Europe

hybrid libraries
SN *Combination of physical and virtual*
collections and information resources.
BT libraries

hybrid search engines
SN *Search engines, such as Yahoo!, that*
combine the results of automated searches
with results generated by human editors.
BT search engines

hybrid systems
BT computer systems

hyperdocuments
USE hypertext

hyperlinks
USE hypermedia links

hypermedia
USE hypertext

hypermedia authoring
SN *For writing of linear texts, use "authorship."*
BT authorship
RT authoring software
    hypertext

hypermedia links
UF hyperlinks
    hypertext links
    link markers
BT access points
RT frames
    hypertext
    indexing term links
    link analysis

hypertext
SN *Documents containing links which allow*
immediate shifting between documents or
parts of documents.
UF hyperdocuments
    hypermedia
    metadocuments
BT (documents by availability, access,
    organization)
RT HTML
    hypermedia authoring
    hypermedia links
    World Wide Web

hypertext links
USE hypermedia links

hypertext markup language
USE HTML

hypertext transfer protocol
USE http

HyTime
USE metadata standards

I&R services
USE community information services

IAC
USE information analysis centers

iconography
USE images

icons
SN *Graphical interface objects.*
BT information representations
RT graphical user interfaces
    symbols

identification
BT general activities
RT computer access control
    security
    smart cards

identifiers
USE keywords

ideographs
BT writing systems
RT romanization

idioms
UF figurative language
    figures of speech
    tropes
BT human language
    information representations

ILL (interlibrary loans)
USE interlibrary loans

illiteracy
USE literacy

illustrations
BT graphics
RT graphics

illustrations (cont.)
    image information systems
    images

image analysis
BT image processing
RT image enhancement
    image indexing
    images

image compression
USE images

image data
USE images

image databases
BT nonbibliographic databases
RT image indexing
    images

image enhancement
BT image processing
RT image analysis

image indexing
BT (indexing by feature indexed)
RT content based indexing
    image analysis
    image databases
    image retrieval
    images

image information systems
UF pictorial information systems
BT database management systems
RT electronic document management systems
    geographic information systems
    illustrations
    image retrieval
    images

image processing
BT information processing
NT image analysis
    image enhancement
RT facsimile transmission
    images
    imaging
    signal processing

image retrieval
BT information retrieval
RT image indexing
    image information systems
    images

image servers
BT file servers

images
UF iconography
    image compression
    image data
BT visual materials
NT bit-mapped images
    digitized images
    filmstrips
    photo CD
    photographic slides
    photographs
RT computer graphics
    data
    graphics
    illustrations
    image analysis
    image databases
    image indexing
    image information systems
    image processing
    image retrieval
    imaging
    multimedia
    pictures

imaging
UF electronic imaging
BT general activities
NT holography
RT image processing
    images

impact factor
SN *Measure of citations to a given journal or*
    article, roughly interpreted as reflecting the
    influence and quality of journal or article.
BT citation analysis
RT journal productivity

implied knowledge
BT knowledge

incunabula
SN *Works of art or of human industry, of an*
    early epoch; especially, a book printed before
    CE 1500.
UF early books
BT rare materials

indecent materials
USE obscene materials

index entries
USE entries

index language construction
UF classification construction
   taxonomy construction
   thesaurus construction
BT organization of information
NT notation synthesis
RT automatic taxonomy generation
   classification schemes
   facet analysis
   index languages
   literary warrant
   semantic relationships
   thesauri
   thesaurus management
   vocabulary control

index language specificity
USE indexing specificity

index languages
UF indexing languages
   indexing vocabularies
   retrieval languages
   search languages
BT language types
NT classification schemes
   controlled vocabularies
RT index language construction
   index terms
   indexing
   indexing term links
   information retrieval
   information retrieval indexes
   role indicators
   subject indexing

index term weighting
USE weighting

index terms
SN *Terms used in subject indexing.*
UF indexing terms
   subject index terms
   used terms
BT terms
NT descriptors
   keyword spam
   keywords
   modifiers
   qualifiers
   subject headings
   top terms
RT citation order

index terms (cont.)
   classification
   concepts
   headings
   index languages
   indexing
   search terms
   subject indexes
   thesauri
   weighting

indexer consistency
SN *The extent to which different indexers, or the
   same indexer at different times, assign the
   same index terms to a given document.*
UF consistency, indexer
BT (human attributes)
RT effectiveness
   evaluation
   indexing
   reliability

indexing
BT organization of information
NT (indexing by feature indexed)
   (indexing by item indexed)
   (indexing by method used)
RT abstracting and indexing service bureaus
   authority files
   classification
   classification schemes
   facet analysis
   index languages
   index terms
   indexer consistency
   indexing exhaustivity
   indexing specificity
   information retrieval indexes
   literary warrant
   weighting

indexing depth
SN *The combination of the average number of
   terms assigned to documents in an indexing
   system and the specificity of those terms.*
BT (attributes of information and data)
RT indexing exhaustivity
   indexing specificity

indexing discrimination
SN *Degree to which an indexing term
   contributes to how well documents are
   distinguished from each other through
   indexing.*
BT (attributes of information and data)

indexing exhaustivity
SN *The average number of terms assigned to each document in an indexing system.*
BT (attributes of information and data)
RT indexing
    indexing depth
    indexing specificity

indexing languages
USE index languages

indexing services
USE abstracting and indexing service bureaus

indexing specificity
SN *The extent to which the breadth of the terms assigned to documents matches the breadth of the subjects of the documents; specificity is independent of the breadth of the terms themselves.*
UF index language specificity
BT (attributes of information and data)
RT indexing
    indexing depth
    indexing exhaustivity
    subject indexing

indexing term links
SN *Indications that two index terms assigned to the same document are connected in some way.*
BT knowledge organization systems
RT hypermedia links
    index languages
    link analysis
    postcoordinate indexing
    role indicators
    subject indexing

indexing terms
USE index terms

indexing vocabularies
USE index languages

India
BT Asia

Indians (American)
USE Native Americans

indicators
UF economic indicators
BT information content
RT economics

indirect collective references
SN *References made to all references cited in a directly cited publication, e.g. "and references therein."*
BT bibliographic references

individual differences
UF personal styles
BT psychological aspects
RT cognitive styles

induction
BT reasoning

industry
USE business

inference
UF deduction
BT reasoning

infixes
USE affixes

infometrics
USE informetrics

informal communication
BT human communications
RT organizational communication
    spoken communication

informatics
SN *An area of activity which represents the conjunction of information science and information technology.*
BT information science
NT bioinformatics
    museum informatics
    social informatics
RT information technology
    informetrics

information access
UF availability of information
BT access to resources
NT subject access
RT bibliographic access
    freedom of information
    library access

information age
USE information society

information analysis centers
UF clearinghouses (information analysis)

63

information analysis centers (cont.)
> IAC
> information centers (information analysis)

BT (product and service providers)

information and reference skills
SN *Skills used in finding information, searching,*
> *etc.*

BT skills
RT bibliographic instruction
> information literacy
> librarianship

information and referral services
USE community information services

information architects
BT information professionals
RT information architecture

information architecture
SN *The design, organization, and labeling of*
> *web sites, intranets, online communities and*
> *software to enable users to locate and*
> *manage information.*

BT information science
RT information architects
> information discovery
> taxonomies

information associations
BT professional associations

information attribution
BT information operations

information brokers
BT (product and service providers)
RT information industry
> information professionals

information centers (information analysis)
USE information analysis centers

information centers (libraries)
USE libraries

information centers (special libraries)
USE special libraries

information channels
BT (communications media)
RT information flow

information content
UF content

information content (cont.)
BT (knowledge and information)
NT algorithms
> concepts
> contextual information
> criteria
> data
> default values
> domain information
> factual information
> false information
> indicators
> knowledge
> news
> proper names
> topics
> trade secrets

RT content analysis
> information use

information discovery
SN *Process of searching for and finding*
> *information. For extracting patterns within*
> *data, use "knowledge discovery."*

BT information operations
NT information retrieval
> information seeking

RT information architecture

information dissemination
SN *Active and intentional sharing of*
> *information; contrast with "information*
> *flow."*

UF dissemination, information
> electronic information dissemination
> information distribution

BT information operations
RT information flow
> information resources management
> information transfer
> publishing
> resource sharing
> scholarly communication
> SDI services

information distribution
USE information dissemination

information economics
USE economics of information

information engineering
USE knowledge engineering

information entropy
SN *Movement toward disorder or randomness of*

information entropy (cont.)
   information.
BT (information and data processes)
RT information theory

information exchange
USE information transfer

information exchange formats
USE interchange formats

information explosion
UF publication explosion
BT (information and data processes)
RT information overload
   publishing

information extraction
USE data mining

information filtering
UF filtering, information
BT information operations
NT collaborative filtering
   content filtering
RT boundary spanners
   censorship
   gatekeepers
   information overload
   invisible colleges
   SDI services
   social networking

information flow
SN *Passive and unintentional spread of*
   information; contrast with "information
   dissemination."
BT (information and data processes)
NT cross disciplinary fertilization
   transborder data flow
RT boundary spanners
   gatekeepers
   information channels
   information dissemination
   information resources management
   information transfer
   interdisciplinarity
   invisible colleges
   social networking

information gathering
USE information retrieval

information harvesting
USE knowledge discovery

information highway
USE telecommunications networks

information industry
BT (product and service providers)
NT online industry
RT database producers
   information brokers
   information infrastructure
   information sector
   information utilities
   publishers
   search services
   telecommunications industry

information infrastructure
BT socioeconomic aspects
RT abstracting and indexing service bureaus
   database producers
   information industry
   information utilities
   libraries
   publishers
   search services

information life cycle
BT (information and data processes)
RT aging of materials
   obsolescence

information literacy
UF information skills
BT literacy
RT bibliographic instruction
   computer literacy
   information and reference skills
   information needs
   information use
   user training

information management
USE information resources management

information mapping
SN *Use for, e.g., mapping of queries to*
   documents, or of one vocabulary to another.
UF metamapping
   subject switching
BT information operations
RT controlled vocabularies
   cross matching
   searching
   switching languages

information models
BT analytic models

information models (cont.)
NT cognitive models
  information space
  spreading activation
RT information theory

information needs
UF user information needs
  user needs
BT (human attributes)
RT information literacy
  information resources management
  information seeking
  information use
  needs assessment
  users

information networks
USE telecommunications networks

information objects
USE data objects

information operation closings
USE library closings

information operations
BT (activities and operations)
NT information attribution
  information discovery
  information dissemination
  information filtering
  information mapping
  information production
  information resources management
  information transfer
  information use
  organization of information
  summarization
  translation
  transliteration

information overload
UF overload, information
BT psychological aspects
RT information explosion
  information filtering
  information society
  information use

information policy
BT public policy
RT data security
  information society
  legal aspects
  political aspects

information policy (cont.)
  privacy

information processing
BT computer operations
NT graph processing
  image processing
  query processing
  text processing
RT automatic indexing
  information science
  knowledge representation

information production
UF knowledge production
BT information operations
RT data processing
  information transfer
  publishing

information products
USE publications

information professionals
UF information professions
  information specialists
  professionals, information
BT information workers
NT archivists
  computer programmers
  editors
  information architects
  information scientists
  intermediaries
  librarians
  media specialists
  records managers
  translators
  web designers
RT career development
  information brokers
  professional competencies

information professions
USE information professionals

information representations
BT (knowledge and information)
NT abbreviations
  acronyms
  anaphora
  bar codes
  breadcrumbs
  character sets
  chemical connection tables
  chemical structure models

information representations (cont.)
    diacriticals
    document titles
    graphs
    icons
    idioms
    keyframes
    metaphors
    multilingual information
    node labels
    notation
    search histories
    symbols
    terminology
    trademarks
    writing systems

information resources
BT (documents by information content, purpose)
NT databases
    human information resources
    Internet information resources
    reference materials
RT information resources management
    information storage and retrieval systems
    publications

information resources management
UF information management
    IRM
    resource management (information)
BT information operations management
NT collection management
    content management
    database management
    document management
    records management
    thesaurus management
RT information dissemination
    information flow
    information needs
    information resources
    library management

information retrieval
UF information gathering
BT information discovery
NT answer passage retrieval
    audio retrieval
    document retrieval
    image retrieval
    multilingual retrieval
RT document retrieval
    index languages
    information retrieval models
    information retrieval software

information retrieval (cont.)
    information science
    information storage and retrieval systems
    natural language processing
    retrieval effectiveness

information retrieval agents
USE intelligent agents

information retrieval indexes
BT (documents by information content, purpose)
NT alphabetico classed indexes
    author indexes
    author-prepared indexes
    book indexes
    citation indexes
    cumulative indexes
    keyword indexes
    periodical indexes
    subject indexes
RT abstracting and indexing service bureaus
    bibliographic databases
    bibliographies
    catalogs (bibliographic)
    index languages
    indexing
    overlap

information retrieval models
SN *Models and techniques underlying*
    information retrieval systems. Contrast with
    "search strategies" which focuses on the user.
BT analytic models
NT associative retrieval
    Bayesian functions
    Boolean logic
    inverse document frequency
    latent semantic analysis
    probabilistic retrieval
    unified retrieval models
    vector space models
RT algorithms
    information retrieval

information retrieval noise
UF false drops
BT (attributes of information and data)
RT evaluation
    failure analysis
    fallout
    precision
    recall
    relevance
    retrieval effectiveness

information retrieval software
UF retrieval software
BT computer software applications
NT gophers
information storage and retrieval systems
intelligent agents
search engines
RT document retrieval
information retrieval
online searching

information reuse
SN *Use of existing components of information
or content to develop new documents.*
BT information use

information science
SN *Study of the gathering, organizing, storing,
retrieving, and dissemination of information.
Note: Use sparingly only for materials
pertaining broadly to the topic.*
UF library and information science
LIS
BT (fields and disciplines)
NT archival science
domain naming system
economics of information
informatics
information architecture
information science history
information theory
knowledge management
RT cognitive science
computer science
cybernetics
information processing
information retrieval
information science education
information scientists
information technology
librarianship
linguistics

information science education
BT education
RT information science
information science schools
library education

information science history
BT history
information science

information science schools
UF information studies schools
schools of information science

information science schools (cont.)
BT colleges and universities
RT information science education
library schools

information scientists
BT information professionals
RT information science

information sector
BT economic sectors
RT information industry
information society
information workers

information seeking
BT information discovery
NT browsing
navigation
searching
RT information needs
information use
social networking

information seeking behavior
USE search behavior

information services
SN *For publishing and production services, use
"database producers" or "abstracting and
indexing services."*
UF expert services
BT library operations
NT community information services
current awareness services
home information services
litigation support
RT abstracting and indexing service bureaus
database producers
library and archival services
library closings
reference services
value added

information skills
USE information literacy

information society
SN *The concept of society in which information
is the driving force of the economy, with
global availability of communication and
large-scale production of information.*
UF global village
information age
BT socioeconomic aspects
RT economics of information

information society (cont.)
    end users
    information overload
    information policy
    information sector
    social aspects

information space
SN *The set of objects and relations among them*
    held by an information system, e.g. a
    database or the World Wide Web.
BT information models
RT topic maps
    vector space models

information specialists
USE information professionals

information storage and retrieval systems
UF content management systems
    electronic information systems
    file systems
    information systems
    online information retrieval systems
    online systems
    search systems
BT information retrieval software
    information technology
NT fact retrieval systems
    fuzzy retrieval systems
    management information systems
    paper based information systems
    personal information systems
    reference retrieval systems
RT aboutness
    content management
    information resources
    information retrieval
    online searching
    pertinence
    relevance

information studies schools
USE information science schools

information superhighway
USE telecommunications networks

information systems
USE information storage and retrieval systems

information technology
SN *Encompasses all forms of technology used to*
    create, store, exchange, and use information
    in its various forms. Usually includes
    computer technology and telecommunication

information technology (cont.)
    systems. Note: Use sparingly only for
    materials pertaining broadly to the topic.
BT (hardware, software, and equipment)
NT information storage and retrieval systems
RT informatics
    information science
    library equipment
    telecommunications

information theory
UF communications theory
BT information science
RT epistemology
    information entropy
    information models

information transfer
UF information exchange
    knowledge transfer
    transfer of information
BT information operations
RT information dissemination
    information flow
    information production
    information use

information use
UF data utilization
    document use
    information utilization
    library use
    use of information
BT information operations
NT information reuse
RT bibliometrics
    frequency of use
    information content
    information literacy
    information needs
    information overload
    information seeking
    information transfer
    library users
    user studies
    users

information user studies
USE user studies

information users
USE users

information utilities
BT (product and service providers)
RT bibliographic utilities

information utilities (cont.)
    information industry
    information infrastructure
    online industry
    search services

information utilization
USE information use

information visualization
USE electronic visualization

information workers
UF knowledge workers
BT (persons and informal groups)
NT information professionals
    library personnel
RT employment
    human resources management
    information sector
    volunteers

informetrics
SN *Statistical and mathematical treatment of*
    library, documentation and information
    problems.
UF cliometrics
    infometrics
BT measurement
NT bibliometrics
    scientometrics
    sociometrics
    webometrics
RT informatics

initialisms
USE acronyms

injury
BT (human processes)
NT repetitive stress injury

innovation
UF technological innovation
BT socioeconomic activities
NT diffusion of innovation
RT change
    diffusion of innovation
    early adopters
    entrepreneurship
    patents
    technology impact

input equipment
BT computer peripherals
NT joysticks

input equipment (cont.)
    keyboards
    light pens
    pointing devices
    scanners
RT sensors
    video display terminals

instant messaging
BT message systems

institutional libraries
BT libraries
NT prison libraries

instruction
USE education

instructional technology
USE educational technology

instrumentation
BT (hardware, software, and equipment)
NT sensors
RT display devices
    lasers

integrated circuits
BT computer equipment
NT LSI
RT microcomputers
    microprocessors

integrated library systems
UF integrated online library systems
BT integrated systems
RT library automation

integrated online library systems
USE integrated library systems

integrated systems
BT (hardware, software, and equipment)
NT integrated library systems
RT computer systems
    systems integration

integration
UF fusion
BT general activities

integration, systems
USE systems integration

intellectual assets
USE intellectual property

intellectual capital
USE intellectual property

intellectual freedom
BT civil rights
NT academic freedom
   freedom of information
   freedom of speech
   freedom to read
RT banned materials
   censorship

intellectual property
SN *Intellectual material that has commercial*
   value.
UF intellectual assets
   intellectual capital
BT legal aspects
NT copyright
   fair use
   public domain
   public lending right
RT copyright piracy
   patents
   plagiarism
   trade secrets
   trademarks

intelligence
BT psychological aspects
RT creativity
   military intelligence

intelligent agents
SN *Retrieval tools which routinely scan*
   networks and systems for information
   meeting specified criteria and present the
   retrieved information to the user.
UF information retrieval agents
   knowbots
   search agents
BT information retrieval software
RT artificial intelligence
   message filtering

intelligent interfaces
BT interfaces
RT artificial intelligence
   natural language interfaces

interactive design
USE computer aided design

interactive systems
SN *Limit to discussions in which interactivity is*
   the primary issue. Do not use for all systems

interactive systems (cont.)
   which happen to be interactive.
BT computer systems
RT interfaces

interchange formats
UF electronic document interchange formats
   exchange formats
   information exchange formats
BT data formats
NT MARC formats
   Open Document Architecture
RT electronic data interchange

interdisciplinarity
BT (attributes of information and data)
RT boundary spanners
   cross disciplinary fertilization
   information flow
   multidisciplinary information

interfaces
SN *Limited to interfaces between humans and*
   computers.
UF computer human interfaces
   human computer interfaces
   man machine interfaces
   user system interfaces
BT computer systems
NT audio interfaces
   command driven interfaces
   direct manipulation interfaces
   error messages
   front ends
   graphical user interfaces
   help systems
   intelligent interfaces
   menu based interfaces
   natural language interfaces
   portals
   touch screen interfaces
RT command languages
   cybernetics
   external cognition
   human computer interaction
   interactive systems
   navigation
   screen design

interlibrary loans
UF ILL (interlibrary loans)
BT document delivery
   library technical services
RT collaboration
   resource sharing

intermediaries
SN *Information professionals who perform a task on behalf of an end user.*
BT information professionals

intermediate index languages
USE switching languages

intermediate lexicons
USE switching languages

international aspects
UF global aspects
BT geopolitical aspects
RT (countries and regions)
international librarianship
language barriers
transborder data flow

international data flow
USE transborder data flow

international librarianship
BT librarianship
RT comparative librarianship
international aspects

International Patent Classification
UF IPC
BT classification schemes

International Standard Bibliographic Description
SN *Specifies the requirements for description and identification of information resources. Maintained by the International Federation of Library Associations and Institutions - Section on Cataloguing.*
UF ISBD
BT standards

International Standard Book Number
USE ISBN

International Standard Film Number
USE ISFN

International Standard Music Number
USE ISMN

International Standard Record Code
USE ISRC

International Standard Serial Number
USE ISSN

Internet
UF cyberspace
information highway
information superhighway
BT telecommunications networks
NT World Wide Web
RT e-mail list servers
ftp
gophers
Internet search systems
National Research and Education Network
network computers
newsgroups
telnet
Web TV

Internet computers
USE network computers

Internet information resources
BT information resources

Internet search systems
SN *Systems which search Internet files, such as Web pages and newsgroups, and retrieve information in response to queries.*
UF bots
crawlers
spiders (automatic searching)
wanderers
webbots
BT search engines
RT Internet
World Wide Web

Internet service providers
UF ISPs
BT telecommunications industry

Internet telephony
SN *Transmission of telephone calls over the Internet.*
BT telephony
RT telephones

interoperability
BT (attributes of systems and equipment)
RT Open Archives Initiative
Protocol for Metadata Harvesting specification

interpretation (linguistic)
USE translation

interpreters (linguistic)
USE translators

interviews
BT spoken communication
NT presearch interviews
   reference interviews

intranets
BT (communications networks)

intrusion prevention and detection
BT security

inventory
BT management operations
RT accounting

inverse document frequency
SN *Frequency of a particular term appearing across all documents in a collection. Unique words have a high IDF, while common words have a low IDF.*
BT information retrieval models

inverted files
SN *For each term that appears in a collection of documents, a list of document numbers containing that term.*
BT (documents by information content, purpose)
RT organization of information

invisible colleges
BT academic communities
RT boundary spanners
   gatekeepers
   human information resources
   information filtering
   information flow
   social networking
   subject experts

invisible web
SN *Data freely reachable through the Web, but not covered by the search engines.*
UF deep web
   hidden web
BT World Wide Web

IPC
USE International Patent Classification

Ireland
BT Europe

IRM
USE information resources management

ISBD
USE International Standard Bibliographic
   Description

ISBN
UF International Standard Book Number
   standard book numbers
BT document surrogates
RT books
   standards

ISFN
UF International Standard Film Number
   standard film numbers
BT document surrogates
RT motion picture films
   standards

ISMN
UF International Standard Music Number
   standard music numbers
BT document surrogates
RT music
   standards

ISO
USE standards developing
   organizations

ISPs
USE Internet service providers

ISRC
UF International Standard Record Code
   standard record codes
BT document surrogates
RT audio recordings
   standards

ISSN
UF International Standard Serial Number
   standard serial numbers
BT document surrogates
RT serials
   standards

Italy
BT Europe

jail libraries
USE prison libraries

Japan
BT Asia

jargon
BT human language

jobbers
UF book jobbers
BT vendors
RT book vendors
    materials acquisitions

joint authorship
UF coauthorship
BT authorship
RT collaboration

journal articles
USE periodical articles

journal indexes
USE periodical indexes

journal productivity
SN *Measure of the number of articles*
    contributed to the literature on a topic by a
    given journal.
UF productivity (journals)
BT bibliometrics
RT frequency of use
    half life measures
    impact factor
    journals

journals
SN Scholarly journals.
UF scholarly journals
BT periodicals
NT electronic journals
RT journal productivity
    periodical articles
    periodical indexes
    primary literature
    refereeing
    reprints
    scholarly publishing

joysticks
BT input equipment
RT video games

judgment
BT mental processes

jukeboxes (CD-ROM drives)
USE multidisk drives

junior high schools
USE middle schools

KDD
USE knowledge discovery

Kenya
BT Africa

key words
USE keywords

keyboarding errors
USE typographical errors

keyboarding
USE data entry

keyboards
BT input equipment
RT repetitive stress injury

keyframes
SN *Single video frames used to represent a video*
    or to reference subsequent frames.
BT information representations
RT keywords
    video clips

keying
USE data entry

keyphrases
USE keywords

keyword in context indexes
USE KWIC indexes

keyword indexes
UF natural language indexes
BT information retrieval indexes
NT concordances
    KWIC indexes
    KWOC indexes
    permuted indexes
RT keywords

keyword out of context indexes
USE KWOC indexes

keyword searching
BT searching
RT full text searching
    keywords

keyword spam
SN *Spurious or repeated keywords in website*
    meta data to create intentionally irrelevant
    search results.

keyword spam (cont.)
UF search engine persuasion
  spamdexing
BT index terms
RT relevance ranking

keyword tagging
USE subject indexing

keywords
SN *Terms, frequently single words, used in uncontrolled indexing.*
UF identifiers
  key words
  keyphrases
  natural language indexing
  subject metadata
  uncontrolled indexing
BT index terms
RT full text databases
  keyframes
  keyword indexes
  keyword searching
  stoplists
  subject headings
  subject indexing

kiosks
SN *Small, stand-alone structures which provide public information by means of a computer display and keyboard or touch screen.*
BT (hardware, software, and equipment)

KM
USE knowledge management

knowbots
USE intelligent agents

knowledge
SN *Meaning attached to information.*
BT information content
NT common sense knowledge
  domain knowledge
  implied knowledge
  situated knowledge
  system knowledge
  task knowledge
RT concepts
  domain information
  knowledge bases
  knowledge engineering

knowledge acquisition
SN *Acquisition of knowledge modeled on that of a domain expert for use in expert systems.*

knowledge acquisition (cont.)
BT knowledge engineering
RT expert systems
  knowledge bases
  learning

knowledge based systems
USE knowledge bases

knowledge bases
UF frame based systems
  knowledge based systems
  knowledgebase management systems
  knowledgebases
  rule based systems
BT knowledge organization systems
RT artificial intelligence
  common sense knowledge
  databases
  domain knowledge
  expert systems
  knowledge
  knowledge acquisition
  knowledge engineering

knowledge discovery
SN *Process of generating patterns in a large group of data to predict future behavior. Includes acquisition, representation, storage, analysis, visualization, interpretation, and deployment.*
UF information harvesting
  KDD
BT automatic extracting
NT data mining
  text mining
  web mining
RT pattern recognition

knowledge engineering
SN *Branch of artificial intelligence focused on building intelligent systems to model the knowledge and problem solving techniques of the domain expert.*
UF information engineering
BT artificial intelligence
NT knowledge acquisition
  knowledge modeling
  knowledge representation
RT artificial intelligence
  expert systems
  knowledge
  knowledge bases

knowledge management
SN *Activities involved in discovering or*

knowledge management (cont.)
*acquiring, organizing, disseminating, and
implementing knowledge.*
UF KM
BT information science

knowledge modeling
SN *Developing abstract models of a knowledge
domain or behavior, drawing on ontologies of
entities, concepts or actions and their
relationships.*
BT knowledge engineering
RT domain knowledge
   ontologies

knowledge organization systems
BT (knowledge and information)
NT access points
   arrangement
   call numbers
   cataloging rules
   categories
   data formats
   data structures
   facets
   file structures
   hierarchies
   indexing term links
   knowledge bases
   locators
   matrices
   paradigms
   persistent identifiers
   role indicators
   sort sequences
   topic threads
RT organization of information
   search strategies

knowledge production
USE information production

knowledge representation
SN *Subfield of artificial intelligence concerned
with designing and using systems for storing
knowledge, the facts and rules about a subject
and its associations. Resulting
representations serve as surrogates of an
entity, concept, or action, rendered in a
computer usable form.*
UF data representation
   representation, knowledge
BT knowledge engineering
RT classification
   data presentation
   domain analysis

knowledge representation (cont.)
information processing
ontologies

knowledge transfer
USE information transfer

knowledge workers
USE information workers

knowledgebase management systems
USE knowledge bases

knowledgebases
USE knowledge bases

known item searching
BT searching

Korea
BT Asia

KWIC indexes
UF keyword in context indexes
   rotated term indexes
BT keyword indexes
RT document titles

KWOC indexes
UF keyword out of context indexes
BT keyword indexes
RT document titles

labor unions
UF unions, labor
BT (organizations)
RT employees
   employment

LAN
USE local area networks

language
BT (language)
RT linguistic analysis
   linguistics

language barriers
BT cultural aspects
RT cross cultural aspects
   international aspects
   multilingual retrieval
   multilingualism
   non English languages

language types
BT (language)
NT command languages
    data definition languages
    human language
    index languages
    markup languages
    programming languages
    query languages
    sublanguages

language understanding
USE natural language comprehension

laptop computers
USE personal computers

large print materials
BT print publications
RT books
    visually impaired persons

large scale grammars
BT grammars

large scale integration
USE LSI

laser disks
USE optical disks

lasers
BT (hardware, software, and equipment)
RT instrumentation
    optical disks

latent semantic analysis
SN *Statistical technique to improve information*
    retrieval by inducing similarities among
    terms through revealing indirect associations
    between data.
UF LSA
    semantic indexing
BT information retrieval models
RT data mining

Latin America
BT regions
RT Mexico
    South America

Latinos
USE Hispanics

law
UF criminal justice

law (cont.)
    legislation
    regulations
BT (fields and disciplines)
RT contracts
    copyright
    crime
    law libraries
    legal aspects
    legal information
    legislative libraries and reference services
    litigation support
    social sciences

law libraries
BT special libraries
NT legislative libraries and reference services
RT law

LCD panels
UF liquid crystal displays
BT flat panel displays

leadership
BT psychological aspects

learned society publishers
BT publishers

learning
SN *Human learning; for artificial or machine*
    learning, use "machine learning."
BT educational activities
NT distance learning
    lifelong learning
    perceptual learning
RT knowledge acquisition
    machine learning

learning centers
USE media centers

learning disabled persons
BT disabled persons

learning resource centers
USE media centers

leasing, database
USE database leasing

legal aspects
BT (sociocultural aspects)
NT admissibility of records
    censorship
    crime

legal aspects (cont.)
 human rights
 intellectual property
 legal deposit
 liability
 litigation
 security
 usage agreements
RT digital rights management
 information policy
 law
 legal information

legal deposit
SN *For copyright purposes.*
UF compulsory deposit
BT legal aspects
RT copyright

legal information
BT domain information
RT law
 legal aspects

legibility
BT (attributes of information and data)
RT character sets

legislation
USE law

legislative libraries and reference services
BT law libraries
RT law

lending (library materials)
USE library circulation

lesbians
USE gays and lesbians

letter by letter arrangement
BT alphabetical arrangement

letters
USE correspondence

lexemes
USE word roots

lexical analysis
BT linguistic analysis
RT lexicography

lexicography
BT (fields and disciplines)

lexicography (cont.)
NT computational lexicography
RT dictionaries
 lexical analysis
 linguistics
 thesauri
 words

liability
BT legal aspects

liaison agents
USE gatekeepers

librarians
SN *For librarians in specific types of libraries,*
 also use the type of library, e.g., "special
 libraries."
BT information professionals
 library personnel
NT reference librarians
RT library associations

librarianship
SN *For specific types of librarianship, also use*
 the type, e.g., "academic libraries."
UF library science
BT (fields and disciplines)
NT comparative librarianship
 international librarianship
RT information and reference skills
 information science
 libraries
 library schools

libraries
UF information centers (libraries)
 learning centers
BT (product and service providers)
NT academic libraries
 branch libraries
 central libraries
 children's libraries
 depository libraries
 digital libraries
 government libraries
 hybrid libraries
 institutional libraries
 media centers
 mobile libraries
 public libraries
 research libraries
 small libraries
 special libraries
 virtual libraries
RT archives

libraries (cont.)
 friends of libraries
 information infrastructure
 librarianship
 library access
 library and archival services
 library associations
 library automation
 library buildings
 library management
 library materials
 library networks
 problem patrons

library access
BT access to resources
RT information access
 libraries

library acquisitions
USE materials acquisitions

library administration
USE library management

library administrators
USE managers

library and archival services
BT library operations
NT children's services
 library outreach services
 library programs
 library technical services
 off campus library services
 reader services
 reference services
 young adult services
RT archival science
 archives
 archivists
 information services
 libraries
 library automation
 storytelling

library and information science
USE information science

library assistants
USE paraprofessional library personnel

library associations
BT professional associations
RT librarians
 libraries

library automation
UF electronic libraries
BT computer applications
NT computerized cataloging
RT integrated library systems
 libraries
 library and archival services
 virtual libraries

library binding
BT binding

library boards
UF boards (library)
 library trustees
 trustees (library)
BT library management

library buildings
BT buildings
RT libraries
 library equipment

library circulation
UF borrowing (library materials)
 charging systems
 lending (library materials)
 library circulation
 loans (library materials)
BT library technical services
RT overdue materials
 reader services

library closings
UF branch library closings
 information operation
 closings
BT library operations
RT information services

library collections
UF book collections
 book stock
 holdings (library)
BT collections
RT library materials

library education
BT education
RT information science education
 library schools

library equipment
BT (hardware, software, and equipment)
NT library security systems
 library shelving

library equipment (cont.)
RT information technology
    library buildings
    library suppliers
    library supplies
    materials storage

library exhibits and displays
UF displays (library)
    exhibits and displays (library)
BT library operations

library extension
USE library outreach services

library fines
BT funding
    library operations
RT overdue materials

library instruction
USE bibliographic instruction

library management
UF library administration
BT management
NT library boards
RT information resources management
    libraries

library materials
BT (documents by availability, access,
    organization)
NT overdue materials
RT banned materials
    collection management
    libraries
    library collections

library networks
UF library systems
BT (communications networks)
RT academic libraries
    collaboration
    libraries
    telecommunications networks

Library of Congress Classification
BT classification schemes

Library of Congress Subject Headings
BT subject heading lists

library operations
BT (activities and operations)
NT access to resources

library operations (cont.)
    backlogs
    bibliographic control
    bibliography construction
    bibliotherapy
    book collecting
    database leasing
    document delivery
    document handling
    document retrieval
    documentation
    information services
    library and archival services
    library closings
    library exhibits and displays
    library fines
    library user profiles
    materials preservation
    output reformatting
    photocopying

library outreach services
UF community based library services
    library extension
BT library and archival services
RT community information services

library patrons
USE library users

library personnel
UF library staff
BT information workers
NT librarians
    paraprofessional library personnel
RT media specialists

library policy
BT policy

library programs
SN *Services for users. For library-oriented*
    software use "library automation."
UF adult programs
BT library and archival services

library reserves
BT access to resources
NT electronic reserves

library schools
BT colleges and universities
RT information science schools
    librarianship
    library education

library science
USE librarianship

library security systems
UF book detection systems
   theft detection systems
BT library equipment
RT library security

library security
UF book security
BT security
RT library security systems

library shelving
UF compact shelving
   library stacks
   mobile shelving
   movable shelving
   rolling stacks
   shelving, library
   stacks, library
BT library equipment
RT materials storage

library stacks
USE library shelving

library staff
USE library personnel

library suppliers
BT vendors
RT library equipment
   library supplies

library supplies
BT (hardware, software, and equipment)
NT chalk
RT library equipment
   library suppliers

library support staff
USE paraprofessional library
   personnel

library surveys
BT surveys
RT user studies

library systems
USE library networks

library technical assistants
USE paraprofessional library personnel

library technical services
BT library and archival services
NT cataloging
   collection management
   interlibrary loans
   library circulation
   materials processing
RT backlogs
   binding
   materials preservation

library technicians
USE paraprofessional library
   personnel

library trustees
USE library boards

library use
USE information use

library user profiles
UF search profiles
BT library operations
   personal information
   user profiles
RT search strategies
   SDI serviccs

library user services
USE reader services

library users
UF borrowers
   library patrons
   patrons, library
BT users
NT homebound patrons
   problem patrons
RT information use

library weeks
BT promotional activities

licenses
BT (documents by information content, purpose)
RT contracts

life sciences
USE natural sciences

lifelong learning
BT learning
RT adult education
   continuing education
   distance learning

light pens
UF light wands
BT input equipment

light wands
USE light pens

likeness
USE similarity

limited area networks
USE local area networks

limited cataloging
USE minimal cataloging

linear programming
UF linear systems
BT mathematical methods

linear systems
USE linear programming

linguistic analysis
BT mental processes
   text processing
NT disambiguation
   lexical analysis
   morphological analysis
   semantic analysis
   syntactic analysis
RT language
   linguistics

linguistic elements
BT (language)
NT adjectives
   adverbs
   capitalization
   morphemes
   nouns
   orthography
   paragraphs
   phonemes
   phrases
   punctuation
   sentences
   verbs
   word roots
   words

linguistic parsing
USE syntactic analysis

linguistics
BT (fields and disciplines)

linguistics (cont.)
NT computational linguistics
   etymology
   grammars
   phonetics
   pragmatics
   semantics
   sublanguages
   syntactics
RT cognitive science
   information science
   language
   lexicography
   linguistic analysis
   semiotics

link analysis
BT webometrics
RT hypermedia links
   indexing term links

link markers
USE hypermedia links

liquid crystal displays
USE LCD panels

LIS
USE information science

listservs
USE e-mail list servers

literacy
SN *The ability to read and write; for the ability*
   to employ information effectively use
   "information literacy"; for the ability to
   employ computers use "computer literacy."
UF adult literacy
   functional literacy
   illiteracy
BT cultural aspects
NT computer literacy
   information literacy

literary reviews
USE book reviews

literary warrant
SN *Justification for inclusion of a term for a*
   concept in an indexing language on the basis
   of its occurrence in the literature.
BT warrant
RT index language construction
   indexing
   user warrant

literary warrant (cont.)
　　vocabulary control

literature
UF belles lettres
BT humanities
NT fiction
　　nonfiction
　　poetry
RT nonfiction

literature reviews
SN *More or less comprehensive studies of the*
　　publications of a subject.
UF reviews of the literature
BT reviews
RT summarization

litigation
SN *Restricted to litigation within the information*
　　industry.
BT legal aspects

litigation support
BT information services
RT law

live reference services
USE electronic reference services

loans (library materials)
USE library circulation

local area networks
UF LAN
　　limited area networks
　　local networks
BT telecommunications networks
RT file servers
　　office automation

local networks
USE local area networks

location breadcrumbs
SN *Display of the location of an item of content*
　　metadata in a taxonomy.
BT breadcrumbs

locators
SN *Devices which indicate the position of*
　　information items within files.
UF page references
　　reference locators
BT knowledge organization systems
NT URL

locators (cont.)
RT call numbers
　　URI

logic
BT humanities
NT Boolean logic
　　predicate logic
　　propositional logic
RT logic programming
　　mathematics

logic programming
BT computer programming
RT logic

logical operators
USE Boolean logic

long term memory
BT human memory

longitudinal studies
BT research methods

loose leaf services
BT reference materials

Lotka's law
SN *A bibliometric principle which describes*
　　author productivity quantitatively.
BT bibliometrics
RT authorship
　　human productivity
　　Zipf's law

LSA
USE latent semantic analysis

LSI
UF large scale integration
BT integrated circuits
NT VLSI

LTA
USE paraprofessional library personnel

machine aided indexing
UF MAI
　　computer aided indexing
BT (indexing by method used)
　　computer applications
RT automatic indexing

machine aided translation
USE machine translation

machine intelligence
USE artificial intelligence

machine learning
UF computer learning
BT artificial intelligence
NT font learning
RT learning

machine readable cataloging formats
USE MARC formats

machine readable cataloging records
USE MARC records

machine readable data
SN *Limit to information emphasizing the aspect*
of machine readability, and also use a term
for the specific kind of information, e.g.,
"dictionaries." Prefer "electronic texts," if
appropriate.
BT data
RT electronic books

machine readable records
USE records

machine translation
UF automatic translation
computer aided translation
computer translation
machine aided translation
MT
BT computer applications
translation

machine vision
USE computer vision

magazines
USE periodicals

magnetic disks
UF discs
disks
BT magnetic media
NT floppy disks
hard disks
magneto-optical disks

magnetic media
BT (physical media)
NT magnetic disks
magnetic tapes
smart cards
RT data storage devices

magnetic media (cont.)
magnetic recording
recording equipment

magnetic recording
BT recording
RT magnetic media

magnetic tapes
BT magnetic media
NT audiotapes
RT videocassettes

magneto-optical disks
BT magnetic disks
optical disks

MAI
USE machine aided indexing

main libraries
USE central libraries

mainframe computers
BT computers
RT computer centers

maintainability
BT (attributes of systems and equipment)
RT durability
maintenance
quality
reliability

maintenance
BT general activities
NT updating
RT maintainability

malicious software
UF malware
BT computer software
NT computer viruses
computer worms
Trojan horses

malware
USE malicious software

man machine interfaces
USE interfaces

management
UF administration
BT management operations
NT computing resource management

84

management (cont.)
    digital rights management
    financial management
    human resources management
    information resources management
    library management
RT administrative records
    decision support systems
    management information systems
    managers
    organization charts
    planning
    scheduling

management information systems
SN *An integrated, user-machine system for*
    providing information to support operations,
    management, and decision-making functions
    in an organization. The system draws on
    models for analysis planning, control and
    decision making; and a database.
UF EIS
    executive information systems
    MIS
BT information storage and retrieval systems
RT decision support systems
    management

management operations
BT (activities and operations)
NT accounting
    business
    centralization
    decentralization
    funding
    inventory
    management
    marketing
    materials storage
    moving
    outsourcing
    planning
    scheduling
    security classification
    systems integration

managers
UF administrators
    library administrators
BT (persons and informal groups)
RT management

manual indexing
UF human indexing
BT (indexing by method used)

manuals
USE handbooks

manuscripts
BT (documents by medium, physical form)
RT archives
    rare materials

mapping (cartography)
USE cartography

maps
BT visual materials
RT atlases
    cartography
    visual materials

MARC formats
UF machine readable cataloging formats
BT interchange formats
RT MARC records

MARC records
UF machine readable cataloging records
BT bibliographic records
RT MARC formats

marginalia
BT (documents by information content, purpose)
RT annotations

marketing
BT management operations
NT advertising
    promotional activities
    telemarketing
RT commerce
    focus groups
    public relations

Markov chains
USE Markov models

Markov models
SN *Models in which the probabilities of future*
    events depend only on the current state of
    the model, and not on how the model
    reached that state.
UF Markov chains
    Markov processes
BT mathematical models

Markov processes
USE Markov models

markup languages
SN *Coding systems permitting identification of the various elements of a machine readable text.*
BT language types
NT HDML
    HTML
    SGML
    WML
    XML
RT editing

mass communications
USE mass media

mass media
UF mass communications
BT (communications media)
NT news media
    radio
    television
    World Wide Web

massively parallel processing
USE parallel processing

materials acquisitions
UF acquisitions (of materials)
    library acquisitions
BT collection development
NT accessions
    approval plans
    gifts and exchanges
    materials claims
    materials orders
    subscriptions
RT book vendors
    jobbers
    subscription agencies
    subscription cancellation

materials claims
BT materials acquisitions
RT subscriptions

materials conservation
SN *Protection of library and archive materials from damage and decay.*
UF conservation of materials
BT materials preservation
NT deacidification
RT aging of materials

materials orders
BT materials acquisitions
NT blanket orders

materials orders (cont.)
    standing orders

materials preservation
SN Preservation of both documents and the information they contain.
BT library operations
NT binding
    digital object preservation
    materials conservation
    restoration
RT aging of materials
    library technical services

materials processing
UF technical processes
BT library technical services

materials selection
UF book selection
BT collection development
    selection

materials storage
UF document storage
    shelving
BT management operations
NT compact storage
    data warehousing
RT library equipment
    library shelving
    moving
    records management

mathematical methods
BT quantitative analysis
NT Fourier analysis
    factor analysis
    finite element analysis
    linear programming
    nonlinear programming
    statistical methods
    vector analysis
RT mathematical models
    mathematics
    matrices

mathematical models
BT analytic models
NT chaos theory
    game theory
    graph theory
    Markov models
    set theory
    stochastic models
RT mathematics

mathematics
SN *The discipline; for applications in research and analysis, use "mathematical methods."*
BT (fields and disciplines)
NT algebra
   statistics
RT game theory
   graph theory
   logic
   mathematical methods
   mathematical models
   set theory
   statistical methods

matrices
BT knowledge organization systems
RT mathematical methods

meaning
USE semantics

measurement
SN *Also use quality being measured, e.g., "similarity," if applicable.*
UF metrics
BT quantitative analysis
NT econometrics
   informetrics
   photogrammetry
   psychometrics
   telemetry
RT remote sensing

media
SN *Use the specific kind of medium, e.g., "journals," "books," "films."*
BT (documents by medium, physical form)

media centers
UF learning centers
   learning resource centers
   resource centers
   school libraries
   school media centers
BT libraries
RT schools

media instruction
USE bibliographic instruction

media materials
USE nonprint media

media specialists
BT information professionals
RT library personnel

medical informatics
UF health informatics
BT bioinformatics
RT biomedical information
   medical libraries
   medical records
   medical science
   MeSH

medical information
USE biomedical information

medical libraries
BT special libraries
RT biomedical information
   medical informatics
   medical science

medical personnel
BT (persons and informal groups)
NT physicians

medical records
BT records
RT confidential records
   medical informatics

medical science
UF health sciences
BT natural sciences
RT biomedical information
   medical informatics
   medical libraries
   pharmacology
   physicians

Medical Subject Headings
USE MeSH

meetings
UF conferences
BT spoken communication
NT workshops
RT computer conferencing
   conference proceedings
   electronic conferencing
   spoken communication
   teleconferencing
   video teleconferencing

memoranda
USE correspondence

men
BT (persons and informal groups)
RT gender

mental models
USE cognitive models

mental processes
BT (human processes)
NT abstraction
    affect
    cognition
    cognitive perception
    comprehension
    concept association
    concept discrimination
    generalization
    human memory
    judgment
    linguistic analysis
    mental visualization
    reasoning
    sensory perception
RT cognitive science

mental visualization
SN *A mental process. For computer-based visualization, use "visualization (electronic)."*
BT mental processes
RT electronic visualization
    visual memory

mentoring
BT educational activities
RT career development
    employees

menu based interfaces
UF menus
BT interfaces
RT graphical user interfaces

menus
USE menu based interfaces

MeSH
UF Medical Subject Headings
BT thesauri
RT biomedical information
    medical informatics

message filtering
SN *Automatic methods for assuring that messages received, e.g., by email or Usenet, meet certain criteria.*
BT computer operations
RT e-mail
    intelligent agents
    newsgroups

message systems
UF messaging systems
BT computer mediated communications
NT bulletin board systems
    chat rooms
    e-mail
    e-mail list servers
    instant messaging
    text messaging
    voice mail

messaging systems
USE message systems

meta analysis
UF meta-analysis
BT data analysis

meta search engines
SN *Search engines which query multiple primary search engines and collate the highest ranking returns from each.*
UF metasearch engines
BT search engines

meta-analysis
USE meta analysis

metadata
UF metatags
    semantic headers
BT data
RT Open Archives Initiative Protocol for Metadata Harvesting specification
    OpenURL
    bibliographic cataloging
    bibliographic records
    database design
    databases
    metadata standards

metadata standards
UF Dublin Core
    HyTime
BT standards
RT metadata

metadocuments
USE hypertext

metamapping
USE information mapping

metaphors
UF analogies
BT information representations

metaphors (cont.)
NT desktop metaphor

metasearch engines
USE meta search engines

metatags
USE metadata

metathesauri
BT thesauri

metrics
USE measurement

Mexico
BT North America
RT Latin America

mice
UF mouse (computer peripheral)
BT pointing devices
RT graphical user interfaces
   trackballs

microcomputers
SN *Computers built around microprocessors on*
   integrated circuit chips. For microcomputers
   designed for individual desktop or travel use,
   use "personal computers."
BT computers
NT pen based computers
   personal computers
   personal digital assistants
   Web TV
RT integrated circuits
   microprocessors

microfiche
BT microforms

microfilm
BT microforms
RT computer output microforms

microforms
UF micrographics
BT (physical media)
NT computer output microforms
   microfiche
   microfilm
RT data storage devices
   micropublishing

micrographics
USE microforms

microprocessors
UF microtechnology
BT computer processing units
RT integrated circuits
   microcomputers

microproduction
USE micropublishing

micropublishing
UF microproduction
BT publishing
RT microforms

microtechnology
USE microprocessors

microthesauri
SN *Thesauri which are subsets, usually limited*
   to a specialized topic, of larger thesauri.
UF minithesauri
BT thesauri

Middle East
BT regions

middle schools
UF junior high schools
BT schools

migration
SN *Transitioning digital objects created on one*
   system for maintenance, access, and display
   to a different system.
BT digital object preservation

military intelligence
BT domain information
RT armed forces
   intelligence
   security classification

military services
USE armed forces

minicomputers
BT computers

minimal cataloging
UF limited cataloging
BT cataloging

minithesauri
USE microthesauri

minorities and ethnic groups
UF ethnic groups
BT (persons and informal groups)
NT African Americans
    disabled persons
    gays and lesbians
    Hispanics
    Native Americans
RT affirmative action
    cultural diversity
    demographics
    social discrimination

mirror sites
BT web sites

MIS
USE management information systems

misinformation
USE false information

mission oriented research
BT research and development

misspellings
USE typographical errors

mixed media
USE multimedia

mobile communications
BT telecommunications
NT cellular communications

mobile libraries
BT libraries
NT bookmobiles

mobile shelving
USE library shelving

mobile telephones
USE cellular communications

mobility impaired persons
BT disabled persons

modeling
USE analytic models

modems
BT telecommunications equipment
RT transmission speed

modification
SN *Use with area of change if appropriate, e.g.*
    "user behavior."
BT general activities
NT reengineering
    repurposing
RT change

modifiers
SN *Terms or phrases, usually applied ad hoc,*
    which differentiate among the entries under a
    main term in an index.
UF subdivisions (indexing)
    subheadings
BT index terms

modularity
BT (attributes of systems and equipment)
RT computer programming
    systems design

monitoring
UF surveillance
BT general activities
RT evaluation

monographs
BT publications
RT books
    primary literature
    scholarly publishing

Monte Carlo method
BT statistical methods
RT probability

morals
USE ethics

morphemes
BT linguistic elements
NT affixes
RT morphological analysis
    semantics

morphological analysis
BT linguistic analysis
RT morphemes

motion picture films
SN *Use for information recorded in film form;*
    for the physical material use "photographic
    films."
UF motion pictures
    movies
BT video recordings

motion picture films (cont.)
RT ISFN
   filmstrips
   photographic films
   records

motion pictures
USE motion picture films

motion video
UF full motion video
BT video communications
NT video clips
RT data streaming
   video recordings
   video teleconferencing

motion video streaming
USE data streaming

motivation
BT psychological aspects

mouse (computer peripheral)
USE mice

movable shelving
USE library shelving

movies
USE motion picture films

moving
BT management operations
RT materials storage

MT
USE machine translation

MUDs
USE multiuser Internet games

multidimensional scaling
BT statistical methods
RT dimensionality reduction

multidisciplinary information
BT domain information
RT interdisciplinarity

multidisk drives
UF jukeboxes (CD-ROM drives)
BT disk drives

multilingual information
BT information representations

multilingual information (cont.)
RT multilingual retrieval
   non English languages

multilingual retrieval
UF cross lingual retrieval
BT information retrieval
RT language barriers
   multilingual information
   multilingual subject indexing
   multilingual thesauri
   multilingualism

multilingual subject indexing
BT subject indexing
RT multilingual retrieval
   multilingual thesauri
   non English languages

multilingual thesauri
UF bilingual thesauri
BT thesauri
RT multilingual retrieval
   multilingual subject indexing
   multilingualism
   non English language materials
   non English languages

multilingualism
UF bilingualism
BT cultural aspects
RT human language
   language barriers
   multilingual retrieval
   multilingual thesauri
   non English languages

multimedia
SN *Communication of information by means of*
   simultaneous use of more than one medium,
   e.g., both sound and image.
UF mixed media
BT (documents by medium, physical form)
RT images

multiple access communications
BT telecommunications

multiplexing
SN *Transmission of several lower-speed data*
   streams simultaneously over a single
   higher-speed line.
BT telecommunications

multiprocessing
BT data processing

multiprocessing (cont.)
RT multiprocessors

multiprocessors
BT computer processing units
RT multiprocessing

multiuser Internet games
UF MUDs
BT computer mediated communications
RT video games
    virtual reality

multivariate analysis
BT statistical methods

municipal libraries
USE public libraries

museum informatics
BT informatics
RT museums

museums
BT (product and service providers)
RT museum informatics

music
BT fine arts
RT ISMN

name indexing
UF corporate name indexing
    personal name indexing
BT (indexing by feature indexed)
RT author indexes
    corporate names
    personal names
    proper names

names
USE proper names

narratives
BT spoken communication

narrower term references
USE cross references

narrower term relationships
USE hierarchical relationships

national archives
BT archives
RT national libraries

national aspects
BT geopolitical aspects
RT (countries and regions)
    regional aspects

national bibliographies
BT bibliographies

national libraries
BT government libraries
RT national archives

National Research and Education Network
BT telecommunications networks
RT Internet

national security
BT security
RT political aspects

Native Americans
UF American Indians
    Indians (American)
BT minorities and ethnic groups

natural disasters
USE disasters

natural language comprehension
UF language understanding
    understanding (natural language)
BT natural language processing

natural language indexes
USE keyword indexes

natural language indexing
USE keywords

natural language interfaces
BT interfaces
RT intelligent interfaces
    natural language processing

natural language processing
SN *Computer understanding, analysis,*
    manipulation, and/or generation of natural
    language.
UF automated language processing
    NLP
BT artificial intelligence
NT discourse analysis
    discourse generation
    natural language comprehension
    sentence generation
    speech recognition

natural language processing (cont.)
 speech synthesis
RT automatic indexing
 computational lexicography
 computational linguistics
 full text searching
 information retrieval
 natural language interfaces
 probabilistic indexing
 relevance ranking
 text processing

natural language searching
USE full text searching

natural sciences
UF life sciences
BT (fields and disciplines)
NT biology
 geography
 medical science
 pharmacology
RT scientific and technical information
 scientometrics

navigation
SN *Finding one's way around a website,*
 taxonomy, etc. to locate desired information.
BT information seeking
RT breadcrumbs
 interfaces
 path breadcrumbs

navy
USE armed forces

NC (network computers)
USE network computers

nearest neighbor
USE relevance ranking

near-published literature
USE grey literature

near-synonymous relationships
USE quasi-synonymous relationships

needs assessment
UF assessment, needs
BT (research and analytic methods)
RT information needs

negotiation
BT human communications

net computers
USE network computers

Netherlands
BT Europe

netiquette
USE etiquette

netometrics
USE webometrics

network analysis
BT data analysis

network computers
SN *Computers designed primarily for accessing*
 information via the Internet or other network;
 usually relying on remote access to both
 software and data.
UF Internet computers
 NC (network computers)
 net computers
BT computers
RT Internet
 Web TV
 World Wide Web

network protocols
USE communications protocols

network security
BT computer security
RT telecommunications networks

network servers
USE file servers

network structures
BT data structures
RT semantic networks

neural nets
USE neural networks

neural networks
UF artificial neural networks
 neural nets
BT artificial intelligence
RT spreading activation

New Zealand
BT (countries and regions)

news
BT information content

news (cont.)
RT news media
   newsletters
   newspapers
   newswire services

news media
BT mass media
NT newsletters
   newspapers
   newswire services
RT news

news wire services
USE newswire services

newsgroups
SN *A network of discussion groups, on a wide variety of subjects, available over the Internet.*
UF discussion groups
   Usenet newsgroups
BT computer mediated communications
RT Internet
   message filtering

newsletters
BT news media
   periodicals
RT news

newspapers
BT news media
   serials
RT news

newswire services
UF news wire services
   wire services
BT news media
RT news

Nigeria
BT Africa

NISO
USE standards developing organizations

NLP
USE natural language processing

node labels
UF facet indicators
   guide terms
BT information representations
RT faceted classification

node labels (cont.)
   facets

nodes
SN *A terminal of any branch of a network or an interconnecting point of two or more branches of a network.*
BT (communications networks)

nomenclature
USE terminology

nomenclature, chemical
USE chemical nomenclature

non English language materials
SN *Use for information about non-English language materials, not for materials in languages other than English.*
UF foreign language materials
BT (documents by availability, access, organization)
RT multilingual thesauri
   non English languages

non English languages
UF foreign languages
BT human language
NT Chinese language
RT language barriers
   multilingual information
   multilingual subject indexing
   multilingual thesauri
   multilingualism
   non English language materials

non text-based materials
USE nonprint media

nonbibliographic databases
BT databases
NT community resource files
   fact databases
   human resource files
   image databases
   numeric databases

nonfiction
BT literature
NT biography
RT books
   literature

nonhierarchical relationships
USE associative relationships

nonlinear programming
BT mathematical methods

nonpreferred term references
USE cross references

nonpreferred terms
USE synonyms

nonprint media
UF audio visual materials
   audiovisual aids
   audiovisual materials
   media materials
   non text-based materials
BT (documents by medium, physical form)
NT audio recordings
   video recordings
   visual materials

nonprofit sector
BT economic sectors

nonroman scripts
BT writing systems
RT romanization
   transliteration

nonverbal communication
BT human communications

normal distribution
BT data distribution
RT probability

normalization
BT data processing
RT data models
   stemming

North America
BT (countries and regions)
NT Canada
   Mexico
   United States

Northern Ireland
BT United Kingdom

notation
BT information representations
RT classification
   classification schemes
   notation synthesis

notation synthesis
UF synthesis, notation
BT index language construction
RT notation

notebook computers
USE personal computers

nothing before something arrangement
USE word by word arrangement

nouns
BT linguistic elements

novels
USE fiction

novice users
BT end users
RT user expertise

NREN
USE National Research and Education Network

NT references
USE cross references

NT relationships
USE hierarchical relationships

numeric data
UF statistical data
BT data
RT numeric databases
   spreadsheets

numeric databases
UF data sets
   statistical databases
BT nonbibliographic databases
RT numeric data

numeric range searching
USE range searching

object oriented databases
BT databases
RT data objects
   object oriented programming

object oriented programming
UF OOP
BT computer programming
RT data objects
   object oriented databases

object recognition
BT pattern recognition

objectives
USE goals

objects (physical)
USE physical objects

obscene materials
UF indecent materials
BT (documents by information content, purpose)
NT pornographic materials

observational research
BT research methods
RT qualitative analysis

obsolescence
UF aging of literatures
BT (general attributes)
RT half life measures
    information life cycle

Oceania
UF Pacific islands
BT regions

OCR
USE optical character recognition

off campus education
UF extension campuses
BT education
RT adult education
    distance learning

off campus library services
BT library and archival services

off site access
USE remote access

office automation
UF electronic offices
BT computer applications
RT local area networks

offsite access
USE remote access

on line databases
USE online databases

one person libraries
USE small libraries

online catalogs
USE OPACs

online databases
UF on line databases
BT databases
NT OPACs
RT online searching

online industry
BT information industry
RT database producers
    domain naming system
    information utilities
    online searching
    search services

online information retrieval
USE online searching

online information retrieval systems
USE information storage and retrieval systems

online public access catalogs
USE OPACs

online searching
UF online information retrieval
BT computer applications
    searching
RT downloading
    full text searching
    information retrieval software
    information storage and retrieval systems
    online databases
    online industry
    output reformatting
    search strategies
    subject searching

online systems
USE information storage and retrieval systems

ontologies
SN *Collections of definitions of words and
    concepts representing an area of knowledge,
    including relationships, properties, and
    functions, formatted to facilitate information
    sharing, especially between computers.*
BT controlled vocabularies
RT knowledge modeling
    knowledge representation
    semantic networks

OOP
USE object oriented programming

OPACs
UF online catalogs
    online public access catalogs
BT bibliographic databases
    catalogs (bibliographic)
    online databases

open access publications
SN *Publications for which the author and*
    copyright holder grant users free use and
    right to copy the work, subject to proper
    attribution of authorship. A complete copy of
    the work must be deposited in a repository.
BT publications
RT copyright
    public domain

Open Archives Initiative Protocol for
    Metadata Harvesting specification
BT standards
RT interoperability
    metadata
    scholarly communication

Open Document Architecture
SN *ISO standard (8613) for describing*
    documents, which enables transfer of text,
    graphics, and facsimile documents between
    different systems.
BT interchange formats

open source
SN *Software source code that is freely available*
    for volunteers to use, modify, and improve.
BT computer software

OpenURL
SN *Standard for specifying URLs containing*
    extended information about a document to
    facilitate retrieval from any one of multiple
    locations.
BT standards
RT data transmission
    metadata

operating systems
BT computer software

operations research
SN *Application of information technology for*
    informed decision-making and optimization
    of system performance; draws heavily on
    mathematical and computer models of
    organizational systems.
BT systems analysis
RT analytic models

operations research (cont.)
    decision making
    decision theory
    optimization

optical character recognition
UF character recognition
    OCR
BT pattern recognition
NT feature extraction
    font learning
RT scanning

optical computers
BT computers
    optical equipment

optical disks
UF discs
    disks
    laser disks
BT optical media
NT compact disks
    erasable optical disks
    floptical disks
    magneto-optical disks
    videodisks
    WORM disks
RT lasers

optical equipment
BT (hardware, software, and equipment)
NT optical computers
    optical media
RT cameras
    fiber optics
    optical recording

optical fibers
USE fiber optics

optical media
BT (physical media)
    optical equipment
NT optical disks
    optical tape
RT data storage devices
    optical recording

optical recognition
BT pattern recognition

optical recording
BT recording
RT optical equipment
    optical media

optical scanners
USE scanners

optical scanning
USE scanning

optical tape
BT optical media

optimization
BT (research and analytic methods)
NT search engine optimization
RT operations research

oral communications
USE spoken communication

oral history
BT history
RT biography
    history

organization charts
BT graphics
RT management

organization names
USE corporate names

organization of information
BT information operations
NT cataloging
    classification
    database design
    domain analysis
    facet analysis
    index language construction
    indexing
    relevance ranking
    vocabulary control
RT inverted files
    knowledge organization systems

organization productivity
SN *Reflection of the number of articles*
    originating from a specific group, e.g. a
    university or company.
BT citation analysis
RT corporate authorship

organization theory
BT sociology
RT (organizations)
    organizational culture
    organizational environment

organizational communication
BT human communications
RT (organizations)
    informal communication
    organizational culture
    organizational environment
    social networking

organizational culture
SN *Pertains to the manner in which members of*
    an organization interact, internally influenced
    by the norms and conventions of the
    organization.
UF corporate culture
BT cultural aspects
RT (organizations)
    organization theory
    organizational communication
    organizational environment

organizational environment
SN *Pertains to external influences on an*
    organization.
BT cultural aspects
RT (organizations)
    organization theory
    organizational communication
    organizational culture

organizational intelligence
USE company information

orthography
UF spelling
BT linguistic elements
RT homography

out of print publications
BT publications
RT rare materials

output equipment
BT computer peripherals
NT printers
RT video display terminals

output reformatting
BT library operations
RT downloading
    online searching

outsourcing
SN *Contracting out work or services to an*
    outside provider in order to cut costs.
BT management operations

overdue materials
BT library materials
RT library circulation
　　library fines

overhead costs
BT costs

overlap
SN *In scope or coverage.*
BT (attributes of information and data)
RT abstracting and indexing service bureaus
　　database producers
　　information retrieval indexes

overload, information
USE information overload

overviews
USE abstracts

Pacific islands
USE Oceania

Pacific Rim
BT regions

packet switching
BT telecommunications

page references
USE locators

palmtop computers
USE personal computers

pamphlets
BT publications
RT ephemera
　　vertical files

paper
BT (physical media)
NT permanent paper

paper based information systems
BT information storage and retrieval systems

paperbacks
BT books

paperwork management
USE records management

paradigms
BT knowledge organization systems

paradigms (cont.)
RT cognitive models

paragraphs
BT linguistic elements

Paraguay
BT South America

parallel architecture
USE parallel processors

parallel processing
UF concurrent processing
　　massively parallel processing
BT data processing
RT parallel processors

parallel processors
UF parallel architecture
BT computer processing units
RT parallel processing

paraprofessional library personnel
UF library assistants
　　library support staff
　　library technical assistants
　　library technicians
　　LTA
　　support staff, library
BT library personnel

Pareto principle
UF 80/20 rule
BT data distribution
RT Zipf's law

Pareto-Zipf law
USE Zipf's law

part whole relationships
BT hierarchical relationships
RT cross references

partial match retrieval systems
USE fuzzy retrieval systems

passages
USE document surrogates

password control
USE computer access control

patents
SN *Use for information about patents, not for
　　examples of patents.*

patents (cont.)
BT (documents by information content, purpose)
RT innovation
    intellectual property

path breadcrumbs
SN *Display of the navigational route a user took*
    to arrive at a particular website.
BT breadcrumbs
RT navigation

Pathfinder networks
SN *Spatial representation of underlying patterns*
    in proximity data.
UF PFnet
BT data maps
RT statistical methods

patrons, library
USE library users

patrons
USE users

pattern matching
USE pattern recognition

pattern recognition
UF pattern matching
BT data processing
NT object recognition
    optical character recognition
    optical recognition
    word recognition
RT bar codes
    knowledge discovery

payments, electronic
USE electronic cash

PC
USE personal computers

PDAs
USE personal digital assistants

peer groups
BT communities

peer review
USE refereeing

peer to peer file sharing
BT resource sharing
RT digital objects

pen based computers
UF hand held computers
    handwritten input
BT microcomputers

perceptions (attitudes)
USE attitudes

perceptual learning
BT learning
RT sensory perception

performance
BT (general attributes)
RT bandwidth
    costs
    durability
    effectiveness
    quality
    reliability
    response time
    search time

performing arts
BT fine arts

periodical articles
UF articles, periodical
    journal articles
BT periodicals
RT journals
    reprints

periodical indexes
UF journal indexes
BT information retrieval indexes
RT abstracting and indexing service bureaus
    databases
    journals
    periodical indexing
    periodicals

periodical indexing
BT (indexing by item indexed)
RT database indexing
    periodical indexes
    periodicals

periodicals
UF magazines
BT serials
NT journals
    newsletters
    periodical articles
RT periodical indexes
    periodical indexing

peripherals, computer
USE computer peripherals

permanence
BT (general attributes)
RT durability
quality
reliability

permanent paper
UF acid free paper
alkaline paper
BT paper

permuted indexes
UF rotated indexes
BT keyword indexes

persistent identifiers
BT knowledge organization systems
NT URI
digital object identifiers

personal authorship
BT authorship

personal collections
BT collections
RT personal files

personal computers
SN *Microcomputers intended for individual desktop or travel use.*
UF desktop computers
laptop computers
notebook computers
palmtop computers
PC
BT microcomputers
RT personal digital assistants
workstations

personal digital assistants
UF PDAs
hand held computers
BT microcomputers
RT personal computers

personal files
SN *Files compiled for an individual's own use. For files containing personal information about individuals use "personal data."*
UF customized materials
BT (documents by information content, purpose)
RT personal collections
personal information systems

personal information
SN *Data and information about individual persons. For data compiled for an individual's own use, use "personal files."*
BT domain information
NT library user profiles
RT confidential records
data security
privacy

personal information systems
BT information storage and retrieval systems
RT personal files

personal name indexing
USE name indexing

personal names
UF forenames
surnames
BT proper names
RT authority files
name indexing
pseudonyms

personal networking
USE social networking

personal styles
USE individual differences

personality, matter, energy, space, and time
USE PMEST facets

personalization
USE customization

personnel
USE employees

pertinence
SN *In retrieval evaluation, the extent to which a retrieved document is a useful response to the query, taking into consideration the user's existing state of knowledge.*
BT (attributes of information and data)
RT evaluation
information storage and retrieval systems
relevance
retrieval effectiveness

Peru
BT South America

PFnet
USE Pathfinder networks

pharmacology
UF drugs
BT natural sciences
RT chemistry
    medical science

Philippines
BT Asia

philosophy
BT humanities
NT epistemology

phonemes
BT linguistic elements
RT phonetics

phonetics
BT linguistics
RT phonemes

photo CD
BT compact disks
    images

photocopiers
UF copiers
BT (hardware, software, and
    equipment)
RT photocopying

photocopying
UF copying
BT library operations
RT photocopiers

photogrammetry
BT measurement
RT remote sensing

photographic films
SN *Materials used to make photographic*
    negatives or transparencies.
BT (physical media)
RT motion picture films
    photographic slides
    photographs

photographic slides
BT images
RT photographic films
    photographs

photographs
BT images
RT photographic films

photographs (cont.)
    photographic slides
    pictures

phrases
BT linguistic elements
RT syntactic analysis

physical attributes
BT (general attributes)
NT color
    shape
    texture
RT acoustic data

physical objects
UF objects (physical)
    realia
BT (documents by medium, physical form)
RT artifacts

physical sciences
BT (fields and disciplines)
NT astronomy
    chemistry
    earth sciences
    physics
RT scientific and technical
    information
    scientometrics

physically challenged persons
USE disabled persons

physicians
BT medical personnel
RT medical science

physics
BT physical sciences

pictorial information systems
USE image information systems

picture telephones
USE videotelephones

pictures
BT visual materials
RT images
    photographs

plagiarism
BT fraud
RT intellectual property

planning
BT management operations
NT critical incident method
   critical path method
   strategic planning
RT backlogs
   environmental scanning
   forecasting
   goals
   management
   scheduling

PMEST facets
UF personality, matter, energy, space, and time
BT facets
RT citation order
   Colon Classification
   faceted classification

poetry
BT literature

pointing devices
BT input equipment
NT mice
   trackballs
RT graphical user interfaces

Poland
BT Europe

policy
BT political aspects
NT editorial policy
   library policy
   public policy
RT censorship

policy, public
USE public policy

political aspects
UF democracy
BT (sociocultural aspects)
NT government
   policy
RT information policy
   national security
   political science

political science
BT social sciences
RT political aspects
   public policy

polysemy
USE homography

popular culture
BT cultural aspects

popular materials
BT (documents by information content, purpose)
RT fiction

population
USE demographics

pornographic materials
BT obscene materials
RT erotic materials

portals
SN *Web sites that are commonly used as*
   gateways to other Web sites.
UF gateways
BT interfaces
   web sites

postcoordinate indexing
UF coordinate indexing
   uniterm indexing
BT subject indexing
RT indexing term links
   role indicators

practical methods
SN *Non-research "how to" methods.*
BT (research and analytic methods)
NT critical incident method
   critical path method

pragmatics
SN *Pertains to the relationship between words*
   or signs and their senders and receivers, i.e.,
   to the way in which signals are used to
   communicate.
BT linguistics
   semiotics

precision
SN *The percentage of relevant documents in a*
   retrieved set.
BT (attributes of information and data)
RT evaluation
   fallout
   information retrieval noise
   recall
   relevance
   retrieval effectiveness

precoordinate indexing
BT subject indexing

predicate calculus
USE predicate logic

predicate logic
UF predicate calculus
BT logic

prediction
USE forecasting

predictive models
UF probabilistic models
BT analytic models
RT forecasting
    probability

preferred order
USE citation order

preferred term references
USE cross references

prefixes
USE affixes

preprints
SN *Use for information about preprints, not for*
    examples of preprints.
BT (documents by availability, access,
    organization)
RT grey literature
    primary literature

presearch interviews
BT interviews

Presidential libraries
BT research libraries
    special libraries

prices
USE pricing

pricing
UF charges
    prices
BT financial management
NT fees for service
    royalties

primary literature
SN *Literature written by scholars, for scholars,*
    to report new and original research.

primary literature (cont.)
UF scholarly literature
    scientific literature
BT (documents by information content, purpose)
RT conference proceedings
    journals
    monographs
    preprints
    technical reports

print materials
USE print publications

print publications
UF print materials
BT publications
NT large print materials

printers
BT output equipment
NT color printers

printing
BT technical and manufacturing operations
RT publishing
    typesetting
    typography

prison libraries
UF correctional institution libraries
    jail libraries
BT institutional libraries

privacy
UF confidentiality
BT civil rights
RT confidential records
    data security
    disclosure
    encryption
    information policy
    personal information
    security

private copying
USE fair use

private sector
BT economic sectors
RT competition
    public sector

probabilistic indexing
SN *Algorithmic indexing of terms in a*
    document, using weights to show the
    importance of individual terms to the

104

probabilistic indexing (cont.)
   document.
BT subject indexing
RT associative retrieval
   natural language processing
   probabilistic retrieval
   probability

probabilistic models
USE predictive models

probabilistic retrieval
SN *Assignment of weights to documents*
   retrieved in response to a query to indicate
   the probable relevance of the documents to
   the query.
UF statistical retrieval
BT information retrieval models
RT associative retrieval
   probabilistic indexing
   probability
   relevance ranking

probability
BT (general attributes)
RT Bayesian functions
   Monte Carlo method
   normal distribution
   predictive models
   probabilistic indexing
   probabilistic retrieval
   queuing
   statistical methods
   stochastic processes
   uncertainty

problem patrons
UF problem users
BT library users
RT libraries

problem solving
BT (research and analytic methods)
NT heuristics
RT decision making
   decision support systems
   decision theory
   decision trees

problem users
USE problem patrons

proceedings (conference)
USE conference proceedings

productivity (journals)
USE journal productivity

professional associations
UF associations
   professional societies
   scientific societies
   societies
BT (organizations)
NT information associations
   library associations

professional competencies
SN *Set of knowledge and skills that are highly*
   relevant for a specific professional area.
UF core competencies
   professional skills
BT skills
RT computer literacy
   information professionals

professional skills
USE professional competencies

professional societies
USE professional associations

professionals, information
USE information professionals

professors
USE faculty

programming (computer)
USE computer programming

programming languages
UF computer languages
BT computer science
   language types
NT high level languages
RT computer programming
   computer software

programs, computer
USE computer software

promotional activities
UF publicity
BT marketing
NT library weeks

proofreading
BT editing

proper names
UF names
   surnames
BT information content
NT corporate names
   personal names
   pseudonyms
RT authority files
   name indexing

proposed descriptors
USE candidate descriptors

propositional logic
BT logic

protocols
USE standards

prototypes
USE prototyping

prototyping
UF prototypes
BT testing
RT design

proximity
BT (general attributes)
RT proximity searching

proximity searching
UF adjacency searching
BT searching
RT proximity
   string searching

pseudonyms
BT proper names
RT personal names

psychological aspects
SN *Of information and information use. For the*
   discipline, use "psychology."
BT (sociocultural aspects)
NT attitudes
   cognitive styles
   creativity
   ethics
   goals
   human behavior
   individual differences
   information overload
   intelligence
   leadership
   motivation

psychological aspects (cont.)
   trust
RT psychology

psychology
SN *The discipline; for applications to*
   information use, use "psychological aspects."
BT behavioral sciences
NT cognitive science
   psychometrics
   social psychology
RT human behavior
   psychological aspects

psychometrics
BT measurement
   psychology

public agencies
USE government agencies

public domain
SN *Documents or property with rights held by*
   the public at large, without protection of
   patent or copyright.
BT (documents by availability, access,
   organization)
   intellectual property
RT open access publications

public domain information
SN *The status of publications, products, and*
   processes that are not protected under patent
   or copyright.
BT domain information
RT public records

public lending right
BT intellectual property
RT copyright
   royalties

public libraries
UF municipal libraries
BT libraries
RT branch libraries
   research libraries
   state library agencies

public policy
UF government policy
   policy, public
BT policy
NT information policy
RT government
   political science

public records
BT records
RT freedom of information
   public domain information

public relations
BT human communications
RT marketing

public sector
BT economic sectors
RT government agencies
   private sector

publication explosion
USE information explosion

publications
SN *Very general term. Prefer specific type, e.g.,*
   "journals," "books."
UF information products
BT (documents by availability, access,
   organization)
NT alternative publications
   bestsellers
   books
   conference proceedings
   electronic publications
   government publications
   monographs
   open access publications
   out of print publications
   pamphlets
   print publications
   reprints
   serials
   series
RT information resources
   publishing

publicity
USE promotional activities

publishers
BT (product and service providers)
NT commercial publishers
   database producers
   learned society publishers
   secondary publishers
   small presses
   university presses
RT information industry
   information infrastructure
   publishing

publishing
BT human communications
NT desktop publishing
   electronic publishing
   micropublishing
   scholarly publishing
   self publishing
RT editing
   information dissemination
   information explosion
   information production
   printing
   publications
   publishers
   software industry

punctuation
BT linguistic elements

QBE
USE query by example

qualifiers
SN *Delimiters used to distinguish different*
   homographs or meanings of words.
BT index terms
RT homography

qualitative analysis
SN *Research providing detailed narrative*
   descriptions and explanations of phenomena
   investigated, with lesser emphasis given to
   numerical quantification.
UF description (research method)
BT (research and analytic methods)
RT observational research

quality assurance
BT technical and manufacturing
   operations
RT quality
   quality control

quality control
BT technical and manufacturing
   operations
NT duplicate detection
   error correction
   error detection
RT evaluation
   quality
   quality assurance

quality
BT (general attributes)
RT evaluation

quality (cont.)
    maintainability
    performance
    permanence
    quality assurance
    quality control

quantitative analysis
BT (research and analytic methods)
NT mathematical methods
    measurement
RT empirical studies

quasi-synonymous relationships
UF near-synonymous relationships
BT equivalence relationships
RT synonyms

query analysis
USE query processing

query by example
UF QBE
    document as query
    relevance feedback
BT searching
RT feedback

query expansion
BT query formulation

query formulation
UF search formulation
BT searching
NT query expansion
    query refinement
RT query refinement
    search strategies
    search terms

query languages
BT language types
NT SDQL
    SQL
RT query processing

query processing
UF query analysis
BT information processing
RT query languages

query refinement
UF query reformulation
BT query formulation
RT assisted searching
    query formulation

query reformulation
USE query refinement

query weighting
USE weighting

question answering retrieval
USE answer passage retrieval

question answering systems
USE fact retrieval systems

questionnaires
BT (documents by information content, purpose)
    research methods

queuing
BT stochastic processes
RT probability

radio
BT mass media
RT broadcasting

RAM
USE random access memory

random access memory
UF RAM
BT computer memory
NT DRAM

random processes
USE stochastic processes

randomness
BT (general attributes)

range searching
UF numeric range searching
BT searching

ranking
UF seriation
BT hierarchical models
NT density ranking
    relevance ranking

ranking (relevance)
USE relevance ranking

rare materials
UF antiquarian materials
BT (documents by availability, access,
    organization)
NT incunabula

rare materials (cont.)
RT archives
  book collecting
  manuscripts
  out of print publications
  special collections

rating scales
BT research design

RDF
USE Resource Description Framework

read only memory
UF ROM
BT computer memory

reader services
UF library user services
  reading guidance
BT library and archival services
RT library circulation
  reference services

reading
BT human communications
RT bibliotherapy
  education

reading disabled persons
UF dyslexia
  reading handicapped persons
BT disabled persons

reading guidance
USE reader services

reading handicapped persons
USE reading disabled persons

ready reference materials
BT reference materials

real time processing
BT data processing

realia
USE physical objects

reasoning
BT mental processes
NT induction
  inference

recall
SN *The ratio of the relevant documents retrieved*

recall (cont.)
  by a query to the total number of relevant
  documents in the system.
BT (attributes of information and data)
RT evaluation
  fallout
  information retrieval noise
  precision
  retrieval effectiveness

recording
BT technical and manufacturing operations
NT magnetic recording
  optical recording

recording equipment
BT audiovisual equipment
NT audio recorders
  video recorders
RT magnetic media

recordings, sound
USE audio recordings

recordings, video
USE video recordings

recordkeeping
USE records management

records
SN *Collections of information items, each*
  collection referring to a particular entity. For
  recordings, use "video recordings" or "sound
  recordings."
UF machine readable records
BT (documents by information content, purpose)
NT administrative records
  bibliographic records
  confidential records
  duplicate records
  medical records
  public records
  usage records
RT admissibility of records
  data
  motion picture films
  records management

records handling
USE records management

records management
UF paperwork management
  recordkeeping
  records handling

records management (cont.)
BT information resources management
NT document retention
RT archives
    collection management
    correspondence
    materials storage
    records
    records managers

records managers
BT information professionals
RT records management

recreation
USE entertainment

reduced instruction set computers
USE RISC

redundancy
BT (general attributes)

reengineering
BT modification

refereeing
UF peer review
BT evaluation
RT grants
    journals
    scholarly publishing

reference interviews
BT interviews
    reference services

reference librarians
BT librarians
RT reference services

reference locators
USE locators

reference management software
USE bibliographic software

reference materials
BT information resources
NT almanacs
    atlases
    dictionaries
    directories
    encyclopedias
    handbooks
    loose leaf services

reference materials (cont.)
    ready reference materials
    yearbooks

reference retrieval systems
UF bibliographic retrieval systems
BT information storage and retrieval systems
RT bibliographic databases
    bibliographic references

reference services
BT library and archival services
NT electronic reference services
    reference interviews
RT information services
    reader services
    reference librarians

referral services
USE community information services

regional aspects
BT geopolitical aspects
RT (countries and regions)
    geography
    national aspects

regions
BT (countries and regions)
NT Caribbean region
    European Union
    Latin America
    Middle East
    Oceania
    Pacific Rim
    Scandinavia
    Southeast Asia

regulations
USE law

related term references
USE cross references

related term relationships
USE associative relationships

relational databases
BT databases
RT relational models

relational models
BT database models
RT relational databases

relevance
SN *Applicability of retrieved documents or information to the subject of a query.*
BT (attributes of information and data)
RT contextual information
    evaluation
    fallout
    information retrieval noise
    information storage and retrieval systems
    pertinence
    precision
    relevance ranking
    retrieval effectiveness
    similarity

relevance feedback
USE query by example

relevance ranking
UF nearest neighbor
    ranking (relevance)
BT organization of information
    ranking
RT fuzzy retrieval systems
    keyword spam
    natural language processing
    probabilistic retrieval
    relevance

reliability
BT (general attributes)
RT complexity
    data corruption
    durability
    error correction
    error detection
    error rates
    errors
    fault tolerance
    file integrity
    indexer consistency
    maintainability
    performance
    permanence
    validity

religion
BT humanities

remote access
SN *To information systems.*
UF off site access
    offsite access
BT access to resources
NT wireless access
RT ftp

remote access (cont.)
    gophers
    telnet
    World Wide Web

remote control
BT control systems
NT telerobotics

remote sensing
BT (research and analytic methods)
RT measurement
    photogrammetry
    telemetry

repetitive stress injury
BT injury
RT data entry
    ergonomics
    human factors
    keyboards

replicative studies
BT research methods

reports, technical
USE technical reports

representation, knowledge
USE knowledge representation

reprints
BT publications
RT journals
    periodical articles

repurposing
BT modification

research and development
BT (research and analytic methods)
NT mission oriented research
    research design
    systems development
RT evaluation
    testing

research design
BT research and development
NT rating scales
    research variables
RT experiments
    research methods

research libraries
BT libraries

research libraries (cont.)
NT Presidential libraries
RT academic libraries
    public libraries

research methods
BT (research and analytic methods)
NT case studies
    Delphi studies
    empirical studies
    experiments
    longitudinal studies
    observational research
    questionnaires
    replicative studies
    surveys
    usage studies
    user studies
RT research design
    statistical methods

research variables
BT research design

researchers
USE scholars

resource centers
USE media centers

Resource Description Framework
UF RDF
BT XML

resource management (computing)
USE computing resource management

resource management (information)
USE information resources management

resource sharing
UF shared library resources
BT collaboration
NT peer to peer file sharing
RT information dissemination
    interlibrary loans

response time
UF retrieval speed
BT (attributes of systems and equipment)
RT bandwidth
    performance
    search time
    telecommunications traffic

restoration
BT materials preservation

retrieval effectiveness
BT effectiveness
RT evaluation
    fallout
    information retrieval
    information retrieval noise
    pertinence
    precision
    recall
    relevance

retrieval languages
USE index languages

retrieval software
USE information retrieval software

retrieval speed
USE response time

retrospective cataloging
BT cataloging

retrospective conversion
SN *Of data to machine-readable form.*
BT data conversion
RT digitization

reviewing
SN *Post-publication. For pre-publication reviewing, use "refereeing."*
BT evaluation

reviews
BT (documents by information content, purpose)
NT book reviews
    literature reviews

reviews of the literature
USE literature reviews

rewritable optical disks
USE erasable optical disks

RISC
UF reduced instruction set computers
BT computers

robotics
SN *The study of machines that interact with their environment by moving around in it and/or manipulating it, in what could be considered an intelligent manner.*

robotics (cont.)
BT computer science
NT telerobotics
RT computer vision
    robots

robots
BT (hardware, software, and equipment)
RT computer applications
    computer vision
    computers
    robotics

role indicators
SN *Codes used to explicate syntactic*
    relationships among the index terms assigned
    to a document.
BT knowledge organization systems
RT index languages
    indexing term links
    postcoordinate indexing
    subject indexing

rolling stacks
USE library shelving

ROM
USE read only memory

romanization
BT transliteration
RT ideographs
    nonroman scripts
    translation
    transliteration
    writing systems

rotated indexes
USE permuted indexes

rotated term indexes
USE KWIC indexes

rough set theory
SN *A method for representing uncertain or*
    imprecise knowledge, where certain items are
    known to belong in a rough set, while
    additional items may possibly belong to the
    rough set.
BT set theory
RT fuzzy logic

royalties
BT pricing
RT copyright
    public lending right

RT references
USE cross references

RT relationships
USE associative relationships

rule based systems
USE knowledge bases

Russia
BT Europe

sampling
BT statistical methods

satellite communications
UF communications satellites
BT (communications media)
    telecommunications
RT aerospace

satisfaction
USE user satisfaction

scalability
BT (attributes of systems and equipment)

Scandinavia
BT regions

scanners
UF optical scanners
BT input equipment
RT scanning

scanning
UF optical scanning
BT data processing
RT optical character recognition
    scanners

scheduling
BT management operations
RT backlogs
    management
    planning
    strategic planning

schemata
USE cognitive space

scholarly communication
SN *Reporting, discussion, and distribution of*
    nonpublished research.
BT human communications
RT Open Archives Initiative Protocol for

scholarly communication (cont.)
    Metadata Harvesting specification
    information dissemination
    scholarly publishing

scholarly journals
USE journals

scholarly literature
USE primary literature

scholarly publishing
UF academic publishing
BT publishing
RT journals
    monographs
    refereeing
    scholarly communication
    university presses

scholars
UF researchers
BT academic communities
RT faculty

school libraries
USE media centers

school media centers
USE media centers

schools
BT (organizations)
NT elementary schools
    high schools
    middle schools
RT accreditation
    colleges and universities
    media centers
    students

schools of information science
USE information science schools

scientific and technical information
UF STI
    technical information
BT domain information
NT biomedical information
    chemical information
    environmental information
RT natural sciences
    physical sciences
    scientometrics

scientific literature
USE primary literature

scientific societies
USE professional associations

scientists
BT (persons and informal groups)

scientometrics
BT informetrics
RT bioinformatics
    natural sciences
    physical sciences
    scientific and technical
    information

scope notes
SN *Statements providing guidance to the usage*
    or meaning of a term in a particular index
    language.
UF SN
BT syndetic structures

Scotland
BT Great Britain

screen design
BT design
RT human computer interaction
    interfaces
    video display terminals
    web sites

scripts (writing systems)
USE writing systems

SDI services
SN *Services which alert registered users to the*
    latest publications in specified field(s) of
    interest.
UF selective dissemination of information
BT current awareness services
RT contents lists
    e-mail list servers
    information dissemination
    information filtering
    library user profiles

SDQL
UF standard document query language
BT query languages
RT DSSSL
    SGML

search agents
USE intelligent agents

search behavior
UF information seeking behavior
BT user behavior
RT end user searching
    searching

search engine optimization
BT optimization

search engine persuasion
USE keyword spam

search engines
SN *Software which performs searches of queries*
    submitted to it; it may analyze the query
    and/or rank the results.
UF Google
BT information retrieval software
NT Internet search systems
    hybrid search engines
    meta search engines
RT full text searching

search formulation
USE query formulation

search hedges
SN *Strings of terms used concurrently in an*
    online search query.
BT search strategies

search histories
BT information representations
RT breadcrumbs
    searching
    usage records

search languages
USE index languages

search profiles
USE library user profiles

search services
SN *Organizations which sell, lease, or provide*
    access to databases produced by other
    organizations.
UF aggregators
    database hosts
    database vendors
    host computers
    host services
BT vendors

search services (cont.)
RT database leasing
    database producers
    information industry
    information infrastructure
    information utilities
    online industry

search statements
USE search terms

search strategies
BT searching
NT search hedges
    truncation
    weighting
RT knowledge organization systems
    library user profiles
    online searching
    query formulation
    searching

search systems
USE information storage and retrieval systems

search term weighting
USE weighting

search terms
UF search statements
BT terms
RT index terms
    query formulation
    searching
    weighting

search time
SN *Time expended by a user in searching; not*
    system "response time."
BT (attributes of systems and equipment)
RT performance
    response time
    searching

searching
BT information seeking
NT Boolean searching
    assisted searching
    citation searching
    end user searching
    federated searching
    full text searching
    keyword searching
    known item searching
    online searching
    proximity searching

searching (cont.)
    query by example
    query formulation
    range searching
    search strategies
    string searching
    subject searching
RT fuzzy retrieval systems
    information mapping
    search behavior
    search histories
    search strategies
    search terms
    search time

Sears Subject Headings
BT subject heading lists

secondary information services
USE secondary publishers

secondary literature
USE text editors

secondary publishers
UF secondary information services
BT publishers
RT abstracting and indexing service
    bureaus

security
BT legal aspects
NT computer security
    data security
    intrusion prevention and detection
    library security
    national security
RT crime
    disasters
    disclosure
    identification
    privacy
    security classification

security classification
UF classified information
BT management operations
RT confidential records
    military intelligence
    security

see also references
USE cross references

see references
USE cross references

selection
BT general activities
NT materials selection

selective dissemination of information
USE SDI services

self citation
BT citation analysis

self organizing maps
SN *Data visualization technique which reduces*
    the dimensions of data and displays data
    clustered on the basis of their similarities.
BT data maps
RT algorithms
    dimensionality reduction

self publishing
BT publishing

semantic analysis
BT linguistic analysis
RT semantic relationships
    semantics

semantic headers
USE metadata

semantic indexing
USE latent semantic analysis

semantic nets
USE semantic networks

semantic networks
SN *Graphic representations. For discussion of*
    relationships in meaning, use "semantic
    relationships."
UF semantic nets
BT artificial intelligence
    data maps
RT network structures
    ontologies
    semantic relationships
    semantics

semantic relationships
UF conceptual relationships
BT semantics
NT antonymy
    associative relationships
    equivalence relationships
    hierarchical relationships
    homography
RT categories

semantic relationships (cont.)
  index language construction
  semantic analysis
  semantic networks
  semantics

semantic web
SN *Abstract representation of documents as a
    web, with elements defined so they can be
    processed by machines following RDF and
    other standards.*
BT World Wide Web

semantics
UF meaning
BT linguistics
  semiotics
NT semantic relationships
RT morphemes
  semantic analysis
  semantic networks
  semantic relationships

semiology
USE semiotics

semiotics
SN *Theory and study of signs and symbols,
    especially as elements of language or other
    systems of communication.*
UF semiology
BT (fields and disciplines)
NT pragmatics
  semantics
  syntactics
RT linguistics

sensors
BT instrumentation
RT data collection
  input equipment

sensory perception
SN *Conscious awareness of a sensory stimulus.*
BT mental processes
RT perceptual learning
  sensory processes

sensory processes
BT (human processes)
NT hearing
  touch
  vision
RT sensory perception

sentence generation
SN *Generation of natural language sentences
    from other representations.*
BT natural language processing
RT sentences

sentences
BT linguistic elements
RT sentence generation
  syntactic analysis

serendipity
SN *Unexpected discovery of useful information
    through browsing.*
BT browsing

serial conversion
SN *Changing digital objects incrementally to be
    compatible with later versions of the original
    software used for their creation, maintenance,
    access, and display.*
UF backward compatibility
BT digital object preservation

serials
BT publications
NT newspapers
  periodicals
  yearbooks
RT conference proceedings
  ISSN
  series
  subscriptions

seriation
USE ranking

series
BT publications
RT serials

service bureaus
BT (product and service providers)
NT abstracting and indexing service bureaus
RT vendors

set mapping
BT set theory

set theory
BT mathematical models
NT fuzzy logic
  rough set theory
  set mapping
RT mathematics

sex
USE gender

sex discrimination
USE social discrimination

SGML
UF standard generalized markup language
BT markup languages
RT DSSSL
   SDQL

shape
BT physical attributes
RT touch

shared cataloging
BT cataloging
   collaboration

shared library resources
USE resource sharing

shareware
SN *Software distributed without charge for*
   which users can pay voluntarily.
UF freeware
BT computer software

shelving
USE materials storage

shelving, library
USE library shelving

shopping, computer
USE teleshopping

short term memory
UF working memory
BT human memory

sight
USE vision

signal boundary detection
UF signal detection
BT signal processing
RT data segmentation

signal detection
USE signal boundary detection

signal processing
BT computer operations
NT signal boundary detection

signal processing (cont.)
RT compression
   image processing
   telecommunications

similarity
UF congruence
   likeness
BT (attributes of information and data)
RT feedback
   relevance

simulation
BT (research and analytic methods)
NT computer simulation
RT analytic models

situated knowledge
SN *Relativist perspective of knowledge*
   associated to place, time, conditions,
   practices, and understandings.
BT knowledge
RT contextual information

skewed distribution
BT data distribution

skills
BT (human attributes)
NT communication skills
   information and reference skills
   professional competencies

skills databases
USE human resource files

small libraries
UF one person libraries
   solo librarians
BT libraries

small presses
UF underground presses
BT publishers
RT alternative publications

smart cards
BT magnetic media
RT electronic cash
   identification

smart paper
USE electronic paper

SN
USE scope notes

social aspects
SN *Of information and information use. For the discipline, use "social sciences" and its narrower terms.*
UF folklore
BT (sociocultural aspects)
NT etiquette
RT communities
    human behavior
    information society
    social sciences
    sociology

social discrimination
UF sex discrimination
BT cultural aspects
RT affirmative action
    cultural diversity
    disabled persons
    employment
    gender
    minorities and ethnic groups
    social equity

social equity
BT socioeconomic aspects
RT digital divide
    ethics
    social discrimination
    socioeconomic status

social filtering
USE collaborative filtering

social informatics
SN *The interdisciplinary study of the design, uses and consequences of information technologies that takes into account their interaction with institutional and cultural contexts.*
BT informatics
RT sociometrics

social networking
SN *Contacts among individuals. For networks of organizations or equipment, use "networks" or the appropriate specific term, e.g., "telecommunications networks."*
UF personal networking
BT cultural aspects
RT boundary spanners
    gatekeepers
    human behavior
    human communications
    human information resources
    information filtering

social networking (cont.)
    information flow
    information seeking
    invisible colleges
    organizational communication
    social psychology
    sociograms
    sociology
    sociometrics

social psychology
BT psychology
    social sciences
RT social networking

social sciences
BT (fields and disciplines)
NT anthropology
    economics
    education
    political science
    social psychology
    socioeconomics
    sociology
RT area studies
    behavioral sciences
    demographics
    law
    social aspects
    sociometrics

social systems
USE sociology

societies
USE professional associations

socioeconomic activities
BT (activities and operations)
NT affirmative action
    career development
    commerce
    competition
    employment
    entrepreneurship
    innovation
    technology transfer
RT socioeconomics

socioeconomic aspects
BT (sociocultural aspects)
NT demographics
    digital divide
    economic sectors
    information infrastructure
    information society

socioeconomic aspects (cont.)
    social equity
    technology impact
RT sociology

socioeconomic status
BT demographics
RT digital divide
    social equity
    socioeconomics

socioeconomics
BT economics
    social sciences
RT socioeconomic activities
    socioeconomic status
    sociology

sociograms
BT graphs
RT social networking
    sociometrics

sociology
UF social systems
BT behavioral sciences
    social sciences
NT organization theory
    sociometrics
RT social aspects
    social networking
    socioeconomic aspects
    socioeconomics

sociometrics
BT informetrics
    sociology
RT social informatics
    social networking
    social sciences
    sociograms

software development
USE software engineering

software engineering
UF software development
    software programming
BT computer programming engineering
NT computer aided software engineering
RT computer science

software industry
UF software publishers
BT (product and service providers)
RT computer industry

software industry (cont.)
    computer software
    publishing

software programming
USE software engineering

software publishers
USE software industry

software reuse
BT computer operations
RT computer programming
    standardization

software, computer
USE computer software

solo librarians
USE small libraries

sort sequences
BT knowledge organization systems
RT alphabetical arrangement
    arrangement
    sorting

sorting
BT data processing
RT arrangement
    data parsing
    sort sequences

sound
USE acoustic data

sound recorders
USE audio recorders

sound recordings
USE audio recordings

source materials
BT (documents by availability, access,
    organization)
RT bibliographic citations

South Africa
BT Africa

South America
BT (countries and regions)
NT Argentina
    Bolivia
    Brazil
    Chile

South America (cont.)
   Colombia
   Ecuador
   Guyana
   Paraguay
   Peru
   Suriname
   Uruguay
   Venezuela
RT Latin America

Southeast Asia
BT Asia
   regions

Spain
BT Europe

spam
USE unsolicited e-mail

spamdexing
USE keyword spam

spatial information
BT domain information
NT geospatial information

special collections
BT collections
RT rare materials

special libraries
UF clearinghouses (special libraries)
   information centers (special libraries)
BT libraries
NT corporate libraries
   law libraries
   medical libraries
   Presidential libraries

speech recognition
SN *Mechanical conversion of human speech*
   sounds into words which can be processed as
   text.
UF speech understanding
   voice recognition
BT natural language processing
RT audio interfaces
   human speech

speech synthesis
SN *Mechanical generation of human speech.*
UF artificial speech production
   synthesis, speech
   voice synthesis

speech synthesis (cont.)
BT natural language processing
RT audio interfaces
   human speech

speech understanding
USE speech recognition

spell checkers
USE spelling checkers

spelling
USE orthography

spelling checkers
UF spell checkers
BT computer software applications
RT typographical errors
   word processing

spelling errors
USE typographical errors

spiders (automatic searching)
USE Internet search systems

spoken communication
UF oral communications
BT human communications
NT face to face communication
   interviews
   meetings
   narratives
   storytelling
RT acoustic data
   human speech
   informal communication
   meetings

spreading activation
SN *Theory of sequential retrieval of informally*
   linked concepts in a mental map prompted by
   an initial stimulus.
BT information models
RT neural networks

spreadsheets
BT (documents by information content, purpose)
RT numeric data

SQL
UF structured query language
BT query languages

stacks, library
USE library shelving

staff development
BT educational activities
RT employees
    training

stakeholders
BT (persons and informal groups)

standard book numbers
USE ISBN

standard document query language
USE SDQL

standard film numbers
USE ISFN

standard generalized markup language
USE SGML

standard music numbers
USE ISMN

standard record codes
USE ISRC

standard serial numbers
USE ISSN

standardization
BT general activities
RT benchmarks
    evaluation
    software reuse
    standards
    standards developing organizations

standards
UF guidelines
    protocols
BT (documents by information content, purpose)
NT International Standard Bibliographic
    Description
    Open Archives Initiative Protocol for
      Metadata Harvesting specification
    OpenURL
    benchmarks
    communications protocols
    metadata standards
RT ISBN
    ISFN
    ISMN
    ISRC
    ISSN
    standardization
    standards developing organizations

standards developing organizations
UF ANSI
    ISO
    NISO
    W3C
BT (organizations)
RT standardization
    standards

standing orders
UF till forbid orders
BT materials orders

state agencies
USE government agencies

state libraries
USE state library agencies

state library agencies
UF state libraries
BT government agencies
    government libraries
RT government libraries
    public libraries

statistical analysis
USE statistical methods

statistical data
USE numeric data

statistical databases
USE numeric databases

statistical methods
UF statistical analysis
BT mathematical methods
NT analysis of variance
    Bayesian functions
    canonical correlation
    Monte Carlo method
    multidimensional scaling
    multivariate analysis
    sampling
RT factor analysis
    mathematics
    Pathfinder networks
    probability
    research methods
    statistics

statistical retrieval
USE probabilistic retrieval

statistics
BT mathematics
NT decision theory
RT statistical methods

stemming
SN *Truncation of words, disregarding prefixes and/or suffixes; may be used either in algorithmic indexing or in retrieval.*
BT truncation
RT affixes
   normalization
   word roots

STI
USE scientific and technical information

stochastic models
BT mathematical models
RT stochastic processes

stochastic processes
SN *Processes that involve a random variable, i.e., a variable that changes over time.*
UF random processes
BT (general processes)
NT queuing
RT cybernetics
   probability
   stochastic models

stop lists
USE stoplists

stop words
USE stoplists

stoplists
UF stop lists
   stop words
BT (documents by information content, purpose)
RT derivative indexing
   full text searching
   keywords

storytelling
BT spoken communication
RT children's services
   library and archival services

strategic planning
BT planning
RT forecasting
   scheduling

streaming audio
USE data streaming

streaming media
USE data streaming

streaming video
USE data streaming

string indexing
SN *Indexing methods which generate a string or set of articulated index terms for each entry.*
BT subject indexing

string searching
BT searching
RT proximity searching

structured query language
USE SQL

students
BT academic communities
RT education
   schools

subdivisions (indexing)
USE modifiers

subheadings
USE modifiers

subject access
BT information access
RT subject searching

subject cataloging
BT cataloging
RT subject heading lists
   subject indexing

subject expertise
USE domain knowledge

subject experts
UF experts, subject
BT human information resources
RT invisible colleges

subject heading lists
BT controlled vocabularies
NT Library of Congress Subject Headings
   Sears Subject Headings
RT subject cataloging
   subject headings
   thesauri

subject headings
SN *Words, phrases, and modifiers used to indicate the content of documents or parts of documents; typically using precoordinated terms for complex concepts.*
BT index terms
RT descriptors
    keywords
    subject heading lists
    vocabulary control

subject index terms
USE index terms

subject indexes
BT information retrieval indexes
RT index terms
    subject indexing
    subject searching

subject indexing
UF content tagging
    keyword tagging
    subject metadata
BT (indexing by feature indexed)
NT assignment indexing
    chain indexing
    derivative indexing
    generic posting
    multilingual subject indexing
    postcoordinate indexing
    precoordinate indexing
    probabilistic indexing
    string indexing
RT aboutness
    index languages
    indexing specificity
    indexing term links
    keywords
    role indicators
    subject cataloging
    subject indexes

subject metadata
USE subject indexing

subject searching
BT searching
RT full text searching
    online searching
    subject access
    subject indexes

subject switching
USE information mapping

sublanguages
SN *Specialized vernacular used within a discourse community.*
BT language types
    linguistics

subscription agencies
BT vendors
RT materials acquisitions
    subscriptions

subscription cancellation
BT collection management
RT deselection
    materials acquisitions
    subscriptions

subscriptions
BT materials acquisitions
RT materials claims
    serials
    subscription agencies
    subscription cancellation

subsidies
BT funding
NT grants

suffixes
USE affixes

summaries
USE digests

summarization
UF gist
BT information operations
NT abstracting
    extracting
RT literature reviews

supercomputers
UF high performance computing
BT computers

superimposed coding
BT encoding

suppliers
USE vendors

support staff, library
USE paraprofessional library personnel

Suriname
BT South America

surnames
USE proper names

surveillance
USE monitoring

surveys
BT (documents by information content, purpose)
    research methods
NT library surveys

switching languages
UF intermediate index languages
    intermediate lexicons
BT controlled vocabularies
RT information mapping

symbols
BT information representations
RT icons

syndetic structures
BT controlled vocabularies
NT cross references
    scope notes

synonyms
UF nonpreferred terms
BT terms
RT equivalence relationships
    quasi-synonymous relationships
    words

syntactic analysis
UF linguistic parsing
BT linguistic analysis
RT phrases
    sentences
    syntactics

syntactics
SN *Pertains to the rules of syntax, the formal*
    relationships between words or signs,
    independent of their meaning.
BT linguistics
    semiotics
RT affixes
    anaphora
    syntactic analysis

synthesis, notation
USE notation synthesis

synthesis, speech
USE speech synthesis

synthetic classification
BT classification

system knowledge
BT knowledge

systematic arrangement
UF classified arrangement
BT arrangement
RT classification
    classification schemes
    classified catalogs

systems analysis
BT systems development
NT flow charting
    operations research
RT systems design
    systems development
    work flow analysis

systems design
BT systems development
RT flow charting
    modularity
    systems analysis
    systems development

systems development
BT research and development
NT systems analysis
    systems design
RT systems analysis
    systems design
    systems integration

systems integration
UF integration, systems
BT management operations
RT integrated systems
    systems development

table of contents lists
USE contents lists

tagging, automatic
USE automatic categorization

talking books
BT audio recordings
    books

tape leasing
USE database leasing

tape recorders
USE audio recorders

task analysis
BT (research and analytic methods)
NT work flow analysis

task knowledge
BT knowledge
RT domain knowledge

taxonomies
SN *Arrangements of ordered groups or*
categories in a hierarchical structure.
BT controlled vocabularies
RT automatic taxonomy generation
classification schemes
information architecture
thesauri

taxonomy construction
USE index language construction

teachers
USE faculty

teaching
USE education

technical and manufacturing operations
BT (activities and operations)
NT computer aided engineering
computer aided manufacturing
computer integrated manufacturing
flexible manufacturing systems
printing
quality assurance
quality control
recording
typesetting
typography

technical information
USE scientific and technical information

technical processes
USE materials processing

technical reports
UF reports, technical
BT (documents by availability, access,
organization)
RT government publications
grey literature
primary literature

technical writing
BT human communications
RT authorship

technological gatekeepers
USE gatekeepers

technological innovation
USE innovation

technology impact
BT socioeconomic aspects
RT innovation
technology transfer

technology transfer
BT socioeconomic activities
RT diffusion of innovation
technology impact

telecommunications
UF telematics
BT communications activities
NT audio communications
broadcasting
computer mediated communications
data transmission
facsimile transmission
mobile communications
multiple access communications
multiplexing
packet switching
satellite communications
telecommunications traffic
teleconferencing
telegraphy
teletext
video communications
videotex
RT communications protocols
information technology
signal processing
telecommunications equipment
telecommunications industry
telecommunications networks
telecommunications traffic
teleshopping
transmission speed

telecommunications equipment
BT (hardware, software, and equipment)
NT coaxial cable
fiber optics
modems
telephones
RT telecommunications

126

telecommunications equipment (cont.)
    telecommunications industry
    television

telecommunications industry
UF common carriers
BT (product and service providers)
NT Internet service providers
RT information industry
    telecommunications
    telecommunications equipment
    telecommunications networks

telecommunications networks
UF communications networks
    computer networks
    information highway
    information networks
    information superhighway
BT (communications networks)
NT common carrier networks
    Internet
    local area networks
    National Research and Education Network
    wide area networks
RT library networks
    network security
    telecommunications
    telecommunications industry

telecommunications traffic
SN *Data or messages conveyed through a*
    telecommunications network.
BT telecommunications
RT response time

telecommuting
UF teleworking
BT employment

teleconferencing
BT telecommunications
NT electronic conferencing
    video teleconferencing
    web conferencing
RT groupware
    meetings

telefacsimile
USE facsimile transmission

telegraphy
BT telecommunications

telemarketing
BT marketing

telematics
USE telecommunications

telemetry
BT measurement
RT remote sensing

telephones
BT telecommunications equipment
NT videotelephones
RT Internet telephony
    voice transmission

telephony
BT audio communications
NT Internet telephony

telerobotics
BT remote control
    robotics

teleshopping
UF shopping, computer
BT computer applications
RT electronic commerce
    telecommunications
    videotex

teletext
SN *Electronic communications system in which*
    printed information is broadcast by television
    signal to sets equipped with decoders.
BT telecommunications
RT videotex

television
BT mass media
    video communications
RT broadcasting
    cameras
    telecommunications equipment

teleworking
USE telecommuting

telnet
BT communications protocols
RT Internet
    computer mediated communications
    remote access

temporal arrangement
UF chronological order
BT arrangement
RT temporal information

temporal currency
UF timeliness
    up to dateness
BT (attributes of information and data)
RT accuracy
    updating

temporal information
UF time data
BT domain information
NT time series data
RT temporal arrangement

term co-occurrence analysis
USE co-occurrence analysis

term frequency
USE word frequency

term weighting
USE weighting

terminals, video display
USE video display terminals

terminology
SN *The collection of terms peculiar to a*
    specialized subject; nomenclature.
UF definitions (of terms)
    nomenclature
BT information representations
NT chemical nomenclature
    terms
RT controlled vocabularies
    dictionaries

terms
SN *Words or phrases used to denote concepts.*
BT terminology
NT index terms
    search terms
    synonyms
RT words

terms of use
USE usage agreements

terrorism
BT crime

test data
UF TREC test collection
BT data

testing
BT (research and analytic methods)

testing (cont.)
NT prototyping
RT evaluation
    experiments
    research and development

text analysis
USE text processing

text databases
USE full text databases

text editors
UF secondary literature
BT computer software applications
RT word processing

text messaging
BT message systems

text mining
SN *Search for patterns in natural language text*
    to extract information for a specific purpose.
BT knowledge discovery

text processing
UF text analysis
BT information processing
NT content analysis
    linguistic analysis
RT data processing
    natural language processing

text retrieval
USE full text searching

textbases
USE full text databases

textbooks
BT books

textual databases
USE full text databases

texture
BT physical attributes
RT touch

theft
USE crime

theft detection systems
USE library security systems

theoretical models
USE analytic models

thesauri
BT controlled vocabularies
NT graphical thesauri
   MeSH
   metathesauri
   microthesauri
   multilingual thesauri
   thesaurus displays
RT associative relationships
   candidate descriptors
   descriptors
   dictionaries
   equivalence relationships
   hierarchical relationships
   index language construction
   index terms
   lexicography
   subjcct heading lists
   taxonomies
   thesaurofacet
   thesaurus management
   vocabulary control

thesaurofacet
SN *An indexing vocabulary which combines an*
   alphabetical thesaurus and a faceted
   classification scheme.
BT controlled vocabularies
RT classification schemes
   faceted classification
   thesauri

thesaurus construction
USE index language construction

thesaurus displays
UF displays (thesauri)
BT thesauri

thesaurus management
UF thesaurus updating
BT information resources management
RT index language construction
   thesauri

thesaurus updating
USE thesaurus management

theses
USE dissertations

thinking
USE cognition

three dimensional imagery
USE holography

thumbnail views
SN *A small graphic representation of a page,*
   image or file.
BT document surrogates

till forbid orders
USE standing orders

time data
USE temporal information

time series data
BT temporal information

timeliness
USE temporal currency

top terms
SN *In thesauri, the broadest terms in*
   hierarchies; terms which have narrower
   terms, but no broader term.
UF TT
BT index terms

topic maps
BT data maps
RT information space

topic threads
BT knowledge organization systems
RT concepts
   e-mail list servers
   topics

topics
BT information content
RT aboutness
   topic thrcads

topology
USE data maps

touch screen interfaces
UF touch terminals
BT interfaces
RT touch
   video display terminals

touch terminals
USE touch screen interfaces

touch
BT sensory processes

touch (cont.)
RT shape
   texture
   touch screen interfaces

trackballs
BT pointing devices
RT graphical user interfaces
   mice

trade secrets
BT information content
RT copyright
   intellectual property

trademark infringement
BT crime
RT copyright piracy
   trademarks

trademarks
BT information representations
RT copyright
   intellectual property
   trademark infringement

training
BT educational activities
NT bibliographic instruction
   tutorials
   user training
RT education
   staff development

transaction logs
USE usage records

transborder data flow
UF crossborder data flow
   international data flow
   transnational data flow
BT information flow
RT international aspects

transfer of information
USE information transfer

translation
UF interpretation (linguistic)
BT information operations
NT machine translation
RT romanization

translators
UF interpreters (linguistic)
BT information professionals

transliteration
SN *Transcription from one alphabet to another.*
BT information operations
NT romanization
RT alphabets
   nonroman scripts
   romanization
   writing systems

transmission speed
UF baud rate
BT (attributes of systems and equipment)
RT modems
   telecommunications

transnational data flow
USE transborder data flow

TREC test collection
USE test data

tree structures
BT data structures

trends
BT change

Trojan horses
BT malicious software

tropes
USE idioms

truncation
SN *In algorithmic indexing or searching,*
   dropping of characters at the beginning, at
   the end and/or within a word, to permit
   matching on all character sequences which
   match the truncated word.
BT search strategies
NT stemming
RT affixes

trust
BT psychological aspects

trustees (library)
USE library boards

TT
USE top terms

turnkey systems
BT computer systems

130

tutorials
BT training
RT user aids

typesetting
UF computer typesetting
BT technical and manufacturing operations
RT printing
    typography

typographical errors
UF keyboarding errors
    misspellings
    spelling errors
BT errors
RT spelling checkers

typography
BT technical and manufacturing operations
RT printing
    typesetting

ubicomp
USE ubiquitous computing

ubiquitous computing
SN *Computer operations carried out through*
many computers available in the physical
environment, but effectively invisible to the
user.
UF ubicomp
BT human computer interaction

UDC
USE Universal Decimal Classification

UF references
USE cross references

UF relationships
USE equivalence relationships

uncertainty
BT (attributes of information and data)
RT ambiguity
    probability

uncontrolled indexing
USE keywords

underground presses
USE small presses

underground publications
USE alternative publications

understanding (comprehension)
USE comprehension

understanding (natural language)
USE natural language comprehension

unified retrieval models
UF data fusion
BT information retrieval models

uniform resource characteristics
SN *Unique metadata describing a networked*
    resource.
UF URC
BT URI

uniform resource identifier
USE URI

uniform resource locators
USE URL

uniform resource names
SN *Unique and permanent identifier of a digital*
    object, independent of its location,
    incorporating in the name its digital object
    identifier and a namespace-specific-string.
UF URN
BT URI
RT digital objects

union catalogs
BT catalogs (bibliographic)

unions, labor
USE labor unions

United Kingdom
BT Europe
NT Great Britain
    Northern Ireland

United States
BT North America

uniterm indexing
USE postcoordinate indexing

universal access
SN *Access to information (as a concept, not*
    technology).
BT access to resources
RT censorship

Universal Decimal Classification
UF UDC

Universal Decimal Classification (cont.)
BT classification schemes

universities
USE colleges and universities

university libraries
USE academic libraries

university presses
BT publishers
RT scholarly publishing

unsolicited bulk e-mail
BT unsolicited e-mail

unsolicited commercial e-mail
BT unsolicited e-mail

unsolicited e-mail
UF spam
BT e-mail
NT unsolicited bulk e-mail
    unsolicited commercial e-mail

up to dateness
USE temporal currency

updating
BT maintenance
RT temporal currency

uploading
BT file transfers

URC
USE uniform resource characteristics

URI
SN *Standardized method for identifying a
    document or digital resource, representing its
    name, location or both.*
UF uniform resource identifier
BT persistent identifiers
NT URL
    uniform resource characteristics
    uniform resource names
RT locators

URL
SN *Standardized addresses for web sites and
    pages, designating where a digital object is
    held at a point in time. Permanence of the
    address is not assured.*
UF uniform resource locators
BT URI

URL (cont.)
    locators
RT digital object identifiers
    domain naming system
    World Wide Web

URN
USE uniform resource names

Uruguay
BT South America

usability
SN *A product's potential to accomplish the goals
    of the user including such features as ease-of-
    use and visual consistency.*
UF ease of use
    user friendliness
BT (general attributes)
RT accuracy
    complexity
    effectiveness
    human factors
    user attributes
    utility

usage agreements
UF browse-wrap
    click-wrap
    terms of use
BT legal aspects

usage frequency
USE frequency of use

usage records
UF transaction logs
BT records
RT search histories

usage studies
BT research methods
NT web usage studies

use instruction
USE bibliographic instruction

use of information
USE information use

use references
USE cross references

use relationships
USE equivalence relationships

use studies
USE user studies

used for references
USE cross references

used for relationships
USE equivalence relationships

used terms
USE index terms

Usenet newsgroups
USE newsgroups

user aids
UF user guides
    user manuals
BT (documents by information content, purpose)
NT help systems
RT documentation
    handbooks
    tutorials
    user training
    users

user attributes
BT (human attributes)
NT user expectations
    user expertise
    user preferences
    user profiles
    user satisfaction
RT usability
    user behavior
    user expectations

user behavior
BT user studies
NT search behavior
RT user attributes
    user expectations
    user training
    users

user education
USE user training

user expectations
BT human factors
    user attributes
RT user attributes
    user behavior
    user satisfaction
    users

user expertise
BT user attributes
RT experienced users
    novice users

user feedback
USE feedback

user friendliness
USE usability

user guides
USE user aids

user information needs
USE information needs

user manuals
USE user aids

user models
SN *Models of users; for users' models of information or objects, use "cognitive models."*
BT analytic models
RT user studies
    users

user multitasking
BT general activities

user needs
USE information needs

user preferences
BT user attributes

user profiles
BT user attributes
NT library user profiles

user satisfaction
UF satisfaction
BT user attributes
RT user expectations
    users

user studies
UF information user studies
    use studies
BT research methods
NT user behavior
RT focus groups
    information use
    library surveys
    user models

user studies (cont.)
    users

user system interfaces
USE interfaces

user training
UF user education
BT training
RT bibliographic instruction
    information literacy
    user aids
    user behavior
    users

user warrant
SN *Justification for inclusion of a term for a*
    concept in an indexing language on the basis
    of requests by users.
BT warrant
RT literary warrant

users
UF information users
    patrons
BT (persons and informal groups)
NT end users
    library users
RT bibliographic instruction
    information needs
    information use
    user aids
    user behavior
    user expectations
    user models
    user satisfaction
    user studies
    user training
    volunteers

utility
BT (general attributes)
RT effectiveness
    usability

utility software
BT computer software applications

validation
BT data processing
RT error correction
    error detection
    error messages
    error rates
    errors
    verification

validity
BT (attributes of information and data)
RT reliability

value added
BT (general attributes)
RT abstracting and indexing service bureaus
    information services

value of information
USE economics of information

vandalism
USE crime

VDT
USE video display terminals

VDU
USE video display terminals

vector analysis
BT mathematical methods
RT vector space models

vector space models
BT information retrieval models
RT data maps
    information space
    vector analysis

vendors
SN *Very broad term; prefer specific product or*
    service, e.g., "book vendors," "consultants."
UF suppliers
BT (product and service providers)
NT book vendors
    jobbers
    library suppliers
    search services
    subscription agencies
RT consultants
    service bureaus

Venezuela
BT South America

verbs
BT linguistic elements

verification
BT data processing
RT error correction
    error detection
    error rates
    errors

verification (cont.)
    validation

vertical files
BT (documents by medium, physical form)
RT ephemera
    pamphlets

very large databases
BT databases

very large scale integration
USE VLSI

video clips
BT motion video
    video recordings
RT keyframes

video communications
UF video streaming
BT telecommunications
NT motion video
    television
    video teleconferencing
RT digital video files

video conferencing
USE video teleconferencing

video display terminals
UF cathode ray tube terminals
    CRT terminals
    graphics terminals
    terminals, video display
    VDT
    VDU
    visual display terminals
BT computer peripherals
    display devices
RT input equipment
    output equipment
    screen design
    touch screen interfaces

video games
UF computer games
BT computer software applications
RT joysticks
    multiuser Internet games

video materials
USE video recordings

video recorders
BT recording equipment

video recordings
SN *Used for recordings of motion video.*
UF recordings, video
    video materials
BT nonprint media
NT motion picture films
    video clips
    videocassettes
RT digital video files
    motion video

video streaming
USE video communications

video teleconferencing
UF video conferencing
BT teleconferencing
    video communications
RT meetings
    motion video

videocassettes
BT video recordings
RT magnetic tapes

videodisks
SN *Magnetic, capacitive, or optical (laser) disks
on which are recorded video signals (with or
without accompanying sound) for play back
on a television monitor or screen.*
BT optical disks

videophones
USE videotelephones

videotelephones
UF picture telephones
    videophones
BT telephones

videotex
SN *An information service in which data is
transmitted over television cables or
telephone lines and displayed on a television
or computer screen in the home.*
BT telecommunications
RT teleshopping
    teletext

virtual communities
UF distributed communities
BT communities

virtual environment
USE virtual reality

virtual libraries
SN *Systems in which information resources are distributed via networks, rather than being physically held in a particular location.*
BT libraries
RT digital libraries
    document delivery
    library automation

virtual memory
BT computer memory

virtual reality
UF virtual environment
BT computer applications
RT multiuser Internet games

virtual reference services
USE electronic reference services

vision
UF sight
BT sensory processes
RT computer vision

visual arts
BT fine arts
RT architecture

visual display terminals
USE video display terminals

visual information
USE visual materials

visual materials
SN *Used for static visual images.*
UF visual information
    visual representation
    visual resources
BT nonprint media
NT images
    maps
    pictures
RT maps

visual memory
BT human memory
RT mental visualization

visual representation
USE visual materials

visual resources
USE visual materials

visually impaired persons
UF blind persons
BT disabled persons
RT braille
    large print materials

VLSI
UF very large scale integration
BT LSI

vocabulary control
BT organization of information
RT assignment indexing
    controlled vocabularies
    index language construction
    literary warrant
    subject headings
    thesauri

vocal interfaces
USE audio interfaces

voice communications
BT audio communications
NT voice mail
RT voice transmission

voice input
USE audio interfaces

voice mail
BT message systems
    voice communications

voice recognition
USE speech recognition

voice synthesis
USE speech synthesis

voice transmission
BT data transmission
RT telephones
    voice communications

volunteers
BT (persons and informal groups)
RT information workers
    users

W3C
USE standards developing
    organizations

Wales
BT Great Britain

WAN
USE wide area networks

wanderers
USE Internet search systems

warrant
BT (attributes of information and data)
NT literary warrant
   user warrant

Web
USE World Wide Web

web bibliometry
USE webometrics

web browsers
BT client server software
RT World Wide Web

web conferencing
BT computer conferencing
   teleconferencing

web content management
BT content management

web designers
BT information professionals
RT web sites

web home pages
SN *Files developed to provide information on*
   subjects of interest to individuals or
   organizations.
BT web pages

web mining
SN *Search for patterns in the hypertext of web*
   sites.
BT knowledge discovery
RT web usage studies
   World Wide Web

web pages
BT web sites
NT web home pages
RT web site traffic

web site traffic
BT frequency of use
RT web pages
   web sites

web sites
BT World Wide Web
NT frames
   mirror sites
   portals
   web pages
RT screen design
   web designers
   web site traffic

Web TV
SN *Equipment designed to work with television*
   sets for Internet access.
BT microcomputers
RT Internet
   network computers
   World Wide Web

web usage studies
UF clickstream analysis
BT usage studies
RT web mining

webbots
USE Internet search systems

webliographies
BT bibliographies

weblogs
SN *Web site of personal or non-commercial*
   origin that uses a dated log format to update
   new information about a particular subject.
UF blogs
BT electronic documents

webometrics
SN *Quantitative study of web-related*
   phenomena.
UF cybermetrics
   netometrics
   web bibliometry
BT informetrics
NT link analysis

weeding
USE deselection

weighting
UF index term weighting
   query weighting
   search term weighting
   term weighting
BT search strategies
RT index terms
   indexing

weighting (cont.)
   search terms

wide area networks
UF WAN
BT telecommunications networks

windows interfaces
USE graphical user interfaces

winnowing
USE faceted browsing

wire services
USE newswire services

wireless access
SN *To information systems and services.*
BT remote access

Wireless Markup Language
USE WML

WML
UF Wireless Markup Language
BT markup languages

women
BT (persons and informal groups)
RT gender

word by word arrangement
UF nothing before something arrangement
BT alphabetical arrangement

word co-occurrence analysis
USE co-occurrence analysis

word frequency
UF term frequency
BT frequency of use
RT Zipf's law

word processing
BT data processing
RT spelling checkers
   text editors

word recognition
BT pattern recognition
RT words

word roots
UF lexemes
BT linguistic elements
RT stemming

words
BT linguistic elements
RT etymology
   lexicography
   synonyms
   terms
   word recognition

work flow analysis
BT task analysis
RT systems analysis

workflow
USE flow charting

workgroup computing
USE groupware

working at home
UF home work
BT employment

working memory
USE short term memory

workshops
BT meetings
RT continuing education

workstations
BT computers
RT personal computers

world knowledge
USE common sense knowledge

World Wide Web
UF Web
   WWW
BT Internet
   mass media
NT invisible web
   semantic web
   web sites
RT HTML
   hypertext
   Internet search systems
   network computers
   remote access
   semantic web
   URL
   web browsers
   web mining
   Web TV

WORM disks
UF write once read many
BT optical disks
NT DRAW

write once read many
USE WORM disks

writers
USE authors

writing systems
UF scripts (writing systems)
BT information representations
NT alphabets
braille
cursive script
ideographs
nonroman scripts
RT romanization
transliteration

writing
USE authorship

WWW
USE World Wide Web

XML
BT markup languages
NT Resource Description Framework

yearbooks
BT reference materials
serials

young adult literature
UF adolescent literature
BT (documents by information content, purpose)
RT adolescents
children's literature
young adult services

young adult services
BT library and archival services
RT young adult literature

youth
BT (persons and informal groups)
NT adolescents
children

Zipf-Mandelbrot law
USE Zipf's law

Zipf's law
UF Pareto-Zipf law
Zipf-Mandelbrot law
BT bibliometrics
RT Bradford's law
Lotka's law
Pareto principle
word frequency

zoomable user interfaces
BT graphical user interfaces

Hierarchical Index of Preferred Terms

(activities and operations)
. communications activities
. . human communications
. . . authorship
. . . . corporate authorship
. . . . hypermedia authoring
. . . . joint authorship
. . . . personal authorship
. . . communication patterns
. . . disclosure
. . . editing
. . . . proofreading
. . explanation
. . . feedback
. . . informal communication
. . . negotiation
. . . nonverbal communication
. . . organizational communication
. . . public relations
. . . publishing
. . . . desktop publishing
. . . . electronic publishing
. . . . micropublishing
. . . . scholarly publishing
. . . . self publishing
. . . reading
. . . scholarly communication
. . . spoken communication
. . . . face to face communication
. . . . interviews
. . . . . presearch interviews
. . . . . reference interviews
. . . . meetings
. . . . . workshops
. . . . narratives
. . . . storytelling
. . . technical writing
. . telecommunications
. . . audio communications
. . . . telephony
. . . . . Internet telephony
. . . . voice communications
. . . . . voice mail
. . . broadcasting
. . . computer mediated communications
. . . . computer conferencing
. . . . . web conferencing
. . . . message systems
. . . . . bulletin board systems
. . . . . chat rooms
. . . . . e-mail
. . . . . . unsolicited e-mail

(activities and operations) (cont.)
. communications activities (cont.)
. . telecommunications (cont.)
. . . computer mediated communications (cont.)
. . . . message systems (cont.)
. . . . . e-mail (cont.)
. . . . . . unsolicited bulk e-mail
. . . . . . unsolicited commercial e-mail
. . . . . e-mail list servers
. . . . . instant messaging
. . . . . text messaging
. . . . . voice mail
. . . . multiuser Internet games
. . . . newsgroups
. . . data transmission
. . . . broadband transmission
. . . . data streaming
. . . . digital communications
. . . . electronic data interchange
. . . . electronic filing
. . . . file transfers
. . . . . downloading
. . . . . uploading
. . . . voice transmission
. . . facsimile transmission
. . . mobile communications
. . . . cellular communications
. . . multiple access communications
. . . multiplexing
. . . packet switching
. . . satellite communications
. . . telecommunications traffic
. . . teleconferencing
. . . . electronic conferencing
. . . . video teleconferencing
. . . . web conferencing
. . . telegraphy
. . . teletext
. . . video communications
. . . . motion video
. . . . . video clips
. . . . television
. . . . video teleconferencing
. . . videotex
. computer operations
. . computer applications
. . . artificial intelligence
. . . . computer vision
. . . . expert systems
. . . . knowledge engineering
. . . . . knowledge acquisition
. . . . . knowledge modeling

(activities and operations) (cont.)
. computer operations (cont.)
. . computer applications (cont.)
. . . artificial intelligence (cont.)
. . . . knowledge engineering (cont.)
. . . . . knowledge representation
. . . . machine learning
. . . . . font learning
. . . . natural language processing
. . . . . discourse analysis
. . . . . discourse generation
. . . . . natural language comprehension
. . . . . sentence generation
. . . . . speech recognition
. . . . . speech synthesis
. . . . neural networks
. . . . semantic networks
. . . automatic abstracting
. . . automatic classification
. . . automatic extracting
. . . . content mining
. . . . knowledge discovery
. . . . . data mining
. . . . . text mining
. . . . . web mining
. . . automatic indexing
. . . . automatic categorization
. . . automatic taxonomy generation
. . . computer aided design
. . . computer aided engineering
. . . computer aided manufacturing
. . . computer assisted instruction
. . . computer graphics
. . . . animation
. . . computer integrated manufacturing
. . . computer mediated communications
. . . . computer conferencing
. . . . . web conferencing
. . . . message systems
. . . . . bulletin board systems
. . . . . chat rooms
. . . . . e-mail
. . . . . . unsolicited e-mail
. . . . unsolicited bulk e-mail
. . . . unsolicited commercial e-mail
. . . . . e-mail list servers
. . . . . instant messaging
. . . . . text messaging
. . . . . voice mail
. . . . multiuser Internet games
. . . . newsgroups
. . . computer simulation
. . . cryptography
. . . . decryption
. . . . encryption
. . . electronic funds transfer

(activities and operations) (cont.)
. computer operations (cont.)
. . computer applications (cont.)
. . . electronic funds transfer (cont.)
. . . . electronic cash
. . . library automation
. . . . computerized cataloging
. . . machine aided indexing
. . . machine translation
. . . office automation
. . . online searching
. . . teleshopping
. . . virtual reality
. . computer programming
. . . logic programming
. . . object oriented programming
. . . software engineering
. . . . computer aided software engineering
. . data processing
. . . batch processing
. . . compression
. . . computer multitasking
. . . cross matching
. . . data conversion
. . . . retrospective conversion
. . . data entry
. . . data parsing
. . . data presentation
. . . data reduction
. . . . dimensionality reduction
. . . decoding
. . . digital to analog conversion
. . . digitization
. . . encoding
. . . . superimposed coding
. . . end user computing
. . . form filling
. . . formatting
. . . hash coding
. . . multiprocessing
. . . normalization
. . . parallel processing
. . . pattern recognition
. . . . object recognition
. . . . optical character recognition
. . . . . feature extraction
. . . . . font learning
. . . . optical recognition
. . . . word recognition
. . . real time processing
. . . scanning
. . . sorting
. . . validation
. . . verification
. . . word processing
. . distributed computing

(activities and operations) (cont.)
. computer operations (cont.)
. . documentation
. . electronic visualization
. . human computer interaction
. . . ubiquitous computing
. . information processing
. . . graph processing
. . . image processing
. . . . image analysis
. . . . image enhancement
. . . query processing
. . . text processing
. . . . content analysis
. . . . linguistic analysis
. . . . . disambiguation
. . . . . lexical analysis
. . . . . morphological analysis
. . . . . semantic analysis
. . . . . syntactic analysis
. . message filtering
. . signal processing
. . . signal boundary detection
. . software reuse
. educational activities
. . accreditation
. . learning
. . . distance learning
. . . . correspondence study
. . . lifelong learning
. . . perceptual learning
. . mentoring
. . staff development
. . training
. . . bibliographic instruction
. . . tutorials
. . . user training
. general activities
. . collaboration
. . . resource sharing
. . . . peer to peer file sharing
. . . shared cataloging
. . customization
. . evaluation
. . . failure analysis
. . . refereeing
. . . reviewing
. . identification
. . imaging
. . . holography
. . integration
. . maintenance
. . . updating
. . modification
. . . reengineering
. . . repurposing

(activities and operations) (cont.)
. general activities (cont.)
. . . monitoring
. . selection
. . . materials selection
. . standardization
. . user multitasking
. information operations
. . information attribution
. . information discovery
. . . information retrieval
. . . . answer passage retrieval
. . . . audio retrieval
. . . . document retrieval
. . . . image retrieval
. . . . multilingual retrieval
. . . information seeking
. . . . browsing
. . . . . faceted browsing
. . . . . serendipity
. . . . navigation
. . . . searching
. . . . . assisted searching
. . . . . Boolean searching
. . . . . citation searching
. . . . . end user searching
. . . . . federated searching
. . . . . full text searching
. . . . . keyword searching
. . . . . known item searching
. . . . . online searching
. . . . . proximity searching
. . . . . query by example
. . . . . query formulation
. . . . . . query expansion
. . . . . . query refinement
. . . . . range searching
. . . . . search strategies
. . . . . . search hedges
. . . . . . truncation
. . . . stemming
. . . . . . weighting
. . . . . string searching
. . . . . subject searching
. . information dissemination
. . information filtering
. . . collaborative filtering
. . . content filtering
. . information mapping
. . information production
. . information resources management
. . . collection management
. . . . collection assessment
. . . . collection development
. . . . . materials acquisitions
. . . . . . accessions

(activities and operations) (cont.)
. information operations (cont.)
. . information resources management (cont.)
. . . collection management (cont.)
. . . . collection development (cont.)
. . . . . materials acquisitions (cont.)
. . . . . . approval plans
. . . . . . gifts and exchanges
. . . . . . materials claims
. . . . . . materials orders
. . . . blanket orders
. . . . standing orders
. . . . . . subscriptions
. . . . . materials selection
. . . . deselection
. . . . subscription cancellation
. . . content management
. . . . web content management
. . . database management
. . . document management
. . . records management
. . . . document retention
. . . thesaurus management
. . information transfer
. . information use
. . . information reuse
. . organization of information
. . . cataloging
. . . . archival cataloging
. . . . bibliographic cataloging
. . . . cataloging in publication
. . . . computerized cataloging
. . . . descriptive cataloging
. . . . minimal cataloging
. . . . retrospective cataloging
. . . . shared cataloging
. . . . subject cataloging
. . . classification
. . . . automatic classification
. . . . faceted classification
. . . . hierarchical classification
. . . . synthetic classification
. . . database design
. . . domain analysis
. . . facet analysis
. . . index language construction
. . . . notation synthesis
. . . indexing
. . . . (indexing by feature indexed)
. . . . . image indexing
. . . . . name indexing
. . . . . subject indexing
. . . . . . assignment indexing
. . . . . . chain indexing
. . . . . . derivative indexing
. . . . . . generic posting

(activities and operations) (cont.)
. information operations (cont.)
. . organization of information (cont.)
. . . indexing (cont.)
. . . . (indexing by feature indexed) (cont.)
. . . . . subject indexing (cont.)
. . . . . . multilingual subject indexing
. . . . . . postcoordinate indexing
. . . . . . precoordinate indexing
. . . . . . probabilistic indexing
. . . . . . string indexing
. . . . (indexing by item indexed)
. . . . . book indexing
. . . . . database indexing
. . . . . periodical indexing
. . . . (indexing by method used)
. . . . . automatic indexing
. . . . . . automatic categorization
. . . . . content based indexing
. . . . . description based indexing
. . . . . machine aided indexing
. . . . . manual indexing
. . . relevance ranking
. . . vocabulary control
. . summarization
. . . abstracting
. . . . automatic abstracting
. . . extracting
. . . . automatic extracting
. . . . . content mining
. . . . . knowledge discovery
. . . . . . data mining
. . . . . . text mining
. . . . . . web mining
. . translation
. . . machine translation
. . transliteration
. . . romanization
. library operations
. . access to resources
. . . bibliographic access
. . . document access
. . . information access
. . . . subject access
. . . library access
. . . library reserves
. . . . electronic reserves
. . . remote access
. . . . wireless access
. . . universal access
. . backlogs
. . bibliographic control
. . bibliography construction
. . . analytical bibliography
. . bibliotherapy
. . book collecting

(activities and operations) (cont.)
. library operations (cont.)
. . database leasing
. . document delivery
. . . facsimile transmission
. . . interlibrary loans
. . document handling
. . document retrieval
. . documentation
. . information services
. . . community information services
. . . current awareness services
. . . . SDI services
. . . home information services
. . . litigation support
. . library and archival services
. . . children's services
. . . library outreach services
. . . library programs
. . . library technical services
. . . . cataloging
. . . . . archival cataloging
. . . . . bibliographic cataloging
. . . . . cataloging in publication
. . . . . computerized cataloging
. . . . . descriptive cataloging
. . . . . minimal cataloging
. . . . . retrospective cataloging
. . . . . shared cataloging
. . . . . subject cataloging
. . . . collection management
. . . . . collection assessment
. . . . . collection development
. . . . . . materials acquisitions
. . . . accessions
. . . . approval plans
. . . . gifts and exchanges
. . . . materials claims
. . . . materials orders
. . . . blanket orders
. . . . standing orders
. . . . subscriptions
. . . . . . materials selection
. . . . . . deselection
. . . . . . subscription cancellation
. . . . interlibrary loans
. . . . library circulation
. . . . materials processing
. . . off campus library services
. . . reader services
. . . reference services
. . . . electronic reference services
. . . . reference interviews
. . . young adult services
. . library closings
. . library exhibits and displays

(activities and operations) (cont.)
. library operations (cont.)
. . library fines
. . library user profiles
. . materials preservation
. . . binding
. . . . library binding
. . . digital object preservation
. . . . emulation
. . . . migration
. . . . serial conversion
. . . materials conservation
. . . . deacidification
. . . restoration
. . output reformatting
. . photocopying
. management operations
. . accounting
. . . auditing
. . business
. . . business models
. . centralization
. . decentralization
. . funding
. . . library fines
. . . subsidies
. . . . grants
. . inventory
. . management
. . . computing resource management
. . . digital rights management
. . . financial management
. . . . budgeting
. . . . cost recovery
. . . . pricing
. . . . . fees for service
. . . . . royalties
. . . human resources management
. . . information resources management
. . . . collection management
. . . . . collection assessment
. . . . . collection development
. . . . . . materials acquisitions
. . . . accessions
. . . . approval plans
. . . . gifts and exchanges
. . . . materials claims
. . . . materials orders
. . . . blanket orders
. . . . standing orders
. . . . subscriptions
. . . . . . materials selection
. . . . . . deselection
. . . . . . subscription cancellation
. . . . content management
. . . . . web content management

(activities and operations) (cont.)
. management operations (cont.)
. . management (cont.)
. . . information resources management (cont.)
. . . . database management
. . . . document management
. . . . records management
. . . . . document retention
. . . . thesaurus management
. . . library management
. . . . library boards
. . marketing
. . . advertising
. . . promotional activities
. . . . library weeks
. . . telemarketing
. . materials storage
. . . compact storage
. . . data warehousing
. . moving
. . outsourcing
. . planning
. . . critical incident method
. . . critical path method
. . . strategic planning
. . scheduling
. . security classification
. . systems integration
. socioeconomic activities
. . affirmative action
. . career development
. . commerce
. . . electronic commerce
. . competition
. . employment
. . . telecommuting
. . . working at home
. . entrepreneurship
. . innovation
. . . diffusion of innovation
. . technology transfer
. technical and manufacturing operations
. . computer aided engineering
. . computer aide manufacturing
. . computer integrated manufacturing
. . flexible manufacturing systems
. . printing
. . quality assurance
. . quality control
. . . duplicate detection
. . . error correction
. . . error detection
. . recording
. . . magnetic recording
. . . optical recording
. . typesetting

(activities and operations) (cont.)
. technical and manufacturing operations (cont.)
. . typography
(attributes)
. (attributes of information and data)
. . aboutness
. . accuracy
. . ambiguity
. . attribute inheritance
. . bibliometric scatter
. . citation order
. . credibility
. . error rates
. . fallout
. . file integrity
. . frequency of use
. . . web site traffic
. . . word frequency
. . indexing depth
. . indexing discrimination
. . indexing exhaustivity
. . indexing specificity
. . information retrieval noise
. . interdisciplinarity
. . legibility
. . overlap
. . pertinence
. . precision
. . recall
. . relevance
. . similarity
. . temporal currency
. . uncertainty
. . validity
. . warrant
. . . literary warrant
. . . user warrant
. (attributes of systems and equipment)
. . bandwidth
. . connectivity
. . fault tolerance
. . interoperability
. . maintainability
. . modularity
. . response time
. . scalability
. . search time
. . transmission speed
. (general attributes)
. . bias
. . compatibility
. . complexity
. . costs
. . . overhead costs
. . design
. . . computer aided design

(attributes) (cont.)
. (general attributes) (cont.)
. . design (cont.)
. . . database design
. . . forms design
. . . screen design
. . durability
. . effectiveness
. . . cost effectiveness
. . . retrieval effectiveness
. . efficiency
. . obsolescence
. . performance
. . permanence
. . physical attributes
. . . color
. . . shape
. . . texture
. . probability
. . proximity
. . quality
. . randomness
. . redundancy
. . reliability
. . usability
. . utility
. . value added
. (human attributes)
. . human productivity
. . indexer consistency
. . information needs
. . skills
. . . communication skills
. . . information and reference skills
. . . professional competencies
. . user attributes
. . . user expectations
. . . user expertise
. . . user preferences
. . . user profiles
. . . . library user profiles
. . . user satisfaction
(buildings and facilities)
. buildings
. . library buildings
. computer centers
. computer laboratories
(communications media)
. information channels
. mass media
. . news media
. . . newsletters
. . . newspapers
. . . newswire services
. . radio
. . television

(communications media) (cont.)
. mass media (cont.)
. . World Wide Web
. . . invisible web
. . . semantic web
. . . web sites
. . . . frames
. . . . mirror sites
. . . . portals
. . . . web pages
. . . . . web home pages
. satellite communications
(communications networks)
. intranets
. library networks
. nodes
. telecommunications networks
. . common carrier networks
. . local area networks
. . Internet
. . . World Wide Web
. . . . invisible web
. . . . semantic web
. . . . web sites
. . . . . frames
. . . . . mirror sites
. . . . . portals
. . . . . web pages
. . . . . . web home pages
. . National Research and Education Network
. . wide area networks
(countries and regions)
. Africa
. . Algeria
. . Kenya
. . Nigeria
. . South Africa
. Asia
. . China
. . India
. . Japan
. . Korea
. . Philippines
. . Southeast Asia
. Australia
. Central America
. developing countries
. Europe
. . France
. . Germany
. . Hungary
. . Ireland
. . Italy
. . Netherlands
. . Poland
. . Russia

(countries and regions) (cont.)
. Europe (cont.)
. . Spain
. . United Kingdom
. . . Great Britain
. . . . England
. . . . Scotland
. . . . Wales
. . . Northern Ireland
. New Zealand
. North America
. . Canada
. . Mexico
. . United States
. regions
. . Caribbean region
. . European Union
. . Latin America
. . Middle East
. . Oceania
. . Pacific Rim
. . Scandinavia
. . Southeast Asia
. South America
. . Argentina
. . Bolivia
. . Brazil
. . Chile
. . Colombia
. . Ecuador
. . Guyana
. . Paraguay
. . Peru
. . Suriname
. . Uruguay
. . Venezuela
(document types)
. (documents by availability, access, organization)
. . banned materials
. . collections
. . . library collections
. . . personal collections
. . . special collections
. . grey literature
. . hypertext
. . library materials
. . . overdue materials
. . non English language materials
. . preprints
. . public domain
. . publications
. . . alternative publications
. . . bestsellers
. . . books
. . . . paperbacks
. . . . talking books

(document types) (cont.)
. (documents by availability, access, organization)
(cont.)
. . publications (cont.)
. . . books (cont.)
. . . . textbooks
. . . conference proceedings
. . . electronic publications
. . . . CD-ROM
. . . . electronic books
. . . . electronic journals
. . . government publications
. . . monographs
. . . open access publications
. . . out of print publications
. . . pamphlets
. . . print publications
. . . . large print materials
. . . reprints
. . . serials
. . . . newspapers
. . . . periodicals
. . . . . journals
. . . . . . electronic journals
. . . . . newsletters
. . . . . periodical articles
. . . . yearbooks
. . . series
. . rare materials
. . . incunabula
. . source materials
. . technical reports
. (documents by information content, purpose)
. . authority files
. . bibliographies
. . . national bibliographies
. . . webliographies
. . catalogs (bibliographic)
. . children's literature
. . contracts
. . core literature
. . correspondence
. . courseware
. . curricula
. . dissertations
. . document surrogates
. . . abstracts
. . . . author abstracts
. . . annotations
. . . ISBN
. . . ISFN
. . . ISMN
. . . ISRC
. . . ISSN
. . . bibliographic records
. . . . bibliographic citations

(document types) (cont.)
. (documents by medium, physical form) (cont.)
. . books (cont.)
. . . textbooks
. . digital objects
. . . digital audio files
. . . digital video files
. . . electronic documents
. . . . electronic publications
. . . . . CD-ROM
. . . . . electronic books
. . . . . electronic journals
. . . . weblogs
. . graphics
. . . computer graphics
. . . . animation
. . . data maps
. . . . citation networks
. . . . ET-maps
. . . . Pathfinder networks
. . . . self organizing maps
. . . . semantic networks
. . . . topic maps
. . . engineering drawings
. . . illustrations
. . . organization charts
. . manuscripts
. . media
. . multimedia
. . nonprint media
. . . audio recordings
. . . . audiotapes
. . . . . audiocassettes
. . . . . digital audio tapes
. . . . talking books
. . . video recordings
. . . . motion picture films
. . . . video clips
. . . . videocassettes
. . . visual materials
. . . . images
. . . . . bit-mapped images
. . . . . digitized images
. . . . . filmstrips
. . . . . photo CD
. . . . . photographic slides
. . . . . photographs
. . . . maps
. . . . pictures
. . physical objects
. . vertical files
(fields and disciplines)
. aerospace
. agriculture
. architecture
. area studies

(fields and disciplines) (cont.)
. behavioral sciences
. . anthropology
. . . cthnography
. . psychology
. . . cognitive science
. . . psychometrics
. . . social psychology
. . sociology
. . . organization theory
. . . sociometrics
. cartography
. computer science
. . automata
. . cybernetics
. . dynamic systems
. . programming languages
. . . high level languages
. . robotics
. . . telerobotics
. engineering
. . ergonomics
. . software engineering
. . . computer aided software engineering
. finance
. fine arts
. . music
. . performing arts
. . visual arts
. human factors
. . ergonomics
. . user expectations
. humanities
. . history
. . . genealogy
. . . information science history
. . . oral history
. . literature
. . . fiction
. . . nonfiction
. . . . biography
. . . poetry
. . logic
. . . Boolean logic
. . . predicate logic
. . . propositional logic
. . philosophy
. . . epistemology
. . religion
. information science
. . archival science
. . domain naming system
. . economics of information
. . informatics
. . . bioinformatics
. . . . medical informatics

(fields and disciplines) (cont.)
. information science (cont.)
. . informatics (cont.)
. . . museum informatics
. . . social informatics
. . information architecture
. . information science history
. . information theory
. . knowledge management
. law
. lexicography
. . computational lexicography
. librarianship
. . comparative librarianship
. . international librarianship
. linguistics
. . computational linguistics
. . . context free languages
. . etymology
. . grammars
. . . case grammar
. . . large scale grammars
. . phonetics
. . pragmatics
. . semantics
. . . semantic relationships
. . . . antonymy
. . . . associative relationships
. . . . equivalence relationships
. . . . . quasi-synonymous relationships
. . . . hierarchical relationships
. . . . . genus species relationships
. . . . . part whole relationships
. . . . homography
. . sublanguages
. . syntactics
. mathematics
. . algebra
. . statistics
. . . decision theory
. natural sciences
. . biology
. . . biochemistry
. . . biotechnology
. . . botany
. . . environmental sciences
. . geography
. . medical science
. . pharmacology
. physical sciences
. . astronomy
. . chemistry
. . . biochemistry
. . earth sciences
. . physics
. semiotics

(fields and disciplines) (cont.)
. semiotics (cont.)
. . pragmatics
. . semantics
. . . semantic relationships
. . . . antonymy
. . . . associative relationships
. . . . equivalence relationships
. . . . . quasi-synonymous relationships
. . . . hierarchical relationships
. . . . . genus species relationships
. . . . . part whole relationships
. . . . homography
. . syntactics
. social sciences
. . anthropology
. . . ethnography
. . economics
. . . econometrics
. . . economics of information
. . . socioeconomics
. . education
. . . adult education
. . . basic education
. . . computer assisted instruction
. . . continuing education
. . . distance learning
. . . . correspondence study
. . . home education
. . . information science education
. . . library education
. . . off campus education
. . political science
. . social psychology
. . socioeconomics
. . sociology
. . . organization theory
. . . sociometrics
(hardware, software, and equipment)
. adaptive technologies
. audiovisual equipment
. . recording equipment
. . . audio recorders
. . . video recorders
. cameras
. computer architecture
. computer equipment
. . computer peripherals
. . . data storage devices
. . . . disk drives
. . . . . CD-ROM drives
. . . . . DVD drives
. . . . . . multidisk drives
. . . . high density data storage
. . . input equipment
. . . . joysticks

(hardware, software, and equipment) (cont.)
. control systems (cont.)
. . remote control (cont.)
. . . telerobotics
. display devices
. . color displays
. . flat panel displays
. . . LCD panels
. . high resolution displays
. . video display terminals
. educational technology
. information technology
. . information storage and retrieval systems
. . . fact retrieval systems
. . . fuzzy retrieval systems
. . . management information systems
. . . paper based information systems
. . . personal information systems
. . . reference retrieval systems
. instrumentation
. . sensors
. integrated systems
. . integrated library systems
. kiosks
. lasers
. library equipment
. . library security systems
. . library shelving
. library supplies
. . chalk
. optical equipment
. . optical computers
. . optical media
. . . optical disks
. . . . compact disks
. . . . . CD-ROM
. . . . . compact disk interactive
. . . . . compact disk recordable
. . . . . . digital video interactive
. . . . . DVD
. . . . . photo CD
. . . . erasable optical disks
. . . . floptical disks
. . . . magneto-optical disks
. . . . videodisks
. . . . WORM disks
. . . . . DRAW
. . . optical tape
. photocopiers
. robots
. telecommunications equipment
. . coaxial cable
. . fiber optics
. . modems
. . telephones
. . . videotelephones

(knowledge and information)
. information content
. . algorithms
. . . decision trees
. . . extension matrices
. . . genetic algorithms
. . concepts
. . contextual information
. . criteria
. . data
. . . acoustic data
. . . analog data
. . . field formatted data
. . . machine readable data
. . . metadata
. . . numeric data
. . . test data
. . default values
. . domain information
. . . business information
. . . company information
. . . competitive intelligence
. . . consumer information
. . . financial information
. . . government information
. . . legal information
. . . military intelligence
. . . multidisciplinary information
. . . personal information
. . . . library user profiles
. . . public domain information
. . . scientific and technical information
. . . . biomedical information
. . . . . genomic information
. . . . chemical information
. . . . . chemical connection tables
. . . . . chemical nomenclature
. . . . . chemical structure models
. . . . environmental information
. . . spatial information
. . . . geospatial information
. . . temporal information
. . . . time series data
. . factual information
. . false information
. . indicators
. . knowledge
. . . common sense knowledge
. . . domain knowledge
. . . implied knowledge
. . . situated knowledge
. . . system knowledge
. . . task knowledge
. . news
. . proper names
. . . corporate names

(language) (cont.)
. language types (cont.)
. . human language
. . . English language
. . . idioms
. . . jargon
. . . non English languages
. . . . Chinese language
. . index languages
. . . classification schemes
. . . . Bliss Bibliographic Classification
. . . . Colon Classification
. . . . Dewey Decimal Classification
. . . . International Patent Classification
. . . . Library of Congress Classification
. . . . Universal Decimal Classification
. . . controlled vocabularies
. . . . ontologies
. . . . subject heading lists
. . . . . Library of Congress Subject Headings
. . . . . Sears Subject Headings
. . . . switching languages
. . . . syndetic structures
. . . . . cross references
. . . . . scope notes
. . . . taxonomies
. . . . thesauri
. . . . . graphical thesauri
. . . . . McSH
. . . . . metathesauri
. . . . . microthesauri
. . . . . multilingual thesauri
. . . . . thesaurus displays
. . . . thesaurofacet
. . markup languages
. . . HDML
. . . HTML
. . . SGML
. . . WML
. . . XML
. . . . Resource Description Framework
. . programming languages
. . . high level languages
. . query languages
. . . SDQL
. . . SQL
. . sublanguages
. linguistic elements
. . adjectives
. . adverbs
. . capitalization
. . morphemes
. . . affixes
. . nouns
. . orthography
. . paragraphs

(language) (cont.)
. linguistic elements (cont.)
. . phonemes
. . phrases
. . punctuation
. . sentences
. . verbs
. . word roots
. . words
(natural processes and events)
. (general processes)
. . aging of materials
. . change
. . . trends
. . disasters
. . growth
. . stochastic processes
. . . queuing
. (human processes)
. . human speech
. . injury
. . . repetitive stress injury
. . mental processes
. . . abstraction
. . . affect
. . . cognition
. . . . external cognition
. . . cognitive perception
. . . comprehension
. . . concept association
. . . concept discrimination
. . . generalization
. . . human memory
. . . . long term memory
. . . . short term memory
. . . . visual memory
. . . judgment
. . . linguistic analysis
. . . . disambiguation
. . . . lexical analysis
. . . . morphological analysis
. . . . semantic analysis
. . . . syntactic analysis
. . . mental visualization
. . . reasoning
. . . . induction
. . . . inference
. . . sensory perception
. . sensory processes
. . . hearing
. . . touch
. . . vision
. (information and data processes)
. . data corruption
. . errors
. . . typographical errors

155

(natural processes and events) (cont.)
. (information and data processes) (cont.)
. . information entropy
. . information explosion
. . information flow
. . . cross disciplinary fertilization
. . . transborder data flow
. . information life cycle
(organizations)
. armed forces
. colleges and universities
. . information science schools
. . library schools
. consortia
. friends of libraries
. labor unions
. professional associations
. . information associations
. . library associations
. schools
. . elementary schools
. . high schools
. . middle schools
. standards developing organizations
(persons and informal groups)
. authors
. communities
. . academic communities
. . . faculty
. . . invisible colleges
. . . scholars
. . . students
. . communities of practice
. . discourse communities
. . peer groups
. . virtual communities
. customers
. early adopters
. employees
. entrepreneurs
. focus groups
. human information resources
. . boundary spanners
. . gatekeepers
. . subject experts
. information workers
. . information professionals
. . . archivists
. . . computer programmers
. . . editors
. . . information architects
. . . information scientists
. . . intermediaries
. . . librarians
. . . . reference librarians
. . . media specialists

(persons and informal groups) (cont.)
. information workers (cont.)
. . information professionals (cont.)
. . . records managers
. . . translators
. . . web designers
. . library personnel
. . . librarians
. . . . reference librarians
. . . paraprofessional library personnel
. managers
. medical personnel
. . physicians
. men
. minorities and ethnic groups
. . African Americans
. . disabled persons
. . . hearing impaired persons
. . . learning disabled persons
. . . mobility impaired persons
. . . reading disabled persons
. . . visually impaired persons
. . gays and lesbians
. . Hispanics
. . Native Americans
. scientists
. stakeholders
. users
. . end users
. . . experienced users
. . . novice users
. . library users
. . . homebound patrons
. . . problem patrons
. volunteers
. women
. youth
. . adolescents
. . children
(physical media)
. artifacts
. electronic ink
. electronic paper
. magnetic media
. . magnetic disks
. . . floppy disks
. . . hard disks
. . . magneto-optical disks
. . magnetic tapes
. . . audiotapes
. . . . audiocassettes
. . . . digital audio tapes
. . smart cards
. microforms
. . computer output microforms
. . microfiche

(physical media) (cont.)
. microforms (cont.)
. . microfilm
. optical media
. . optical disks
. . . compact disks
. . . . CD-ROM
. . . . compact disk interactive
. . . . compact disk recordable
. . . . digital video interactive
. . . . DVD
. . . . photo CD
. . . erasable optical disks
. . . floptical disks
. . . magneto-optical disks
. . . videodisks
. . . WORM disks
. . . . DRAW
. . optical tape
. paper
. . permanent paper
. photographic films
(product and service providers)
. archives
. . national archives
. bibliographic utilities
. binderies
. computer industry
. consultants
. government agencies
. . electronic government
. . state library agencies
. information analysis centers
. information brokers
. information industry
. . online industry
. information utilities
. libraries
. . academic libraries
. . . community college libraries
. . branch libraries
. . central libraries
. . children's libraries
. . depository libraries
. . digital libraries
. . government libraries
. . . national libraries
. . . state library agencies
. . hybrid libraries
. . institutional libraries
. . . prison libraries
. . media centers
. . mobile libraries
. . . bookmobiles
. . public libraries
. . research libraries

(product and service providers) (cont.)
. libraries (cont.)
. . research libraries (cont.)
. . . Presidential libraries
. . small libraries
. . special libraries
. . . corporate libraries
. . . law libraries
. . . . legislative libraries and reference services
. . . medical libraries
. . . Presidential libraries
. . virtual libraries
. museums
. publishers
. . commercial publishers
. . database producers
. . learned society publishers
. . secondary publishers
. . small presses
. . university presses
. service bureaus
. . abstracting and indexing service bureaus
. software industry
. telecommunications industry
. . Internet service providers
. vendors
. . book vendors
. . jobbers
. . library suppliers
. . search services
. . subscription agencies
(research and analytic methods)
. analytic models
. . connectionist models
. . database models
. . . data models
. . . relational models
. . hierarchical models
. . . ranking
. . . . density ranking
. . . . relevance ranking
. . information models
. . . cognitive models
. . . . cognitive space
. . . information space
. . . spreading activation
. . information retrieval models
. . . Bayesian functions
. . . Boolean logic
. . . associative retrieval
. . . inverse document frequency
. . . latent semantic analysis
. . . probabilistic retrieval
. . . unified retrieval models
. . . vector space models
. . mathematical models

(research and analytic methods) (cont.)
. task analysis
. . work flow analysis
. testing
. . prototyping
(sociocultural aspects)
. cultural aspects
. . cross cultural aspects
. . cultural diversity
. . entertainment
. . honors
. . language barriers
. . literacy
. . . computer literacy
. . . information literacy
. . multilingualism
. . organizational culture
. . organizational environment
. . popular culture
. . social discrimination
. . social networking
. geopolitical aspects
. . international aspects
. . national aspects
. . regional aspects
. legal aspects
. . admissibility of records
. . censorship
. . crime
. . . computer crime
. . . . hacking
. . . copyright infringement
. . . . copyright piracy
. . . fraud
. . . . plagiarism
. . . terrorism
. . . trademark infringement
. . human rights
. . . civil rights
. . . . intellectual freedom
. . . . . academic freedom
. . . . . freedom of information
. . . . . freedom of speech
. . . . . freedom to read
. . . . privacy
. . intellectual property
. . . copyright
. . . fair use
. . . public domain
. . . public lending right
. . legal deposit
. . liability
. . litigation
. . security
. . . computer security
. . . . authentication

(sociocultural aspects) (cont.)
. legal aspects (cont.)
. . security (cont.)
. . . computer security (cont.)
. . . . computer access control
. . . . network security
. . . data security
. . . intrusion prevention and detection
. . . library security
. . . national security
. . usage agreements
. political aspects
. . government
. . policy
. . . editorial policy
. . . library policy
. . . public policy
. . . . information policy
. psychological aspects
. . attitudes
. . cognitive styles
. . creativity
. . ethics
. . goals
. . human behavior
. . individual differences
. . information overload
. . intelligence
. . leadership
. . motivation
. . trust
. social aspects
. . etiquette
. socioeconomic aspects
. . demographics
. . . gender
. . . socioeconomic status
. . digital divide
. . economic sectors
. . . information sector
. . . nonprofit sector
. . . private sector
. . . public sector
. . information infrastructure
. . information society
. . social equity
. . technology impact

159

Permuted Display of Terms

3-D representation (Nonpreferred)
80/20 rule (Nonpreferred)
A & I services (Nonpreferred)
AACR (Nonpreferred)
abbreviations
aboutness
abstract data types
abstracting

automatic   abstracting
abstracting and indexing service bureaus
abstraction
abstracts

author   abstracts
academic communities
academic freedom

academic institutions (Nonpreferred)
academic   libraries
academic publishing (Nonpreferred)

bibliographic   access
document   access
information   access
library   access
off site   access (Nonpreferred)
offsite   access (Nonpreferred)
remote   access
subject   access
universal   access
wireless   access
online public   access catalogs (Nonpreferred)
multiple   access communications
computer   access control
access control (computer systems) (Nonpreferred)
random   access memory
dynamic random   access memory (Nonpreferred)
access points
open   access publications
access to resources
access vocabularies (Nonpreferred)
(documents by availability,   access, organization)
accessions
accounting
accreditation
accuracy
acid free paper (Nonpreferred)
acoustic data
acoustics (Nonpreferred)
data   acquisition (Nonpreferred)
knowledge   acquisition
library   acquisitions (Nonpreferred)
materials   acquisitions
acquisitions (of materials) (Nonpreferred)
acronyms

161

affirmative	action
spreading	activation
communications	activities
educational	activities
general	activities
promotional	activities
socioeconomic	activities
	(activities and operations)
	adaptive technologies
value	added
	adjacency searching (Nonpreferred)
	adjectives
	administration (Nonpreferred)
library	*administration (Nonpreferred)*
	administrative records
	administrators (Nonpreferred)
library	*administrators (Nonpreferred)*
	admissibility of records
	adolescent literature (Nonpreferred)
	adolescents
early	adopters
	adult education
	adult literacy (Nonpreferred)
young	adult literature
	adult programs (Nonpreferred)
young	adult services
	adverbs
	advertising
	aerospace
	affect
	affirmative action
	affixes
	Africa
South	Africa
	African Americans
direct read	*after write technology (Nonpreferred)*
information	*age (Nonpreferred)*
government	agencies
public	*agencies (Nonpreferred)*
state	*agencies (Nonpreferred)*
state library	agencies
subscription	agencies
bridge	*agents (Nonpreferred)*
intelligent	agents
information retrieval	*agents (Nonpreferred)*
liaison	*agents (Nonpreferred)*
search	*agents (Nonpreferred)*
	aggregators (Nonpreferred)
	aging of literatures (Nonpreferred)
	aging of materials
usage	agreements
	agriculture
computer	aided design
computer	aided engineering
computer	*aided indexing (Nonpreferred)*

162

machine	aided indexing
computer	*aided instruction (Nonpreferred)*
computer	aided manufacturing
computer	aided software engineering
computer	*aided translation (Nonpreferred)*
machine	*aided translation (Nonpreferred)*
user	aids
audiovisual	*aids (Nonpreferred)*
	air force (Nonpreferred)
	algebra
	Algeria
	algorithms
genetic	algorithms
evolution based	*algorithms (Nonpreferred)*
	alkaline paper (Nonpreferred)
	almanacs
	alphabetic characters (Nonpreferred)
	alphabetic letters
	alphabetical arrangement
	alphabetical order (Nonpreferred)
	alphabetico classed indexes
	alphabetization (Nonpreferred)
	alphabets
see	*also references (Nonpreferred)*
	alternative materials (Nonpreferred)
	alternative publications
	ambiguity
Central	America
Latin	America
North	America
South	America
Anglo	American Cataloguing Rules
	American Indians (Nonpreferred)
Indians	*(American) (Nonpreferred)*
African	Americans
Native	Americans
digital to	analog conversion
	analog data
	analog systems
	analog to digital conversion (Nonpreferred)
	analogies (Nonpreferred)
citation	analysis
clickstream	*analysis (Nonpreferred)*
cluster	analysis
co-citation	analysis
co-word	*analysis (Nonpreferred)*
collocation	*analysis (Nonpreferred)*
content	analysis
cooccurrence	*analysis (Nonpreferred)*
co-occurrence	analysis
cost	analysis
data	analysis
discourse	analysis
domain	analysis
facet	analysis

factor	analysis
failure	analysis
finite element	analysis
Fourier	analysis
image	analysis
latent semantic	analysis
lexical	analysis
linguistic	analysis
link	analysis
meta	analysis
morphological	analysis
multivariate	analysis
network	analysis
qualitative	analysis
quantitative	analysis
query	*analysis (Nonpreferred)*
semantic	analysis
statistical	*analysis (Nonpreferred)*
syntactic	analysis
systems	analysis
task	analysis
term co-occurrence	*analysis (Nonpreferred)*
text	*analysis (Nonpreferred)*
vector	analysis
word co-occurrence	*analysis (Nonpreferred)*
work flow	analysis
information	analysis centers
	analysis of variance
clearinghouses (information	*analysis) (Nonpreferred)*
information centers (information	*analysis) (Nonpreferred)*
(research and	analytic methods)
	analytic models
	analytical bibliography
	anaphora
	Anglo American Cataloguing Rules
	animation
	annotations
	anonymous ftp (Nonpreferred)
	ANOVA (Nonpreferred)
	ANSI (Nonpreferred)
	answer passage retrieval
question	*answering retrieval (Nonpreferred)*
question	*answering systems (Nonpreferred)*
	anthropology
	antiquarian materials (Nonpreferred)
	antonymy
computer	applications
computer software	applications
	approval ordering (Nonpreferred)
	approval plans
information	architects
	architecture
computer	architecture
information	architecture
Open Document	Architecture

parallel	*architecture (Nonpreferred)*
	architectures, computer (Nonpreferred)
	archival cataloging
	archival science
library and	archival services
	archival storage (Nonpreferred)
	archives
national	archives
Open	Archives Initiative Protocol for Metadata Harvesting specification
	archivistics (Nonpreferred)
	archivists
limited	*area networks (Nonpreferred)*
local	area networks
wide	area networks
	area studies
	Argentina
	armed forces
	army (Nonpreferred)
	arrangement
alphabetical	arrangement
classified	*arrangement (Nonpreferred)*
letter by letter	arrangement
nothing before something	*arrangement (Nonpreferred)*
systematic	arrangement
temporal	arrangement
word by word	arrangement
	art (Nonpreferred)
journal	*articles (Nonpreferred)*
periodical	articles
	articles, periodical (Nonpreferred)
	artifacts
	artificial intelligence
	artificial neural networks (Nonpreferred)
	artificial speech production (Nonpreferred)
fine	arts
performing	arts
visual	arts
document	*as query (Nonpreferred)*
	Asia
Southeast	Asia
cross cultural	aspects
cultural	aspects
geopolitical	aspects
global	*aspects (Nonpreferred)*
international	aspects
legal	aspects
national	aspects
political	aspects
psychological	aspects
regional	aspects
social	aspects
socioeconomic	aspects
(sociocultural	aspects)
collection	assessment

needs	assessment
	assessment, needs (Nonpreferred)
intellectual	*assets (Nonpreferred)*
	assigned indexing (Nonpreferred)
	assignment indexing
personal digital	assistants
library	*assistants (Nonpreferred)*
library technical	*assistants (Nonpreferred)*
computer	assisted instruction
	assisted searching
computer	*assisted software engineering (Nonpreferred)*
concept	association
information	associations
library	associations
professiona	associations
	associations (Nonpreferred)
	associative memory
	associative processing (Nonpreferred)
	associative relationships
	associative retrieval
quality	assurance
	astronomy
working	at home
	atlases
	attitudes
perceptions	*(attitudes) (Nonpreferred)*
	attribute breadcrumbs
	attribute inheritance
	(attributes)
	attributes (Nonpreferred)
physical	attributes
user	attributes
	(attributes of information and data)
	(attributes of systems and equipment)
(general	attributes)
(human	attributes)
information	attribution
streaming	*audio (Nonpreferred)*
	audio cassettes (Nonpreferred)
	audio communications
digital	audio files
	audio interfaces
	audio recorders
	audio recordings
	audio retrieval
	audio streaming (Nonpreferred)
digital	audio tapes
	audio tapes (Nonpreferred)
	audio visual materials (Nonpreferred)
	audiocassettes
	audiodisk recordings (Nonpreferred)
cassettes,	*audiotape (Nonpreferred)*
	audiotape cassettes (Nonpreferred)
	audiotapes
	audiovisual aids (Nonpreferred)

	audiovisual equipment
	audiovisual materials (Nonpreferred)
	auditing
	auditory information (Nonpreferred)
	Australia
	authentication
	author abstracts
	author indexes
	author productivity
	author-prepared indexes
hypermedia	authoring
	authoring software
	authority files
	authors
	authorship
corporate	authorship
joint	authorship
personal	authorship
	automata
	automated language processing (Nonpreferred)
categorization,	*automatic (Nonpreferred)*
tagging,	*automatic (Nonpreferred)*
	automatic abstracting
	automatic categorization
	automatic classification
	automatic data processing (Nonpreferred)
	automatic extracting
	automatic indexing
spiders	*(automatic searching) (Nonpreferred)*
	automatic tagging (Nonpreferred)
	automatic taxonomy generation
	automatic thesaurus generation (Nonpreferred)
	automatic translation (Nonpreferred)
library	automation
office	automation
	automation (Nonpreferred)
	availability of information (Nonpreferred)
(documents by	availability, access, organization)
	awards (Nonpreferred)
current	awareness services
current	*awareness systems (Nonpreferred)*
	back end processors
	back of book indexes (Nonpreferred)
	back of book indexing (Nonpreferred)
	backlogs
	backward compatibility (Nonpreferred)
	bandwidth
data	*banks (Nonpreferred)*
	banned materials
	bar codes
language	barriers
evolution	*based algorithms (Nonpreferred)*
pen	based computers
content	based indexing
description	based indexing

paper	based information systems
menu	based interfaces
community	*based library services (Nonpreferred)*
frame	*based systems (Nonpreferred)*
knowledge	*based systems (Nonpreferred)*
rule	*based systems (Nonpreferred)*
knowledge	bases
	basic education
	batch processing
	baud rate (Nonpreferred)
	Bayesian functions
	Bayesian systems (Nonpreferred)
	Bayesian theory (Nonpreferred)
	BBS (Nonpreferred)
nothing	*before something arrangement (Nonpreferred)*
cognitive	*behavior (Nonpreferred)*
human	behavior
information seeking	*behavior (Nonpreferred)*
search	behavior
user	behavior
	behavior, human (Nonpreferred)
	behavioral sciences
	belles lettres (Nonpreferred)
	benchmarks
	bestsellers
	bias
citations,	*bibliographic (Nonpreferred)*
coupling,	*bibliographic (Nonpreferred)*
	bibliographic access
	bibliographic cataloging
	bibliographic citations
Bliss	Bibliographic Classification
	bibliographic control
	bibliographic coupling
	bibliographic data (Nonpreferred)
	bibliographic databases
International Standard	Bibliographic Description
	bibliographic description (Nonpreferred)
	bibliographic families
	bibliographic instruction
	bibliographic records
	bibliographic references
	bibliographic retrieval systems (Nonpreferred)
	bibliographic software
	bibliographic utilities
	bibliographies
national	bibliographies
analytical	bibliography
descriptive	*bibliography (Nonpreferred)*
historical	*bibliography (Nonpreferred)*
	bibliography construction
	bibliometric scatter
	bibliometrics
web	*bibliometry (Nonpreferred)*
	bibliotherapy

	Boolean searching
	borrowers (Nonpreferred)
	borrowing (library materials) (Nonpreferred)
	botany
	bots (Nonpreferred)
signal	boundary detection
	boundary spanners
	Bradford's law
	braille
	branch libraries
	branch library closings (Nonpreferred)
	Brazil
	breadcrumbs
attribute	breadcrumbs
location	breadcrumbs
path	breadcrumbs
	bridge agents (Nonpreferred)
Great	Britain
	broadband transmission
	broadcasting
	broader term references (Nonpreferred)
	broader term relationships (Nonpreferred)
information	brokers
	browse-wrap (Nonpreferred)
web	browsers
	browsing
faceted	browsing
	BT references (Nonpreferred)
	BT relationships (Nonpreferred)
	budgeting
	buildings
library	buildings
	(buildings and facilities)
unsolicited	bulk e-mail
	bulletin board systems
electronic	*bulletin boards (Nonpreferred)*
abstracting and indexing service	bureaus
service	bureaus
	business
	business information
	business intelligence (Nonpreferred)
	business models
(documents	by availability, access, organization)
query	by example
(indexing	by feature indexed)
(documents	by information content, purpose)
(indexing	by item indexed)
letter	by letter arrangement
(documents	by medium, physical form)
(indexing	by method used)
word	by word arrangement
coaxial	cable
	cache
	CAD (Nonpreferred)
	CAE (Nonpreferred)

170

	CAI (Nonpreferred)
predicate	*calculus (Nonpreferred)*
	call numbers
	CAM (Nonpreferred)
	cameras
off	campus education
off	campus library services
extension	*campuses (Nonpreferred)*
	Canada
subscription	cancellation
	candidate descriptors
	canonical correlation
	canonicity (Nonpreferred)
intellectual	*capital (Nonpreferred)*
	capitalization
data	*capture (Nonpreferred)*
	card catalogs
	card files (Nonpreferred)
smart	cards
	career development
	Caribbean region
Monte	Carlo method
common	carrier networks
common	*carriers (Nonpreferred)*
	cartography
mapping	*(cartography) (Nonpreferred)*
	CASE (Nonpreferred)
	case grammar
	case histories (Nonpreferred)
	case studies
electronic	cash
audio	*cassettes (Nonpreferred)*
audiotape	*cassettes (Nonpreferred)*
	cassettes, audiotape (Nonpreferred)
	catalog entries (Nonpreferred)
	catalog records (Nonpreferred)
	cataloging
archival	cataloging
bibliographic	cataloging
computerized	cataloging
descriptive	cataloging
limited	*cataloging (Nonpreferred)*
minimal	cataloging
retrospective	cataloging
shared	cataloging
subject	cataloging
machine readable	*cataloging formats (Nonpreferred)*
	cataloging in publication
machine readable	*cataloging records (Nonpreferred)*
	cataloging rules
card	catalogs
classified	catalogs
online	*catalogs (Nonpreferred)*
online public access	*catalogs (Nonpreferred)*
union	catalogs

Anglo American	Cataloguing Rules
	categories
automatic	categorization
	categorization, automatic (Nonpreferred)
	cathode ray tube terminals (Nonpreferred)
photo	CD
	CD (compact disks) (Nonpreferred)
	CD recordable (Nonpreferred)
	CD-I (Nonpreferred)
	CD-ROM
	CD-ROM drives
jukeboxes	*(CD-ROM drives) (Nonpreferred)*
	cellular communications
	cellular telephones (Nonpreferred)
	censored materials (Nonpreferred)
	censorship
	census data (Nonpreferred)
computer	centers
information analysis	centers
learning	*centers (Nonpreferred)*
learning resource	*centers (Nonpreferred)*
media	centers
resource	*centers (Nonpreferred)*
school media	*centers (Nonpreferred)*
information	*centers (information analysis) (Nonpreferred)*
information	*centers (libraries) (Nonpreferred)*
information	*centers (special libraries) (Nonpreferred)*
	Central America
	central libraries
	central processing units (Nonpreferred)
	centralization
	chain indexing
Markov	*chains (Nonpreferred)*
	chalk
physically	*challenged persons (Nonpreferred)*
	change
information	channels
	chaos theory
	character recognition (Nonpreferred)
optical	character recognition
	character sets
uniform resource	characteristics
alphabetic	*characters (Nonpreferred)*
	charges (Nonpreferred)
	charging systems (Nonpreferred)
flow	charting
organization	charts
	chat reference services (Nonpreferred)
	chat rooms
grammar	checkers
spell	*checkers (Nonpreferred)*
spelling	checkers
nomenclature,	*chemical (Nonpreferred)*
	chemical connection tables
	chemical information

chemical nomenclature
chemical structure models
chemistry
children
children's books (Nonpreferred)
children's librarianship (Nonpreferred)
children's libraries
children's literature
children's services
Chile
China
Chinese language
chronological order (Nonpreferred)
CIM (Nonpreferred)
CIP (Nonpreferred)
integrated circuits
library circulation
self citation
citation analysis
citation coupling (Nonpreferred)
citation frequency (Nonpreferred)
citation indexes
citation maps (Nonpreferred)
citation networks
citation order
citation searching
bibliographic citations
citations, bibliographic (Nonpreferred)
civil rights
materials claims
alphabetico classed indexes
classification
automatic classification
Bliss Bibliographic Classification
Colon Classification
Dewey Decimal Classification
faceted classification
hierarchical classification
International Patent Classification
Library of Congress Classification
security classification
synthetic classification
Universal Decimal Classification
classification construction (Nonpreferred)
classification schemes
classified arrangement (Nonpreferred)
classified catalogs
classified information (Nonpreferred)
clearinghouses (community information) (Nonpreferred)
clearinghouses (information analysis) (Nonpreferred)
clearinghouses (special libraries) (Nonpreferred)
click-wrap (Nonpreferred)
clickstream analysis (Nonpreferred)
client server software
client server systems

	cliometrics (Nonpreferred)
video	clips
branch library	*closings (Nonpreferred)*
information operation	*closings (Nonpreferred)*
library	closings
	cluster analysis
	co-citation analysis
	co-occurrence analysis
term	*co-occurrence analysis (Nonpreferred)*
word	*co-occurrence analysis (Nonpreferred)*
	co-word analysis (Nonpreferred)
	coauthorship (Nonpreferred)
	coaxial cable
International Standard Record	*Code (Nonpreferred)*
	CODEN
bar	codes
standard record	*codes (Nonpreferred)*
hash	coding
superimposed	coding
	cognition
external	cognition
	cognitive behavior (Nonpreferred)
	cognitive controls (Nonpreferred)
	cognitive filtering (Nonpreferred)
	cognitive models
	cognitive perception
	cognitive psychology (Nonpreferred)
	cognitive science
	cognitive space
	cognitive styles
	collaboration
	collaborative filtering
	collaborative work (Nonpreferred)
book	collecting
	collecting, book (Nonpreferred)
book	*collection (Nonpreferred)*
data	collection
TREC test	*collection (Nonpreferred)*
	collection assessment
	collection development
	collection management
	collection reduction (Nonpreferred)
	collections
book	*collections (Nonpreferred)*
library	collections
personal	collections
special	collections
indirect	collective references
	college libraries (Nonpreferred)
community	college libraries
invisible	colleges
	colleges and universities
	collocation analysis (Nonpreferred)
	Colombia
	Colon Classification

	color
	color displays
	color printers
	COM (Nonpreferred)
	command driven interfaces
common	command language
	command languages
	commerce
electronic	commerce
unsolicited	commercial e-mail
	commercial publishers
	common carrier networks
	common carriers (Nonpreferred)
	common command language
	common sense knowledge
face to face	communication
informal	communication
nonverbal	communication
organizational	communication
scholarly	communication
spoken	communication
	communication patterns
	communication skills
audio	communications
cellular	communications
computer mediated	communications
data	*communications (Nonpreferred)*
digital	communications
electronic	*communications (Nonpreferred)*
human	communications
mass	*communications (Nonpreferred)*
mobile	communications
multiple access	communications
oral	*communications (Nonpreferred)*
satellite	communications
video	communications
voice	communications
	communications activities
	(communications media)
	(communications networks)
	communications networks (Nonpreferred)
	communications protocols
	communications satellites (Nonpreferred)
	communications stars (Nonpreferred)
	communications theory (Nonpreferred)
	communities
academic	communities
discourse	communities
distributed	*communities (Nonpreferred)*
virtual	communities
	communities of practice
	community based library services (Nonpreferred)
	community college libraries
	community information services
clearinghouses	*(community information) (Nonpreferred)*

community resource files
compact discs (Nonpreferred)
compact disk interactive
compact disk recordable
compact disks
CD   *(compact disks) (Nonpreferred)*
compact shelving (Nonpreferred)
compact storage
company information
company libraries (Nonpreferred)
comparative librarianship
comparison
compatibility
core   *competencies (Nonpreferred)*
professional   competencies
backward   *compatibility (Nonpreferred)*
competition
competitive intelligence
competitor intelligence (Nonpreferred)
complexity
compound terms
comprehension
natural language   comprehension
understanding   *(comprehension) (Nonpreferred)*
compression
data   *compression (Nonpreferred)*
image   *compression (Nonpreferred)*
compulsory deposit (Nonpreferred)
computational intelligence (Nonpreferred)
computational lexicography
computational linguistics
architectures,   *computer (Nonpreferred)*
hardware,   *computer (Nonpreferred)*
peripherals,   *computer (Nonpreferred)*
programs,   *computer (Nonpreferred)*
shopping,   *computer (Nonpreferred)*
software,   *computer (Nonpreferred)*
computer access control
computer aided design
computer aided engineering
computer aided indexing (Nonpreferred)
computer aided instruction (Nonpreferred)
computer aided manufacturing
computer aided software engineering
computer aided translation (Nonpreferred)
computer applications
computer architecture
computer assisted instruction
computer assisted software engineering (Nonpreferred)
computer centers
computer conferencing
computer crime
computer equipment
computer games (Nonpreferred)
computer graphics

             computer hardware (Nonpreferred)
             computer human interaction (Nonpreferred)
             computer human interfaces (Nonpreferred)
             computer industry
             computer integrated manufacturing
human   computer interaction
human   *computer interfaces (Nonpreferred)*
             computer laboratories
             computer languages (Nonpreferred)
             computer learning (Nonpreferred)
             computer literacy
             computer matching (Nonpreferred)
             computer mediated communications
             computer memory
             computer multitasking
             computer networks (Nonpreferred) .
             computer operations
             computer output microfilm (Nonpreferred)
             computer output microforms
mouse   *(computer peripheral) (Nonpreferred)*
             computer peripherals
             computer processing units
             computer programmers
             computer programming
             computer programs (Nonpreferred)
             computer resource management (Nonpreferred)
             computer science
             computer security
             computer simulation
             computer software
             computer software applications
             computer storage (Nonpreferred)
             computer systems
access control   *(computer systems) (Nonpreferred)*
             computer translation (Nonpreferred)
             computer typesetting (Nonpreferred)
             computer viruses
             computer vision
             computer worms
programming   *(computer) (Nonpreferred)*
             computerized cataloging
             computerized operations (Nonpreferred)
             computers
desktop   *computers (Nonpreferred)*
hand-held   *computers (Nonpreferred)*
host   *computers (Nonpreferred)*
Internet   *computers (Nonpreferred)*
laptop   *computers (Nonpreferred)*
mainframe   computers
net   *computers (Nonpreferred)*
network   computers
notebook   *computers (Nonpreferred)*
optical   computers
palmtop   *computers (Nonpreferred)*
pen based   computers

personal	computers
reduced instruction set	*computers (Nonpreferred)*
NC (network	*computers) (Nonpreferred)*
distributed	computing
end user	computing
high performance	*computing (Nonpreferred)*
ubiquitous	computing
workgroup	*computing (Nonpreferred)*
	computing resource management
resource management	*(computing) (Nonpreferred)*
	concept association
	concept discrimination
	concept formation (Nonpreferred)
	concept space (Nonpreferred)
	concepts
	conceptual models (Nonpreferred)
	conceptual relationships (Nonpreferred)
	conceptual space (Nonpreferred)
	concordances
	concurrent processing (Nonpreferred)
	conference proceedings
proceedings	*(conference) (Nonpreferred)*
	conferences (Nonpreferred)
computer	conferencing
electronic	conferencing
video	*conferencing (Nonpreferred)*
web	conferencing
	confidential records
	confidentiality (Nonpreferred)
	configuration (Nonpreferred)
Library of	Congress Classification
Library of	Congress Subject Headings
	congruence (Nonpreferred)
chemical	connection tables
	connectionist models
	connectivity
materials	conservation
	conservation of materials (Nonpreferred)
indexer	consistency
	consistency, indexer (Nonpreferred)
	consortia
bibliography	construction
classification	*construction (Nonpreferred)*
index language	construction
taxonomy	*construction (Nonpreferred)*
thesaurus	*construction (Nonpreferred)*
	consultants
	consulting services (Nonpreferred)
	consumer information
	content (Nonpreferred)
information	content
	content analysis
	content based indexing
	content filtering
	content management

web	content management
	content management systems (Nonpreferred)
	content mining
	content tagging (Nonpreferred)
(documents by information	content, purpose)
	contents lists
table of	*contents lists (Nonpreferred)*
	context (Nonpreferred)
	context free languages
keyword in	*context indexes (Nonpreferred)*
keyword out of	*context indexes (Nonpreferred)*
	contextual information
	continuing education
	contracts
access	*control (computer systems) (Nonpreferred)*
bibliographic	control
computer access	control
password	*control (Nonpreferred)*
quality	control
remote	control
vocabulary	control
	control systems
	controlled vocabularies
cognitive	*controls (Nonpreferred)*
analog to digital	*conversion (Nonpreferred)*
data	conversion
database	*conversion (Nonpreferred)*
digital to analog	conversion
document	*conversion (Nonpreferred)*
retrospective	conversion
serial	conversion
	cooccurrence analysis (Nonpreferred)
	cooperative work (Nonpreferred)
	coordinate indexing (Nonpreferred)
	coordinate searching (Nonpreferred)
	copiers (Nonpreferred)
	copying (Nonpreferred)
private	*copying (Nonpreferred)*
	copyright
	copyright infringement
Electronic	*Copyright Management Systems (Nonpreferred)*
	copyright piracy
Dublin	*Core (Nonpreferred)*
	core competencies (Nonpreferred)
	core literature
	corporate authorship
	corporate culture (Nonpreferred)
	corporate intelligence (Nonpreferred)
	corporate libraries
	corporate name indexing (Nonpreferred)
	corporate names
error	correction
	correction, error (Nonpreferred)
	correctional institution libraries (Nonpreferred)
canonical	correlation

	correspondence
	correspondence study
data	corruption
	cost analysis
	cost effectiveness
	cost recovery
	costs
overhead	costs
developing	countries
	(countries and regions)
bibliographic	coupling
citation	*coupling (Nonpreferred)*
	coupling, bibliographic (Nonpreferred)
	courseware
	CPM (Nonpreferred)
	CPU (Nonpreferred)
	crawlers (Nonpreferred)
	creativity
	credibility
	crime
computer	crime
	criminal justice (Nonpreferred)
	criteria
	critical incident method
	critical incident technique (Nonpreferred)
	critical path method
	cross cultural aspects
	cross disciplinary fertilization
	cross lingual retrieval (Nonpreferred)
	cross matching
	cross references
	crossborder data flow (Nonpreferred)
	CRT terminals (Nonpreferred)
	crumb trails (Nonpreferred)
	cryptography
liquid	*crystal displays (Nonpreferred)*
	cultural aspects
cross	cultural aspects
	cultural diversity
organizational	culture
popular	culture
corporate	*culture (Nonpreferred)*
	cumulative indexes
temporal	currency
	current awareness services
	current awareness systems (Nonpreferred)
	curricula
	cursive script
	customers
	customization
	customized materials (Nonpreferred)
	cybercash (Nonpreferred)
	cybermetrics (Nonpreferred)
	cybernetics
	cyberspace (Nonpreferred)

information life	cycle
	DAT (Nonpreferred)
	data
acoustic	data
analog	data
bibliographic	*data (Nonpreferred)*
census	*data (Nonpreferred)*
fielded	*data (Nonpreferred)*
field formatted	data
formats,	*data (Nonpreferred)*
image	*data (Nonpreferred)*
machine readable	data
numeric	data
statistical	*data (Nonpreferred)*
test	data
time	*data (Nonpreferred)*
time series	data
	data acquisition (Nonpreferred)
	data analysis
	data banks (Nonpreferred)
	data capture (Nonpreferred)
	data collection
	data communications (Nonpreferred)
	data compression (Nonpreferred)
	data conversion
	data corruption
	data definition languages
	data dictionaries
	data distribution
	data dredging (Nonpreferred)
	data entry
	data files (Nonpreferred)
transborder	data flow
crossborder	*data flow (Nonpreferred)*
international	*data flow (Nonpreferred)*
transnational	*data flow (Nonpreferred)*
	data formats
	data fusion (Nonpreferred)
electronic	data interchange
	data interchange (Nonpreferred)
	data maps
	data mining
	data models
	data objects
	data parsing
	data presentation
(information and	data processes)
	data processing
automatic	*data processing (Nonpreferred)*
electronic	*data processing (Nonpreferred)*
	data processors (Nonpreferred)
	data protection (Nonpreferred)
	data reduction
	data representation (Nonpreferred)
	data security

	data segmentation
	data sets (Nonpreferred)
high density	data storage
	data storage (Nonpreferred)
	data storage devices
	data streaming
	data structures
	data transmission
abstract	data types
	data utilization (Nonpreferred)
	data warehouses (Nonpreferred)
	data warehousing
(attributes of information and	data)
	databanks (Nonpreferred)
leasing,	*database (Nonpreferred)*
	database conversion (Nonpreferred)
	database design
	database hosts (Nonpreferred)
	database indexing
	database leasing
	database machines
	database maintenance (Nonpreferred)
	database management
	database management systems
	database mining (Nonpreferred)
	database models
	database producers
	database tomography
	database vendors (Nonpreferred)
	databases
bibliographic	databases
distributed	databases
fact	databases
factual	*databases (Nonpreferred)*
full text	databases
image	databases
nonbibliographic	databases
numeric	databases
object oriented	databases
on line	*databases (Nonpreferred)*
online	databases
relational	databases
skills	*databases (Nonpreferred)*
statistical	*databases (Nonpreferred)*
text	*databases (Nonpreferred)*
textual	*databases (Nonpreferred)*
very large	databases
up to	*dateness (Nonpreferred)*
	DDC (Nonpreferred)
	deacidification
	deaf persons (Nonpreferred)
	deans (Nonpreferred)
	decentralization
Dewey	Decimal Classification
Universal	Decimal Classification

	decision making
	decision support systems
group	decision support systems
	decision theory
	decision trees
	decoding
	decryption
	dedicated systems
	deduction (Nonpreferred)
	deep web (Nonpreferred)
	default values
data	definition languages
	definitions (of terms) (Nonpreferred)
document	delivery
	delivery of documents (Nonpreferred)
	Delphi studies
	democracy (Nonpreferred)
	demographics
high	density data storage
	density ranking
legal	deposit
compulsory	*deposit (Nonpreferred)*
	depository libraries
indexing	depth
	derivative indexing
International Standard Bibliographic	Description
bibliographic	*description (Nonpreferred)*
	description (research method) (Nonpreferred)
	description based indexing
Resource	Description Framework
document type	*descriptions (Nonpreferred)*
	descriptive bibliography (Nonpreferred)
	descriptive cataloging
	descriptors
candidate	descriptors
proposed	*descriptors (Nonpreferred)*
	deselection
	design
computer aided	design
database	design
forms	design
interactive	*design (Nonpreferred)*
research	design
screen	design
systems	design
web	designers
	desktop computers (Nonpreferred)
	desktop metaphor
	desktop publishing
duplicate	detection
error	detection
intrusion prevention and	detection
signal	*detection (Nonpreferred)*
signal boundary	detection
book	*detection systems (Nonpreferred)*

theft	*detection systems (Nonpreferred)*
	detection, error (Nonpreferred)
	developing countries
standards	developing organizations
career	development
collection	development
research and	development
staff	development
systems	development
software	*development (Nonpreferred)*
Handheld	*Device Markup Language (Nonpreferred)*
data storage	devices
display	devices
pointing	devices
	Dewey Decimal Classification
	diacriticals
	dictionaries
data	dictionaries
individual	differences
	diffusion of innovation
	digests
personal	digital assistants
	digital audio files
	digital audio tapes
	digital communications
analog to	*digital conversion (Nonpreferred)*
	digital divide
	digital documents (Nonpreferred)
	digital ink (Nonpreferred)
	digital libraries
	digital object identifiers
	digital object preservation
	digital objects
	digital paper (Nonpreferred)
	digital preservation (Nonpreferred)
	digital reference services (Nonpreferred)
	digital rights management
	digital to analog conversion
	digital video disks (Nonpreferred)
	digital video files
	digital video interactive
	digitization
	digitized images
three	*dimensional imagery (Nonpreferred)*
	dimensionality reduction
	direct manipulation interfaces
	direct read after write technology (Nonpreferred)
	directories
	disabled persons
learning	disabled persons
reading	disabled persons
	disambiguation
	disasters
natural	*disasters (Nonpreferred)*
cross	disciplinary fertilization

(fields and	disciplines)
	disclosure
	discourse analysis
	discourse communities
	discourse generation
information	discovery
knowledge	discovery
concept	discrimination
indexing	discrimination
social	discrimination
sex	*discrimination (Nonpreferred)*
	discs (Nonpreferred)
compact	*discs (Nonpreferred)*
	discussion groups (Nonpreferred)
	disk drives
compact	disk interactive
compact	disk recordable
	disks (Nonpreferred)
CD (compact	*disks) (Nonpreferred)*
compact	disks
digital video	*disks (Nonpreferred)*
erasable optical	disks
flexible	*disks (Nonpreferred)*
floppy	disks
floptical	disks
hard	disks
laser	*disks (Nonpreferred)*
magnetic	disks
magneto-optical	disks
optical	disks
rewritable optical	*disks (Nonpreferred)*
WORM	disks
terminals, video	*display (Nonpreferred)*
	display devices
video	display terminals
visual	*display terminals (Nonpreferred)*
color	displays
flat panel	displays
flexible electronic	*displays (Nonpreferred)*
high resolution	displays
library exhibits and	displays
liquid crystal	*displays (Nonpreferred)*
thesaurus	displays
	displays (library) (Nonpreferred)
exhibits and	*displays (library) (Nonpreferred)*
	displays (thesauri) (Nonpreferred)
electronic information	*dissemination (Nonpreferred)*
information	dissemination
selective	*dissemination of information (Nonpreferred)*
	dissemination, information (Nonpreferred)
	dissertations
	distance education (Nonpreferred)
	distance learning
	distributed communities (Nonpreferred)
	distributed computing

	distributed databases
	distributed information management system (Nonpreferred)
	distributed processing (Nonpreferred)
data	distribution
information	*distribution (Nonpreferred)*
normal	distribution
skewed	distribution
cultural	diversity
digital	divide
	DNS (Nonpreferred)
	document access
Open	Document Architecture
	document as query (Nonpreferred)
	document conversion (Nonpreferred)
	document delivery
inverse	document frequency
	document handling
electronic	*document interchange formats (Nonpreferred)*
	document management
electronic	document management systems
standard	*document query language (Nonpreferred)*
	document representations (Nonpreferred)
	document retention
	document retrieval
	document schemas
	document storage (Nonpreferred)
	document style semantics and specification language (Nonpreferred)
	document surrogates
	document titles
	document type descriptions (Nonpreferred)
	(document types)
	document use (Nonpreferred)
	documentation
electronic	documents
delivery of	*documents (Nonpreferred)*
digital	*documents (Nonpreferred)*
government	*documents (Nonpreferred)*
	(documents by availability, access, organization)
	(documents by information content, purpose)
	(documents by medium, physical form)
	DOI (Nonpreferred)
public	domain
	domain analysis
	domain information
public	domain information
	domain knowledge
	domain naming system
	downloading
	DP (Nonpreferred)
	DRAM
	DRAW
engineering	drawings
	drawings, engineering (Nonpreferred)
data	*dredging (Nonpreferred)*

186

command	driven interfaces
CD-ROM	drives
disk	drives
DVD	drives
multidisk	drives
jukeboxes (CD-ROM	*drives) (Nonpreferred)*
	DRM (Nonpreferred)
false	*drops (Nonpreferred)*
	drugs (Nonpreferred)
	DSS (Nonpreferred)
	DSSSL
	DTDs
	Dublin Core (Nonpreferred)
	duplicate detection
	duplicate records
	durability
	DV-I (Nonpreferred)
	DVD
	DVD drives
	dynamic random access memory (Nonpreferred)
	dynamic systems
	dyslexia (Nonpreferred)
	e-books (Nonpreferred)
	e-cash (Nonpreferred)
	e-commerce (Nonpreferred)
	e-government (Nonpreferred)
	e-ink (Nonpreferred)
	e-journals (Nonpreferred)
	e-mail
unsolicited	e-mail
unsolicited bulk	e-mail
unsolicited commercial	e-mail
	e-mail list servers
	e-mail software
	e-paper (Nonpreferred)
	e-reserves (Nonpreferred)
	early adopters
	early books (Nonpreferred)
	earth sciences
	ease of use (Nonpreferred)
Middle	East
	ECMS (Nonpreferred)
	econometrics
	economic indicators (Nonpreferred)
	economic sectors
	economics
information	*economics (Nonpreferred)*
	economics of information
	Ecuador
	EDI (Nonpreferred)
	editing
	editorial policy
	editors
text	editors
	EDMS (Nonpreferred)

EDP (Nonpreferred)
education
adult education
basic education
continuing education
distance education (Nonpreferred)
higher education (Nonpreferred)
home education
information science education
library education
off campus education
user education (Nonpreferred)
National Research and Education Network
educational activities
educational technology
effectiveness
cost effectiveness
retrieval effectiveness
efficiency
EFTS (Nonpreferred)
EIS (Nonpreferred)
payments, electronic (Nonpreferred)
electronic books
electronic bulletin boards (Nonpreferred)
electronic cash
electronic commerce
electronic communications (Nonpreferred)
electronic conferencing
Electronic Copyright Management Systems (Nonpreferred)
electronic data interchange
electronic data processing (Nonpreferred)
flexible electronic displays (Nonpreferred)
electronic document interchange formats (Nonpreferred)
electronic document management systems
electronic documents
electronic filing
electronic funds transfer
electronic government
electronic imaging (Nonpreferred)
electronic information dissemination (Nonpreferred)
electronic information products (Nonpreferred)
electronic information systems (Nonpreferred)
electronic ink
electronic journals
electronic libraries (Nonpreferred)
electronic mail (Nonpreferred)
electronic meeting systems (Nonpreferred)
electronic offices (Nonpreferred)
electronic paper
electronic publications
electronic publishing
electronic reference services
electronic reserves
Electronic Rights Management Systems (Nonpreferred)
electronic visualization

finite	element analysis
	elementary schools
linguistic	elements
	email (Nonpreferred)
	emotion (Nonpreferred)
	empirical studies
	employees
	employment
	emulation
	encoding
	encryption
	encyclopedias
back	end processors
	end user computing
	end user searching
	end users
front	ends
personality, matter,	*energy, space, and time (Nonpreferred)*
law	enforcement
search	engine optimization
search	*engine persuasion (Nonpreferred)*
	engineering
computer aided	engineering
computer aided software	engineering
computer assisted software	*engineering (Nonpreferred)*
drawings,	*engineering (Nonpreferred)*
human	*engineering (Nonpreferred)*
human factors	*engineering (Nonpreferred)*
information	*engineering (Nonpreferred)*
knowledge	engineering
software	engineering
	engineering drawings
hybrid search	engines
meta search	engines
search	engines
metasearch	*engines (Nonpreferred)*
	England
	English language
non	English language materials
non	English languages
image	enhancement
	entertainment
	entrepreneurs
	entrepreneurship
	entries
catalog	*entries (Nonpreferred)*
index	*entries (Nonpreferred)*
information	entropy
data	entry
	entry terms (Nonpreferred)
	entry vocabularies
organizational	environment
virtual	*environment (Nonpreferred)*
	environmental information
	environmental scanning

	environmental sciences
	ephemera
	epistemology
audiovisual	equipment
computer	equipment
input	equipment
library	equipment
optical	equipment
output	equipment
recording	equipment
telecommunications	equipment
(attributes of systems and	equipment)
(hardware, software, and	equipment)
social	equity
	equivalence relationships
	erasable optical disks
	ergonomics
	ERMS (Nonpreferred)
	erotic materials
correction,	*error (Nonpreferred)*
detection,	*error (Nonpreferred)*
	error correction
	error detection
	error messages
	error rates
	errors
keyboarding	*errors (Nonpreferred)*
spelling	*errors (Nonpreferred)*
typographical	errors
	ET-maps
	ethics
	ethnic groups (Nonpreferred)
minorities and	ethnic groups
	ethnography
	etiquette
	etymology
	Europe
	European Union
	evaluation
(natural processes and	events)
	evolution based algorithms (Nonpreferred)
query by	example
information	*exchange (Nonpreferred)*
	exchange formats (Nonpreferred)
information	*exchange formats (Nonpreferred)*
gifts and	exchanges
	exchanges (of materials) (Nonpreferred)
	executive information systems (Nonpreferred)
indexing	exhaustivity
	exhibits and displays (library) (Nonpreferred)
library	exhibits and displays
query	expansion
user	expectations
	experienced users
	experiments

	expert services (Nonpreferred)
	expert systems
user	expertise
subject	*expertise (Nonpreferred)*
	experts, subject (Nonpreferred)
subject	experts
	explanation
information	explosion
publication	*explosion (Nonpreferred)*
library	*extension (Nonpreferred)*
	extension campuses (Nonpreferred)
	extension matrices
	external cognition
	extracting
automatic	extracting
feature	extraction
	extraction (Nonpreferred)
information	*extraction (Nonpreferred)*
	face to face communication
	facet analysis
	facet formula (Nonpreferred)
	facet indicators (Nonpreferred)
	faceted browsing
	faceted classification
	faceted navigation (Nonpreferred)
	facets
PMEST	facets
(buildings and	facilities)
	facsimile transmission
	fact databases
	fact retrieval systems
impact	factor
	factor analysis
human	factors
human	*factors engineering (Nonpreferred)*
	factual databases (Nonpreferred)
	factual information
	faculty
	failure analysis
	fair use
	fallout
	false drops (Nonpreferred)
	false information
bibliographic	families
	fault tolerance
	fax (Nonpreferred)
	feature extraction
(indexing by	feature indexed)
	federated searching
	feedback
relevance	*feedback (Nonpreferred)*
user	*feedback (Nonpreferred)*
	fees for service
cross disciplinary	fertilization
	fiber optics

optical	*fibers (Nonpreferred)*
	fiction
	field formatted data
	fielded data (Nonpreferred)
	(fields and disciplines)
	figurative language (Nonpreferred)
	figures of speech (Nonpreferred)
	file integrity
	file servers
peer to peer	file sharing
	file structures
hierarchical	file structures
	file systems (Nonpreferred)
	file transfer protocol (Nonpreferred)
	file transfers
	files (Nonpreferred)
authority	files
card	*files (Nonpreferred)*
community resource	files
data	*files (Nonpreferred)*
digital audio	files
digital video	files
human resource	files
inverted	files
personal	files
vertical	files
	filing (Nonpreferred)
electronic	filing
form	filling
International Standard	*Film Number (Nonpreferred)*
standard	*film numbers (Nonpreferred)*
motion picture	films
photographic	films
	flmstrips
cognitive	*filtering (Nonpreferred)*
collaborative	filtering
content	filtering
information	filtering
message	filtering
social	*filtering (Nonpreferred)*
	filtering, information (Nonpreferred)
	finance
	financial information
	financial management
	fine arts
library	fines
	finite element analysis
	flat panel displays
	flexible disks (Nonpreferred)
	flexible electronic displays (Nonpreferred)
	flexible manufacturing systems
	floppy disks
	floptical disks
information	flow
crossborder data	*flow (Nonpreferred)*

international data	*flow (Nonpreferred)*
transborder data	flow
transnational data	*flow (Nonpreferred)*
work	flow analysis
	flow charting
	focus groups
	folklore (Nonpreferred)
	font learning
till	*forbid orders (Nonpreferred)*
air	*force (Nonpreferred)*
armed	forces
	forecasting
	foreign language materials (Nonpreferred)
	foreign languages (Nonpreferred)
	forenames (Nonpreferred)
	form filling
(documents by medium, physical	form)
concept	*formation (Nonpreferred)*
data	formats
electronic document interchange	*formats (Nonpreferred)*
exchange	*formats (Nonpreferred)*
information exchange	*formats (Nonpreferred)*
interchange	formats
machine readable cataloging	*formats (Nonpreferred)*
MARC	formats
	formats, data (Nonpreferred)
field	formatted data
	formatting
	forms design
facet	*formula (Nonpreferred)*
query	formulation
search	*formulation (Nonpreferred)*
	Fourier analysis
	Fourier transforms (Nonpreferred)
	frame based systems (Nonpreferred)
	frames
Resource Description	Framework
	France
	fraud
context	free languages
acid	*free paper (Nonpreferred)*
	free text indexing (Nonpreferred)
	free text searching (Nonpreferred)
academic	freedom
intellectual	freedom
	freedom of information
	freedom of speech
	freedom to read
	freeware (Nonpreferred)
citation	*frequency (Nonpreferred)*
inverse document	frequency
term	*frequency (Nonpreferred)*
usage	*frequency (Nonpreferred)*
word	frequency
	frequency of use

user	*friendliness (Nonpreferred)*
	friends of libraries
	friends of the library organizations (Nonpreferred)
	front ends
	ftp
anonymous	*ftp (Nonpreferred)*
	fugitive materials (Nonpreferred)
	full motion video (Nonpreferred)
	full text databases
	full text information systems (Nonpreferred)
	full text retrieval (Nonpreferred)
	full text searching
	full text systems (Nonpreferred)
	functional literacy (Nonpreferred)
Bayesian	functions
Boolean	*functions (Nonpreferred)*
	funding
electronic	funds transfer
	fusion (Nonpreferred)
data	*fusion (Nonpreferred)*
	future (Nonpreferred)
	fuzzy logic
	fuzzy retrieval systems
	fuzzy search (Nonpreferred)
	fuzzy set theory (Nonpreferred)
	game theory
computer	*games (Nonpreferred)*
multiuser Internet	games
video	games
	gatekeepers
technological	*gatekeepers (Nonpreferred)*
	gateways (Nonpreferred)
information	*gathering (Nonpreferred)*
	gays and lesbians
	gender
	genealogy
	general activities
	(general attributes)
	(general processes)
	generalization
standard	*generalized markup language (Nonpreferred)*
automatic taxonomy	generation
discourse	generation
sentence	generation
automatic thesaurus	*generation (Nonpreferred)*
	generic posting
	generic relationships (Nonpreferred)
	genetic algorithms
	genomic information
	genus species relationships
	geographic information systems
	geography
	geology (Nonpreferred)
	geopolitical aspects
	geospatial information

	Germany
	gifts and exchanges
	GIS (Nonpreferred)
	gist (Nonpreferred)
	global aspects (Nonpreferred)
	global village (Nonpreferred)
	glossaries (Nonpreferred)
	goals
	Google (Nonpreferred)
	gophers
	government
electronic	government
	government agencies
	government documents (Nonpreferred)
	government information
	government libraries
	government policy (Nonpreferred)
	government publications
	government records (Nonpreferred)
case	grammar
	grammar checkers
	grammars
large scale	grammars
	grants
	graph processing
	graph theory
	graphic images (Nonpreferred)
	graphical representations (Nonpreferred)
	graphical thesauri
	graphical user interfaces
	graphics
computer	graphics
	graphics terminals (Nonpreferred)
	graphs
	gray literature (Nonpreferred)
	Great Britain
	grey literature
	group decision support systems
	group work (Nonpreferred)
discussion	*groups (Nonpreferred)*
ethnic	*groups (Nonpreferred)*
focus	groups
minorities and ethnic	groups
peer	groups
(persons and informal	groups)
	groupware
	growth
	GUI (Nonpreferred)
reading	*guidance (Nonpreferred)*
	guide terms (Nonpreferred)
	guidelines (Nonpreferred)
user	*guides (Nonpreferred)*
	Guyana
	hacking
	half life measures

	hand held computers (Nonpreferred)
	handbooks
	Handheld Device Markup Language (Nonpreferred)
	handicapped persons (Nonpreferred)
reading	*handicapped persons (Nonpreferred)*
document	handling
records	*handling (Nonpreferred)*
	handwritten input (Nonpreferred)
	hard disks
computer	*hardware (Nonpreferred)*
	hardware, computer (Nonpreferred)
	(hardware, software, and equipment)
information	*harvesting (Nonpreferred)*
Open Archives Initiative Protocol for Metadata	Harvesting specification
	hash coding
	hashing (Nonpreferred)
	HCI (Nonpreferred)
	HDML
semantic	*headers (Nonpreferred)*
subject	heading lists
	headings
Library of Congress Subject	Headings
Medical Subject	*Headings (Nonpreferred)*
Sears Subject	Headings
subject	headings
	health informatics (Nonpreferred)
health sciences	*(Nonpreferred)*
	hearing
	hearing impaired persons
search	hedges
hand	*held computers (Nonpreferred)*
	help systems
	heuristics
	hidden web (Nonpreferred)
	hierarchical classification
	hierarchical file structures
	hierarchical models
	hierarchical relationships
	hierarchies
	high density data storage
	high level languages
	high performance computing (Nonpreferred)
	high resolution displays
	high schools
junior	*high schools (Nonpreferred)*
	higher education (Nonpreferred)
information	*highway (Nonpreferred)*
	Hispanics
	historical bibliography (Nonpreferred)
	historical records (Nonpreferred)
search	histories
case	*histories (Nonpreferred)*
	history
information science	history
oral	history

	holdings (library) (Nonpreferred)
	holographic memory
	holography
working at	home
	home education
	home information services
web	home pages
	home schooling (Nonpreferred)
	home work (Nonpreferred)
	homebound patrons
	homography
	honors
Trojan	horses
	host computers (Nonpreferred)
	host services (Nonpreferred)
database	*hosts (Nonpreferred)*
	HTML
	http
behavior,	*human (Nonpreferred)*
	(human attributes)
	human behavior
	human communications
	human computer interaction
	human computer interfaces (Nonpreferred)
	human engineering (Nonpreferred)
	human factors
	human factors engineering (Nonpreferred)
	human indexing (Nonpreferred)
	human information resources
computer	*human interaction (Nonpreferred)*
computer	*human interfaces (Nonpreferred)*
	human language
	human memory
	(human processes)
	human productivity
	human resource files
	human resources management
	human rights
	human speech
	humanities
	Hungary
	hybrid libraries
	hybrid search engines
	hybrid systems
	hyperdocuments (Nonpreferred)
	hyperlinks (Nonpreferred)
	hypermedia (Nonpreferred)
	hypermedia authoring
	hypermedia links
	hypertext
	hypertext links (Nonpreferred)
	hypertext markup language (Nonpreferred)
	hypertext transfer protocol (Nonpreferred)
	HyTime (Nonpreferred)
A &	*I services (Nonpreferred)*

I&R services (Nonpreferred)
IAC (Nonpreferred)
iconography (Nonpreferred)
icons
identification

uniform resource	*identifier (Nonpreferred)*
digital object	identifiers
persistent	identifiers
	identifiers (Nonpreferred)

ideographs
idioms
ILL (interlibrary loans) (Nonpreferred)
illiteracy (Nonpreferred)
illustrations
image analysis
image compression (Nonpreferred)
image data (Nonpreferred)
image databases
image enhancement
image indexing
image information systems
image processing
image retrieval
image servers

three dimensional	*imagery (Nonpreferred)*
	images
bit-mapped	images
digitized	images
graphic	*images (Nonpreferred)*
	imaging
electronic	*imaging (Nonpreferred)*
technology	impact
	impact factor
hearing	impaired persons
mobility	impaired persons
visually	impaired persons
	implied knowledge
critical	incident method
critical	*incident technique (Nonpreferred)*
	incunabula
	indecent materials (Nonpreferred)
	index entries (Nonpreferred)
	index language construction
	index language specificity (Nonpreferred)
	index languages
intermediate	*index languages (Nonpreferred)*
	index term weighting (Nonpreferred)
	index terms
subject	*index terms (Nonpreferred)*
(indexing by feature	indexed)
(indexing by item	indexcd)
consistency,	*indexer (Nonpreferred)*
	indexer consistency
alphabetico classed	indexes
author	indexes

author-prepared	indexes
back of book	*indexes (Nonpreferred)*
book	indexes
citation	indexes
cumulative	indexes
information retrieval	indexes
journal	*indexes (Nonpreferred)*
keyword	indexes
keyword in context	*indexes (Nonpreferred)*
keyword out of context	*indexes (Nonpreferred)*
KWIC	indexes
KWOC	indexes
natural language	*indexes (Nonpreferred)*
periodical	indexes
permuted	indexes
rotated	*indexes (Nonpreferred)*
rotated term	*indexes (Nonpreferred)*
subject	indexes
	indexing
assigned	*indexing (Nonpreferred)*
assignment	indexing
automatic	indexing
back of book	*indexing (Nonpreferred)*
book	indexing
chain	indexing
computer aided	*indexing (Nonpreferred)*
content based	indexing
coordinate	*indexing (Nonpreferred)*
corporate name	*indexing (Nonpreferred)*
database	indexing
derivative	indexing
description based	indexing
free text	*indexing (Nonpreferred)*
human	*indexing (Nonpreferred)*
image	indexing
machine aided	indexing
manual	indexing
multilingual subject	indexing
name	indexing
natural language	*indexing (Nonpreferred)*
periodical	indexing
personal name	*indexing (Nonpreferred)*
postcoordinate	indexing
precoordinate	indexing
probabilistic	indexing
semantic	*indexing (Nonpreferred)*
string	indexing
subject	indexing
uncontrolled	*indexing (Nonpreferred)*
uniterm	*indexing (Nonpreferred)*
	(indexing by feature indexed)
	(indexing by item indexed)
	(indexing by method used)
	indexing depth
	indexing discrimination

	indexing exhaustivity
	indexing languages (Nonpreferred)
abstracting and	indexing service bureaus
	indexing services (Nonpreferred)
	indexing specificity
	indexing term links
	indexing terms (Nonpreferred)
	indexing vocabularies (Nonpreferred)
subdivisions	*(indexing) (Nonpreferred)*
	India
	Indians (American) (Nonpreferred)
American	*Indians (Nonpreferred)*
	indicators
economic	*indicators (Nonpreferred)*
facet	*indicators (Nonpreferred)*
role	indicators
	indirect collective references
	individual differences
	induction
computer	industry
	industry (Nonpreferred)
information	industry
online	industry
software	industry
telecommunications	industry
	inference
	infixes (Nonpreferred)
	infometrics (Nonpreferred)
	informal communication
(persons and	informal groups)
health	*informatics (Nonpreferred)*
	informatics
medical	informatics
museum	informatics
social	informatics
auditory	*information (Nonpreferred)*
availability of	*information (Nonpreferred)*
biomedical	information
business	information
chemical	information
classified	*information (Nonpreferred)*
company	information
consumer	information
contextual	information
dissemination,	*information (Nonpreferred)*
domain	information
economics of	information
environmental	information
factual	information
false	information
filtering,	*information (Nonpreferred)*
financial	information
freedom of	information
genomic	information
geospatial	information

government	information
legal	information
medical	*information (Nonpreferred)*
multidisciplinary	information
multilingual	information
organization of	information
overload,	*information (Nonpreferred)*
personal	information
professionals,	*information (Nonpreferred)*
public domain	information
scientific and technical	information
selective dissemination of	*information (Nonpreferred)*
spatial	information
technical	*information (Nonpreferred)*
temporal	information
transfer of	*information (Nonpreferred)*
use of	*information (Nonpreferred)*
value of	*information (Nonpreferred)*
visual	*information (Nonpreferred)*
	information access
	information age (Nonpreferred)
	information analysis centers
clearinghouses	*(information analysis) (Nonpreferred)*
information centers	*(information analysis) (Nonpreferred)*
	(information and data processes)
(attributes of	information and data)
	information and referral services (Nonpreferred)
	information and reference skills
	information architects
	information architecture
	information associations
	information attribution
	information brokers
	information centers (information analysis) (Nonpreferred)
	information centers (libraries) (Nonpreferred)
	information centers (special libraries) (Nonpreferred)
	information channels
	information content
(documents by	information content, purpose)
	information discovery
	information dissemination
electronic	*information dissemination (Nonpreferred)*
	information distribution (Nonpreferred)
	information economics (Nonpreferred)
	information engineering (Nonpreferred)
	information entropy
	information exchange (Nonpreferred)
	information exchange formats (Nonpreferred)
	information explosion
	information extraction (Nonpreferred)
	information filtering
	information flow
	information gathering (Nonpreferred)
	information harvesting (Nonpreferred)
	information highway (Nonpreferred)

information industry
information infrastructure
information life cycle
information literacy
distributed *information management system (Nonpreferred)*
information management (Nonpreferred)
information mapping
information models
information needs
user *information needs (Nonpreferred)*
information networks (Nonpreferred)
information objects (Nonpreferred)
information operation closings (Nonpreferred)
information operations
information overload
information policy
information processing
information production
information products (Nonpreferred)
electronic *information products (Nonpreferred)*
information professionals
information professions (Nonpreferred)
information representations
information resources
human information resources
Internet information resources
information resources management
information retrieval
online *information retrieval (Nonpreferred)*
information retrieval agents (Nonpreferred)
information retrieval indexes
information retrieval models
information retrieval noise
information retrieval software
online *information retrieval systems (Nonpreferred)*
information reuse
information science
library and *information science (Nonpreferred)*
schools of *information science (Nonpreferred)*
information science education
information science history
information science schools
information scientists
information sector
information seeking
information seeking behavior (Nonpreferred)
information services
community information services
home information services
secondary *information services (Nonpreferred)*
information skills (Nonpreferred)
information society
information space
information specialists (Nonpreferred)
information storage and retrieval systems

	information studies schools (Nonpreferred)
	information superhighway (Nonpreferred)
electronic	*information systems (Nonpreferred)*
executive	*information systems (Nonpreferred)*
full text	*information systems (Nonpreferred)*
geographic	information systems
image	information systems
	information systems (Nonpreferred)
management	information systems
paper based	information systems
personal	information systems
pictorial	*information systems (Nonpreferred)*
	information technology
	information theory
	information transfer
	information use
	information user studies (Nonpreferred)
	information users (Nonpreferred)
	information utilities
	information utilization (Nonpreferred)
	information visualization (Nonpreferred)
	information workers
(knowledge and	information)
resource management	*(information) (Nonpreferred)*
clearinghouses (community	*information) (Nonpreferred)*
	informetrics
information	infrastructure
copyright	infringement
trademark	infringement
attribute	inheritance
	initialisms (Nonpreferred)
Open Archives	Initiative Protocol for Metadata Harvesting specification
	injury
repetitive stress	injury
electronic	ink
digital	*ink (Nonpreferred)*
diffusion of	innovation
	innovation
technological	*innovation (Nonpreferred)*
handwritten	*input (Nonpreferred)*
	input equipment
voice	*input (Nonpreferred)*
	instant messaging
correctional	*institution libraries (Nonpreferred)*
	institutional libraries
academic	*institutions (Nonpreferred)*
bibliographic	instruction
computer aided	*instruction (Nonpreferred)*
computer assisted	instruction
	instruction (Nonpreferred)
library	*instruction (Nonpreferred)*
media	*instruction (Nonpreferred)*
use	*instruction (Nonpreferred)*
reduced	*instruction set computers (Nonpreferred)*
	instructional technology (Nonpreferred)

	instrumentation
	integrated circuits
	integrated library systems
computer	integrated manufacturing
	integrated online library systems (Nonpreferred)
	integrated systems
	integration
large scale	*integration (Nonpreferred)*
systems	integration
very large scale	*integration (Nonpreferred)*
	integration, systems (Nonpreferred)
file	integrity
	intellectual assets (Nonpreferred)
	intellectual capital (Nonpreferred)
	intellectual freedom
	intellectual property
	intelligence
artificial	intelligence
competitive	intelligence
competitor	*intelligence (Nonpreferred)*
computational	*intelligence (Nonpreferred)*
corporate	*intelligence (Nonpreferred)*
machine	*intelligence (Nonpreferred)*
military	intelligence
organizational	*intelligence (Nonpreferred)*
	intelligent agents
	intelligent interfaces
computer human	*interaction (Nonpreferred)*
human computer	interaction
compact disk	interactive
	interactive design (Nonpreferred)
digital video	interactive
	interactive systems
electronic data	interchange
data	*interchange (Nonpreferred)*
	interchange formats
electronic document	*interchange formats (Nonpreferred)*
	interdisciplinarity
	interfaces
audio	interfaces
command driven	interfaces
computer human	*interfaces (Nonpreferred)*
direct manipulation	interfaces
graphical user	interfaces
human computer	*interfaces (Nonpreferred)*
intelligent	interfaces
man machine	*interfaces (Nonpreferred)*
menu based	interfaces
natural language	interfaces
touch screen	interfaces
user system	*interfaces (Nonpreferred)*
vocal	*interfaces (Nonpreferred)*
windows	*interfaces (Nonpreferred)*
zoomable user	interfaces
	interlibrary loans

204

ILL   *(interlibrary loans) (Nonpreferred)*
intermediaries
intermediate index languages (Nonpreferred)
intermediate lexicons (Nonpreferred)
international aspects
international data flow (Nonpreferred)
international librarianship
International Patent Classification
International Standard Bibliographic Description
International Standard Book Number (Nonpreferred)
International Standard Film Number (Nonpreferred)
International Standard Music Number (Nonpreferred)
International Standard Record Code (Nonpreferred)
International Standard Serial Number (Nonpreferred)
Internet
Internet computers (Nonpreferred)
multiuser Internet games
Internet information resources
Internet search systems
Internet service providers
Internet telephony
interoperability
interpretation (linguistic) (Nonpreferred)
interpreters (linguistic) (Nonpreferred)
interviews
presearch interviews
reference interviews
intranets
intrusion prevention and detection
inventory
inverse document frequency
inverted files
invisible colleges
invisible web
IPC (Nonpreferred)
Ireland
Northern Ireland
IRM (Nonpreferred)
ISBD (Nonpreferred)
ISBN
ISFN
Pacific *islands (Nonpreferred)*
ISMN
ISO (Nonpreferred)
ISPs (Nonpreferred)
ISRC
ISSN
Italy
(indexing by item indexed)
known item searching
jail libraries (Nonpreferred)
Japan
jargon
jobbers
book *jobbers (Nonpreferred)*

joint authorship
journal articles (Nonpreferred)
journal indexes (Nonpreferred)
journal productivity
journals
electronic journals
scholarly journals (Nonpreferred)
productivity (journals) (Nonpreferred)
joysticks
judgment
jukeboxes (CD-ROM drives) (Nonpreferred)
junior high schools (Nonpreferred)
criminal justice (Nonpreferred)
KDD (Nonpreferred)
Kenya
key words (Nonpreferred)
keyboarding (Nonpreferred)
keyboarding errors (Nonpreferred)
keyboards
keyframes
keying (Nonpreferred)
keyphrases (Nonpreferred)
keyword in context indexes (Nonpreferred)
keyword indexes
keyword out of context indexes (Nonpreferred)
keyword searching
keyword spam
keyword tagging (Nonpreferred)
keywords
United Kingdom
kiosks
KM (Nonpreferred)
knowbots (Nonpreferred)
knowledge
common sense knowledge
domain knowledge
implied knowledge
representation, knowledge (Nonpreferred)
situated knowledge
system knowledge
task knowledge
world knowledge (Nonpreferred)
knowledge acquisition
(knowledge and information)
knowledge based systems (Nonpreferred)
knowledge bases
knowledge discovery
knowledge engineering
knowledge management
knowledge modeling
knowledge organization systems
knowledge production (Nonpreferred)
knowledge representation
knowledge transfer (Nonpreferred)
knowledge workers (Nonpreferred)

	knowledgebase management systems (Nonpreferred)
	knowledgebases (Nonpreferred)
	known item searching
	Korea
	KWIC indexes
	KWOC indexes
node	labels
unions,	*labor (Nonpreferred)*
	labor unions
computer	laboratories
	LAN (Nonpreferred)
	(language)
	language
Chinese	language
common command	language
document style semantics and specification	*language (Nonpreferred)*
English	language
figurative	*language (Nonpreferred)*
Handheld Device Markup	*Language (Nonpreferred)*
human	language
hypertext markup	*language (Nonpreferred)*
standard document query	*language (Nonpreferred)*
standard generalized markup	*language (Nonpreferred)*
structured query	*language (Nonpreferred)*
Wireless Markup	*Language (Nonpreferred)*
	language barriers
natural	language comprehension
index	language construction
natural	*language indexes (Nonpreferred)*
natural	*language indexing (Nonpreferred)*
natural	language interfaces
non English	language materials
foreign	*language materials (Nonpreferred)*
natural	language processing
automated	*language processing (Nonpreferred)*
natural	*language searching (Nonpreferred)*
index	*language specificity (Nonpreferred)*
	language types
	language understanding (Nonpreferred)
understanding (natural	*language) (Nonpreferred)*
command	languages
computer	*languages (Nonpreferred)*
context free	languages
data definition	languages
foreign	*languages (Nonpreferred)*
high level	languages
index	languages
indexing	*languages (Nonpreferred)*
intermediate index	*languages (Nonpreferred)*
markup	languages
non English	languages
programming	languages
query	languages
retrieval	*languages (Nonpreferred)*
search	*languages (Nonpreferred)*

switching	languages
	laptop computers (Nonpreferred)
very	large databases
	large print materials
	large scale grammars
	large scale integration (Nonpreferred)
very	*large scale integration (Nonpreferred)*
	laser disks (Nonpreferred)
	lasers
	latent semantic analysis
	Latin America
	Latinos (Nonpreferred)
	law
Bradford's	law
Lotka's	law
Pareto-Zipf	*law (Nonpreferred)*
Zipf's	law
Zipf-Mandelbrot	*law (Nonpreferred)*
	law enforcement
	law libraries
	LCD panels
	leadership
loose	leaf services
	learned society publishers
	learning
distance	learning
font	learning
lifelong	learning
machine	learning
perceptual	learning
computer	*learning (Nonpreferred)*
	learning centers (Nonpreferred)
	learning disabled persons
	learning resource centers (Nonpreferred)
database	leasing
tape	*leasing (Nonpreferred)*
	leasing, database (Nonpreferred)
	legal aspects
	legal deposit
	legal information
	legibility
	legislation (Nonpreferred)
	legislative libraries and reference services
	lemmatization (Nonpreferred)
	lending (library materials) (Nonpreferred)
public	lending right
gays and	lesbians
	lesbians (Nonpreferred)
	letter by letter arrangement
alphabetic	letters
	letters (Nonpreferred)
helles	*lettres (Nonpreferred)*
high	level languages
	lexemes (Nonpreferred)
	lexical analysis

	lexicography
computational	lexicography
intermediate	*lexicons (Nonpreferred)*
	liability
	liaison agents (Nonpreferred)
	librarians
reference	librarians
solo	*librarians (Nonpreferred)*
	librarianship
children's	*librarianship (Nonpreferred)*
comparative	librarianship
international	librarianship
	libraries
academic	libraries
branch	libraries
central	libraries
children's	libraries
college	*libraries (Nonpreferred)*
community college	libraries
company	*libraries (Nonpreferred)*
corporate	libraries
correctional institution	*libraries (Nonpreferred)*
depository	libraries
digital	libraries
electronic	*libraries (Nonpreferred)*
friends of	libraries
government	libraries
hybrid	libraries
institutional	libraries
jail	*libraries (Nonpreferred)*
law	libraries
main	*libraries (Nonpreferred)*
medical	libraries
mobile	libraries
municipal	*libraries (Nonpreferred)*
national	libraries
one person	*libraries (Nonpreferred)*
Presidential	libraries
prison	libraries
public	libraries
research	libraries
school	*libraries (Nonpreferred)*
small	libraries
special	libraries
state	*libraries (Nonpreferred)*
university	*libraries (Nonpreferred)*
virtual	libraries
legislative	libraries and reference services
information centers	*(libraries) (Nonpreferred)*
clearinghouses (special	*libraries) (Nonpreferred)*
information centers (special	*libraries) (Nonpreferred)*
patrons,	*library (Nonpreferred)*
shelving,	*library (Nonpreferred)*
stacks,	*library (Nonpreferred)*
support staff,	*library (Nonpreferred)*

	library access
	library acquisitions (Nonpreferred)
	library administration (Nonpreferred)
	library administrators (Nonpreferred)
state	library agencies
	library and archival services
	library and information science (Nonpreferred)
	library assistants (Nonpreferred)
	library associations
	library automation
	library binding
	library boards
	library buildings
	library circulation
	library closings
branch	*library closings (Nonpreferred)*
	library collections
	library education
	library equipment
	library exhibits and displays
	library extension (Nonpreferred)
	library fines
	library instruction (Nonpreferred)
	library management
	library materials
borrowing	*(library materials) (Nonpreferred)*
lending	*(library materials) (Nonpreferred)*
loans	*(library materials) (Nonpreferred)*
	library networks
	Library of Congress Classification
	Library of Congress Subject Headings
	library operations
friends of the	*library organizations (Nonpreferred)*
	library outreach services
	library patrons (Nonpreferred)
	library personnel
paraprofessional	library personnel
	library policy
	library programs
	library reserves
shared	*library resources (Nonpreferred)*
	library schools
	library science (Nonpreferred)
	library security
	library security systems
off campus	library services
community based	*library services (Nonpreferred)*
	library shelving
	library stacks (Nonpreferred)
	library staff (Nonpreferred)
	library suppliers
	library supplies
	library support staff (Nonpreferred)
	library surveys
integrated	library systems

	library systems (Nonpreferred)
integrated online	*library systems (Nonpreferred)*
	library technical assistants (Nonpreferred)
	library technical services
	library technicians (Nonpreferred)
	library trustees (Nonpreferred)
	library use (Nonpreferred)
	library user profiles
	library user services (Nonpreferred)
	library users
	library weeks
boards	*(library) (Nonpreferred)*
displays	*(library) (Nonpreferred)*
exhibits and displays	*(library) (Nonpreferred)*
holdings	*(library) (Nonpreferred)*
trustees	*(library) (Nonpreferred)*
	licenses
information	life cycle
half	life measures
	life sciences (Nonpreferred)
lifelong	learning
	light pens
	light wands (Nonpreferred)
	likeness (Nonpreferred)
	limited area networks (Nonpreferred)
	limited cataloging (Nonpreferred)
on	*line databases (Nonpreferred)*
	linear programming
	linear systems (Nonpreferred)
cross	*lingual retrieval (Nonpreferred)*
	linguistic analysis
	linguistic elements
	linguistic parsing (Nonpreferred)
interpretation	*(linguistic) (Nonpreferred)*
interpreters	*(linguistic) (Nonpreferred)*
	linguistics
computational	linguistics
	link analysis
	link markers (Nonpreferred)
hypermedia	links
indexing term	links
hypertext	*links (Nonpreferred)*
	liquid crystal displays (Nonpreferred)
	LIS (Nonpreferred)
e-mail	list servers
contents	lists
subject heading	lists
stop	*lists (Nonpreferred)*
table of contents	*lists (Nonpreferred)*
	listservs (Nonpreferred)
	literacy
computer	literacy
information	literacy
adult	*literacy (Nonpreferred)*
functional	*literacy (Nonpreferred)*

	literary reviews (Nonpreferred)
	literary warrant
adolescent	*literature (Nonpreferred)*
	literature
children's	literature
core	literature
gray	*literature (Nonpreferred)*
grey	literature
near-published	*literature (Nonpreferred)*
primary	literature
reviews of the	*literature (Nonpreferred)*
scholarly	*literature (Nonpreferred)*
scientific	*literature (Nonpreferred)*
secondary	*literature (Nonpreferred)*
young adult	literature
	literature reviews
aging of	*literatures (Nonpreferred)*
	litigation
	litigation support
	live reference services (Nonpreferred)
interlibrary	loans
	loans (library materials) (Nonpreferred)
ILL (interlibrary	*loans) (Nonpreferred)*
	local area networks
	local networks (Nonpreferred)
	location breadcrumbs
	locators
reference	*locators (Nonpreferred)*
uniform resource	*locators (Nonpreferred)*
	logic
Boolean	logic
fuzzy	logic
predicate	logic
propositional	logic
	logic programming
	logical operators (Nonpreferred)
transaction	*logs (Nonpreferred)*
	long term memory
	longitudinal studies
	loose leaf services
	Lotka's law
	LSA (Nonpreferred)
	LSI
	LTA (Nonpreferred)
	machine aided indexing
	machine aided translation (Nonpreferred)
	machine intelligence (Nonpreferred)
man	*machine interfaces (Nonpreferred)*
	machine learning
	machine readable cataloging formats (Nonpreferred)
	machine readable cataloging records (Nonpreferred)
	machine readable data
	machine readable records (Nonpreferred)
	machine translation
	machine vision (Nonpreferred)

database	machines
	magazines (Nonpreferred)
	magnetic disks
	magnetic media
	magnetic recording
	magnetic tapes
	magneto-optical disks
	MAI (Nonpreferred)
voice	mail
electronic	*mail (Nonpreferred)*
	main libraries (Nonpreferred)
	mainframe computers
	maintainability
	maintenance
database	*maintenance (Nonpreferred)*
decision	making
	malicious software
	malware (Nonpreferred)
	man machine interfaces (Nonpreferred)
	management
collection	management
computer resource	*management (Nonpreferred)*
computing resource	management
content	management
database	management
digital rights	management
document	management
financial	management
human resources	management
information	*management (Nonpreferred)*
information resources	management
knowledge	management
library	management
paperwork	*management (Nonpreferred)*
records	management
thesaurus	management
web content	management
resource	*management (computing) (Nonpreferred)*
resource	*management (information) (Nonpreferred)*
	management information systems
	management operations
reference	*management software (Nonpreferred)*
distributed information	*management system (Nonpreferred)*
content	*management systems (Nonpreferred)*
database	management systems
Electronic Copyright	*Management Systems (Nonpreferred)*
electronic document	management systems
Electronic Rights	*Management Systems (Nonpreferred)*
knowledgebase	*management systems (Nonpreferred)*
	managers
records	managers
direct	manipulation interfaces
	manual indexing
	manuals (Nonpreferred)
user	*manuals (Nonpreferred)*

213

computer aided	manufacturing
computer integrated	manufacturing
technical and	manufacturing operations
flexible	manufacturing systems
	manuscripts
write once read	*many (Nonpreferred)*
information	mapping
set	mapping
	mapping (cartography) (Nonpreferred)
	maps
data	maps
self organizing	maps
topic	maps
citation	*maps (Nonpreferred)*
	MARC formats
	MARC records
	marginalia
link	*markers (Nonpreferred)*
	marketing
	Markov chains (Nonpreferred)
	Markov models
	Markov processes (Nonpreferred)
Handheld Device	*Markup Language (Nonpreferred)*
hypertext	*markup language (Nonpreferred)*
standard generalized	*markup language (Nonpreferred)*
Wireless	*Markup Language (Nonpreferred)*
	markup languages
	mass communications (Nonpreferred)
	mass media
	massively parallel processing (Nonpreferred)
partial	*match retrieval systems (Nonpreferred)*
cross	matching
computer	*matching (Nonpreferred)*
pattern	*matching (Nonpreferred)*
acquisitions (of	*materials) (Nonpreferred)*
aging of	materials
alternative	*materials (Nonpreferred)*
antiquarian	*materials (Nonpreferred)*
audio visual	*materials (Nonpreferred)*
audiovisual	*materials (Nonpreferred)*
banned	materials
borrowing (library	*materials) (Nonpreferred)*
censored	*materials (Nonpreferred)*
conservation of	*materials (Nonpreferred)*
customized	*materials (Nonpreferred)*
erotic	materials
exchanges (of	*materials) (Nonpreferred)*
foreign language	*materials (Nonpreferred)*
fugitive	*materials (Nonpreferred)*
indecent	*materials (Nonpreferred)*
large print	materials
lending (library	*materials) (Nonpreferred)*
library	materials
loans (library	*materials) (Nonpreferred)*
media	*materials (Nonpreferred)*

non English language	materials
non text-based	*materials (Nonpreferred)*
obscene	materials
overdue	materials
popular	materials
pornographic	materials
print	*materials (Nonpreferred)*
rare	materials
ready reference	materials
reference	materials
source	materials
video	*materials (Nonpreferred)*
visual	materials
	materials acquisitions
	materials claims
	materials conservation
	materials orders
	materials preservation
	materials processing
	materials selection
	materials storage
	mathematical methods
	mathematical models
	mathematics
	matrices
extension	matrices
personality,	*matter, energy, space, and time (Nonpreferred)*
	meaning (Nonpreferred)
	measurement
half life	measures
	media
magnetic	media
mass	media
mixed	*media (Nonpreferred)*
news	media
nonprint	media
optical	media
streaming	*media (Nonpreferred)*
	media centers
school	*media centers (Nonpreferred)*
	media instruction (Nonpreferred)
	media materials (Nonpreferred)
	media specialists
(communications	media)
(physical	media)
computer	mediated communications
	medical informatics
	medical information (Nonpreferred)
	medical libraries
	medical personnel
	medical records
	medical science
	Medical Subject Headings (Nonpreferred)
(documents by	medium, physical form)
electronic	*meeting systems (Nonpreferred)*

	meetings
	memoranda (Nonpreferred)
associative	memory
computer	memory
dynamic random access	*memory (Nonpreferred)*
holographic	memory
human	memory
long term	memory
random access	memory
read only	memory
short term	memory
virtual	memory
visual	memory
working	*memory (Nonpreferred)*
	men
	mental models (Nonpreferred)
	mental processes
	mental visualization
	mentoring
	menu based interfaces
	menus (Nonpreferred)
	MeSH
	message filtering
	message systems
error	messages
instant	messaging
text	messaging
	messaging systems (Nonpreferred)
	meta analysis
	meta search engines
	meta-analysis (Nonpreferred)
	metadata
subject	*metadata (Nonpreferred)*
Open Archives Initiative Protocol for	Metadata Harvesting specification
	metadata standards
	metadocuments (Nonpreferred)
	metamapping (Nonpreferred)
desktop	metaphor
	metaphors
	metasearch engines (Nonpreferred)
	metatags (Nonpreferred)
	metathesauri
critical incident	method
critical path	method
Monte Carlo	method
(indexing by	method used)
description (research	*method) (Nonpreferred)*
mathematical	methods
practical	methods
research	methods
statistical	methods
(research and analytic	methods)
	metrics (Nonpreferred)
	Mexico
	mice

	microcomputers
	microfiche
	microfilm
	microforms
computer output	microforms
	micrographics (Nonpreferred)
	microprocessors
	microproduction (Nonpreferred)
	micropublishing
	microtechnology (Nonpreferred)
	microthesauri
	Middle East
	middle schools
	migration
	military intelligence
	military services (Nonpreferred)
	minicomputers
	minimal cataloging
content	mining
data	mining
text	mining
web	mining
database	*mining (Nonpreferred)*
	minithesauri (Nonpreferred)
	minorities and ethnic groups
	mirror sites
	MIS (Nonpreferred)
	misinformation (Nonpreferred)
	mission oriented research
	misspellings (Nonpreferred)
	mixed media (Nonpreferred)
	mobile communications
	mobile libraries
	mobile shelving (Nonpreferred)
	mobile telephones (Nonpreferred)
	mobility impaired persons
knowledge	modeling
	modeling (Nonpreferred)
analytic	models
business	models
chemical structure	models
cognitive	models
conceptual	*models (Nonpreferred)*
connectionist	models
data	models
database	models
hierarchical	models
information	models
information retrieval	models
Markov	models
mathematical	models
mental	*models (Nonpreferred)*
predictive	models
probabilistic	*models (Nonpreferred)*
relational	models

stochastic	models
theoretical	*models (Nonpreferred)*
unified retrieval	models
user	models
vector space	models
	modems
	modification
	modifiers
	modularity
	monitoring
	monographs
	Monte Carlo method
	morals (Nonpreferred)
	morphemes
	morphological analysis
	motion picture films
	motion pictures (Nonpreferred)
full	*motion video (Nonpreferred)*
	motion video
	motion video streaming (Nonpreferred)
	motivation
	mouse (computer peripheral) (Nonpreferred)
	movable shelving (Nonpreferred)
	movies (Nonpreferred)
	moving
	MT (Nonpreferred)
	MUDs (Nonpreferred)
	multidimensional scaling
	multidisciplinary information
	multidisk drives
	multilingual information
	multilingual retrieval
	multilingual subject indexing
	multilingual thesauri
	multilingualism
	multimedia
	multiple access communications
	multiplexing
	multiprocessing
	multiprocessors
computer	multitasking
user	multitasking
	multiuser Internet games
	multivariate analysis
	municipal libraries (Nonpreferred)
	museum informatics
	museums
	music
International Standard	*Music Number (Nonpreferred)*
standard	*music numbers (Nonpreferred)*
corporate	*name indexing (Nonpreferred)*
	name indexing
personal	*name indexing (Nonpreferred)*
corporate	names
	names (Nonpreferred)

organization	*names (Nonpreferred)*
personal	names
proper	names
uniform resource	names
domain	naming system
	narratives
	narrower term references (Nonpreferred)
	narrower term relationships (Nonpreferred)
	national archives
	national aspects
	national bibliographies
	national libraries
	National Research and Education Network
	national security
	Native Americans
	natural disasters (Nonpreferred)
	natural language comprehension
	natural language indexes (Nonpreferred)
	natural language indexing (Nonpreferred)
	natural language interfaces
	natural language processing
	natural language searching (Nonpreferred)
understanding	*(natural language) (Nonpreferred)*
	(natural processes and events)
	natural sciences
	navigation
faceted	*navigation (Nonpreferred)*
	navy (Nonpreferred)
	NC (network computers) (Nonpreferred)
	near-published literature (Nonpreferred)
	near-synonymous relationships (Nonpreferred)
	nearest neighbor (Nonpreferred)
information	needs
assessment,	*needs (Nonpreferred)*
user	*needs (Nonpreferred)*
user information	*needs (Nonpreferred)*
	needs assessment
	negotiation
nearest	*neighbor (Nonpreferred)*
	net computers (Nonpreferred)
	Netherlands
	netiquette (Nonpreferred)
	netometrics (Nonpreferred)
neural	*nets (Nonpreferred)*
semantic	*nets (Nonpreferred)*
National Research and Education	Network
	network analysis
	network computers
NC	*(network computers) (Nonpreferred)*
	network protocols (Nonpreferred)
	network security
	network servers (Nonpreferred)
	network structures
social	networking
personal	*networking (Nonpreferred)*

artificial neural	*networks (Nonpreferred)*
citation	networks
common carrier	networks
communications	*networks (Nonpreferred)*
computer	*networks (Nonpreferred)*
information	*networks (Nonpreferred)*
library	networks
limited area	*networks (Nonpreferred)*
local	*networks (Nonpreferred)*
local area	networks
neural	networks
Pathfinder	networks
semantic	networks
telecommunications	networks
wide area	networks
(communications	networks)
neural	*nets (Nonpreferred)*
neural	networks
artificial neural	*networks (Nonpreferred)*
	New Zealand
	news
	news media
	news wire services (Nonpreferred)
	newsgroups
Usenet	*newsgroups (Nonpreferred)*
	newsletters
	newspapers
	newswire services
	Nigeria
	NISO (Nonpreferred)
	NLP (Nonpreferred)
	node labels
	nodes
information retrieval	noise
chemical	nomenclature
	nomenclature (Nonpreferred)
	nomenclature, chemical (Nonpreferred)
non	English language materials
non	English languages
non	*text-based materials (Nonpreferred)*
	nonbibliographic databases
	nonfiction
	nonhierarchical relationships (Nonpreferred)
	nonlinear programming
	nonpreferred term references (Nonpreferred)
	nonpreferred terms (Nonpreferred)
	nonprint media
	nonprofit sector
	nonroman scripts
	nonverbal communication
	normal distribution
	normalization
	North America
	Northern Ireland
	notation

synthesis,	*notation (Nonpreferred)*
	notation synthesis
	notebook computers (Nonpreferred)
scope	notes
	nothing before something arrangement (Nonpreferred)
	nouns
	novels (Nonpreferred)
	novice users
	NREN (Nonpreferred)
	NT references (Nonpreferred)
	NT relationships (Nonpreferred)
International Standard Book	*Number (Nonpreferred)*
International Standard Film	*Number (Nonpreferred)*
International Standard Music	*Number (Nonpreferred)*
International Standard Serial	*Number (Nonpreferred)*
call	numbers
standard book	*numbers (Nonpreferred)*
standard film	*numbers (Nonpreferred)*
standard music	*numbers (Nonpreferred)*
standard serial	*numbers (Nonpreferred)*
	numeric data
	numeric databases
	numeric range searching (Nonpreferred)
digital	object identifiers
	object oriented databases
	object oriented programming
digital	object preservation
	object recognition
	objectives (Nonpreferred)
data	objects
digital	objects
information	*objects (Nonpreferred)*
physical	objects
	objects (physical) (Nonpreferred)
	obscene materials
	observational research
	obsolescence
	Oceania
	OCR (Nonpreferred)
acquisitions	*(of materials) (Nonpreferred)*
exchanges	*(of materials) (Nonpreferred)*
definitions	*(of terms) (Nonpreferred)*
	off campus education
	off campus library services
	off site access (Nonpreferred)
	office automation
electronic	*offices (Nonpreferred)*
	offsite access (Nonpreferred)
	on line databases (Nonpreferred)
write	*once read many (Nonpreferred)*
	one person libraries (Nonpreferred)
	online catalogs (Nonpreferred)
	online databases
	online industry
	online information retrieval (Nonpreferred)

	online information retrieval systems (Nonpreferred)
integrated	online library systems (Nonpreferred)
	online public access catalogs (Nonpreferred)
	online searching
	online systems (Nonpreferred)
read	only memory
	ontologies
	OOP (Nonpreferred)
	OPACs
	open access publications
	Open Archives Initiative Protocol for Metadata Harvesting specification
	Open Document Architecture
	open source
	OpenURL
	operating systems
information	operation closings (Nonpreferred)
computer	operations
computerized	operations (Nonpreferred)
information	operations
library	operations
management	operations
technical and manufacturing	operations
	operations research
(activities and	operations)
Boolean	operators (Nonpreferred)
logical	operators (Nonpreferred)
	optical character recognition
	optical computers
	optical disks
erasable	optical disks
rewritable	optical disks (Nonpreferred)
	optical equipment
	optical fibers (Nonpreferred)
	optical media
	optical recognition
	optical recording
	optical scanners (Nonpreferred)
	optical scanning (Nonpreferred)
	optical tape
fiber	optics
	optimization
search engine	optimization
	oral communications (Nonpreferred)
	oral history
alphabetical	order (Nonpreferred)
chronological	order (Nonpreferred)
citation	order
preferred	order (Nonpreferred)
approval	ordering (Nonpreferred)
blanket	orders
materials	orders
standing	orders
till forbid	orders (Nonpreferred)
	organization charts

	organization names (Nonpreferred)
	organization of information
	organization productivity
knowledge	organization systems
	organization theory
(documents by availability, access,	organization)
	organizational communication
	organizational culture
	organizational environment
	organizational intelligence (Nonpreferred)
	(organizations)
standards developing	organizations
friends of the library	*organizations (Nonpreferred)*
self	organizing maps
object	oriented databases
object	oriented programming
mission	oriented research
	orthography
keyword	*out of context indexes (Nonpreferred)*
	out of print publications
	output equipment
computer	*output microfilm (Nonpreferred)*
computer	output microforms
	output reformatting
library	outreach services
	outsourcing
	overdue materials
	overhead costs
	overlap
information	overload
	overload, information (Nonpreferred)
	overviews (Nonpreferred)
	Pacific islands (Nonpreferred)
	Pacific Rim
	packet switching
	page references (Nonpreferred)
web	pages
web home	pages
	palmtop computers (Nonpreferred)
	pamphlets
flat	panel displays
LCD	panels
	paper
acid free	*paper (Nonpreferred)*
alkaline	*paper (Nonpreferred)*
digital	*paper (Nonpreferred)*
electronic	paper
permanent	paper
smart	*paper (Nonpreferred)*
	paper based information systems
	paperbacks
	paperwork management (Nonpreferred)
	paradigms
	paragraphs
	Paraguay

223

	parallel architecture (Nonpreferred)
	parallel processing
	parallel processors
	paraprofessional library personnel
	Pareto principle
	Pareto-Zipf law (Nonpreferred)
data	parsing
linguistic	*parsing (Nonpreferred)*
	part whole relationships
	partial match retrieval systems (Nonpreferred)
answer	passage retrieval
	passages (Nonpreferred)
	password control (Nonpreferred)
International	Patent Classification
	patents
	path breadcrumbs
critical	path method
	Pathfinder networks
homebound	patrons
problem	patrons
	patrons (Nonpreferred)
library	*patrons (Nonpreferred)*
	patrons, library (Nonpreferred)
	pattern matching (Nonpreferred)
	pattern recognition
communication	patterns
	payments, electronic (Nonpreferred)
	PC (Nonpreferred)
	PDAs (Nonpreferred)
	peer groups
	peer review (Nonpreferred)
	peer to peer file sharing
	pen based computers
light	pens
cognitive	perception
sensory	perception
	perceptions (attitudes) (Nonpreferred)
	perceptual learning
	performance
high	*performance computing (Nonpreferred)*
	performing arts
articles,	*periodical (Nonpreferred)*
	periodical articles
	periodical indexes
	periodical indexing
	periodicals
mouse (computer	*peripheral) (Nonpreferred)*
computer	peripherals
	peripherals, computer (Nonpreferred)
	permanence
	permanent paper
	permuted indexes
	persistent identifiers
one	*person libraries (Nonpreferred)*
	personal authorship

	personal collections
	personal computers
	personal digital assistants
	personal files
	personal information
	personal information systems
	personal name indexing (Nonpreferred)
	personal names
	personal networking (Nonpreferred)
	personal styles (Nonpreferred)
	personality, matter, energy, space, and time (Nonpreferred)
	personalization (Nonpreferred)
library	personnel
medical	personnel
paraprofessional library	personnel
	personnel (Nonpreferred)
blind	*persons (Nonpreferred)*
deaf	*persons (Nonpreferred)*
disabled	persons
handicapped	*persons (Nonpreferred)*
hearing impaired	persons
learning disabled	persons
mobility impaired	persons
physically challenged	*persons (Nonpreferred)*
reading disabled	persons
reading handicapped	*persons (Nonpreferred)*
visually impaired	persons
	(persons and informal groups)
search engine	*persuasion (Nonpreferred)*
	pertinence
	Peru
	PFnet (Nonpreferred)
	pharmacology
	Philippines
	philosophy
	phonemes
	phonetics
	photo CD
	photocopiers
	photocopying
	photogrammetry
	photographic films
	photographic slides
	photographs
	phrases
	physical attributes
(documents by medium,	physical form)
	(physical media)
	physical objects
	physical sciences
objects	*(physical) (Nonpreferred)*
	physically challenged persons (Nonpreferred)
	physicians
	physics
	pictorial information systems (Nonpreferred)

motion	picture films
	picture telephones (Nonpreferred)
	pictures
motion	*pictures (Nonpreferred)*
copyright	piracy
	plagiarism
	planning
strategic	planning
approval	plans
	PMEST facets
	poetry
	pointing devices
access	points
	Poland
	policy
editorial	policy
government	*policy (Nonpreferred)*
information	policy
library	policy
policy,	*public (Nonpreferred)*
public	policy
	political aspects
	political science
	polysemy (Nonpreferred)
	popular culture
	popular materials
	population (Nonpreferred)
	pornographic materials
	portals
	postcoordinate indexing
generic	posting
	practical methods
communities of	practice
	pragmatics
	precision
	precoordinate indexing
	predicate calculus (Nonpreferred)
	predicate logic
	prediction (Nonpreferred)
	predictive models
user	preferences
	preferred order (Nonpreferred)
	preferred term references (Nonpreferred)
	prefixes (Nonpreferred)
	preprints
	presearch interviews
data	presentation
digital object	preservation
materials	preservation
digital	*preservation (Nonpreferred)*
	Presidential libraries
small	presses
university	presses
underground	*presses (Nonpreferred)*
intrusion	prevention and detection

	prices (Nonpreferred)
	pricing
	primary literature
Pareto	principle
large	print materials
	print materials (Nonpreferred)
	print publications
out of	print publications
	printers
color	printers
	printing
	prison libraries
	privacy
	private copying (Nonpreferred)
	private sector
	probabilistic indexing
	probabilistic models (Nonpreferred)
	probabilistic retrieval
	probability
	problem patrons
	problem solving
	problem users (Nonpreferred)
conference	proceedings
	proceedings (conference) (Nonpreferred)
Markov	*processes (Nonpreferred)*
mental	processes
random	*processes (Nonpreferred)*
sensory	processes
stochastic	processes
technical	*processes (Nonpreferred)*
(natural	processes and events)
(general	processes)
(human	processes)
(information and data	processes)
associative	*processing (Nonpreferred)*
automated language	*processing (Nonpreferred)*
automatic data	*processing (Nonpreferred)*
batch	processing
concurrent	*processing (Nonpreferred)*
data	processing
distributed	*processing (Nonpreferred)*
electronic data	*processing (Nonpreferred)*
graph	processing
image	processing
information	processing
materials	processing
massively parallel	*processing (Nonpreferred)*
natural language	processing
parallel	processing
query	processing
real time	processing
signal	processing
text	processing
word	processing
central	*processing units (Nonpreferred)*

computer	processing units
back end	processors
data	*processors (Nonpreferred)*
parallel	processors
database	producers
(product and service	providers)
artificial speech	*production (Nonpreferred)*
information	production
knowledge	*production (Nonpreferred)*
author	productivity
human	productivity
journal	productivity
organization	productivity
	productivity (journals) (Nonpreferred)
electronic information	*products (Nonpreferred)*
information	*products (Nonpreferred)*
	professional associations
	professional competencies
	professional skills (Nonpreferred)
	professional societies (Nonpreferred)
information	professionals
	professionals, information (Nonpreferred)
information	*professions (Nonpreferred)*
	professors (Nonpreferred)
library user	profiles
search	*profiles (Nonpreferred)*
user	profiles
computer	programmers
computer	programming
linear	programming
logic	programming
nonlinear	programming
object oriented	programming
	programming (computer) (Nonpreferred)
software	*programming (Nonpreferred)*
	programming languages
adult	*programs (Nonpreferred)*
computer	*programs (Nonpreferred)*
library	programs
	programs, computer (Nonpreferred)
	promotional activities
	proofreading
	proper names
intellectual	property
	proposed descriptors (Nonpreferred)
	propositional logic
data	*protection (Nonpreferred)*
file transfer	*protocol (Nonpreferred)*
hypertext transfer	*protocol (Nonpreferred)*
Open Archives Initiative	Protocol for Metadata Harvesting specification
communications	protocols
	protocols (Nonpreferred)
network	*protocols (Nonpreferred)*
	prototypes (Nonpreferred)
	prototyping

Internet service	providers
(product and service	providers)
	proximity
	proximity searching
	pseudonyms
	psychological aspects
	psychology
cognitive	*psychology (Nonpreferred)*
social	psychology
	psychometrics
policy,	*public (Nonpreferred)*
online	*public access catalogs (Nonpreferred)*
	public agencies (Nonpreferred)
	public domain
	public domain information
	public lending right
	public libraries
	public policy
	public records
	public relations
	public sector
cataloging in	publication
	publication explosion (Nonpreferred)
	publications
alternative	publications
electronic	publications
government	publications
open access	publications
out of print	publications
print	publications
underground	*publications (Nonpreferred)*
	publicity (Nonpreferred)
	publishers
commercial	publishers
learned society	publishers
secondary	publishers
software	*publishers (Nonpreferred)*
	publishing
academic	*publishing (Nonpreferred)*
desktop	publishing
electronic	publishing
scholarly	publishing
self	publishing
	punctuation
(documents by information content,	purpose)
	QBE (Nonpreferred)
	qualifiers
	qualitative analysis
	quality
	quality assurance
	quality control
	quantitative analysis
	quasi-synonymous relationships
document as	*query (Nonpreferred)*
	query analysis (Nonpreferred)

query by example
query expansion
query formulation
standard document   *query language (Nonpreferred)*
structured   *query language (Nonpreferred)*
query languages
query processing
query refinement
query reformulation (Nonpreferred)
query weighting (Nonpreferred)
question answering retrieval (Nonpreferred)
question answering systems (Nonpreferred)
questionnaires
queuing
radio
RAM (Nonpreferred)
random access memory
dynamic   *random access memory (Nonpreferred)*
random processes (Nonpreferred)
randomness
range searching
numeric   *range searching (Nonpreferred)*
ranking
density   ranking
relevance   ranking
ranking (relevance) (Nonpreferred)
rare materials
baud   *rate (Nonpreferred)*
error   rates
rating scales
cathode   *ray tube terminals (Nonpreferred)*
RDF (Nonpreferred)
freedom to   read
direct   *read after write technology (Nonpreferred)*
write once   *read many (Nonpreferred)*
read only memory
machine   *readable cataloging formats (Nonpreferred)*
machine   *readable cataloging records (Nonpreferred)*
machine   readable data
machine   *readable records (Nonpreferred)*
reader services
readers
reading
reading disabled persons
reading guidance (Nonpreferred)
reading handicapped persons (Nonpreferred)
ready reference materials
real time processing
realia (Nonpreferred)
virtual   reality
reasoning
recall
character   *recognition (Nonpreferred)*
object   recognition
optical   recognition

230

Permuted Display of Terms

optical character	recognition
pattern	recognition
speech	recognition
voice	*recognition (Nonpreferred)*
word	recognition
International Standard	*Record Code (Nonpreferred)*
standard	*record codes (Nonpreferred)*
compact disk	recordable
CD	*recordable (Nonpreferred)*
audio	recorders
video	recorders
sound	*recorders (Nonpreferred)*
tape	*recorders (Nonpreferred)*
	recording
magnetic	recording
optical	recording
	recording equipment
audio	recordings
audiodisk	*recordings (Nonpreferred)*
sound	*recordings (Nonpreferred)*
video	recordings
	recordings, sound (Nonpreferred)
	recordings, video (Nonpreferred)
	recordkeeping (Nonpreferred)
	records
administrative	records
admissibility of	records
bibliographic	records
catalog	*records (Nonpreferred)*
confidential	records
duplicate	records
government	*records (Nonpreferred)*
historical	*records (Nonpreferred)*
machine readable	*records (Nonpreferred)*
machine readable cataloging	*records (Nonpreferred)*
MARC	records
medical	records
public	records
usage	records
	records handling (Nonpreferred)
	records management
	records managers
cost	recovery
	recreation (Nonpreferred)
	reduced instruction set computers (Nonpreferred)
data	reduction
dimensionality	reduction
collection	*reduction (Nonpreferred)*
	redundancy
	reengineering
	refereeing
	reference interviews
	reference librarians
	reference locators (Nonpreferred)
	reference management software (Nonpreferred)

231

	reference materials
ready	reference materials
	reference retrieval systems
	reference services
chat	*reference services (Nonpreferred)*
digital	*reference services (Nonpreferred)*
electronic	reference services
legislative libraries and	reference services
live	*reference services (Nonpreferred)*
virtual	*reference services (Nonpreferred)*
information and	reference skills
bibliographic	references
broader term	*references (Nonpreferred)*
BT	*references (Nonpreferred)*
cross	references
indirect collective	references
narrower term	*references (Nonpreferred)*
nonpreferred term	*references (Nonpreferred)*
NT	*references (Nonpreferred)*
page	*references (Nonpreferred)*
preferred term	*references (Nonpreferred)*
related term	*references (Nonpreferred)*
RT	*references (Nonpreferred)*
see	*references (Nonpreferred)*
see also	*references (Nonpreferred)*
UF	*references (Nonpreferred)*
use	*references (Nonpreferred)*
used for	*references (Nonpreferred)*
	referral services (Nonpreferred)
information and	*referral services (Nonpreferred)*
query	refinement
output	reformatting
query	*reformulation (Nonpreferred)*
Caribbean	region
	regional aspects
	regions
(countries and	regions)
	regulations (Nonpreferred)
	related term references (Nonpreferred)
	related term relationships (Nonpreferred)
	relational databases
	relational models
public	relations
associative	relationships
broader term	*relationships (Nonpreferred)*
BT	*relationships (Nonpreferred)*
conceptual	*relationships (Nonpreferred)*
equivalence	relationships
generic	*relationships (Nonpreferred)*
genus species	relationships
hierarchical	relationships
narrower term	*relationships (Nonpreferred)*
near-synonymous	*relationships (Nonpreferred)*
nonhierarchical	*relationships (Nonpreferred)*
NT	*relationships (Nonpreferred)*

part whole	relationships
quasi-synonymous	relationships
related term	*relationships (Nonpreferred)*
RT	*relationships (Nonpreferred)*
semantic	relationships
UF	*relationships (Nonpreferred)*
use	*relationships (Nonpreferred)*
used for	*relationships (Nonpreferred)*
	relevance
	relevance feedback (Nonpreferred)
	relevance ranking
ranking	*(relevance) (Nonpreferred)*
	reliability
	religion
	remote access
	remote control
	remote sensing
	repetitive stress injury
	replicative studies
technical	reports
	reports, technical (Nonpreferred)
3-D	*representation (Nonpreferred)*
data	*representation (Nonpreferred)*
knowledge	representation
visual	*representation (Nonpreferred)*
	representation, knowledge (Nonpreferred)
document	*representations (Nonpreferred)*
graphical	*representations (Nonpreferred)*
information	representations
	reprints
	repurposing
mission oriented	research
observational	research
operations	research
	(research and analytic methods)
	research and development
National	Research and Education Network
	research design
	research libraries
description	*(research method) (Nonpreferred)*
	research methods
	research variables
	researchers (Nonpreferred)
electronic	reserves
library	reserves
high	resolution displays
	resource centers (Nonpreferred)
learning	*resource centers (Nonpreferred)*
uniform	resource characteristics
	Resource Description Framework
community	resource files
human	resource files
uniform	*resource identifier (Nonpreferred)*
uniform	*resource locators (Nonpreferred)*
computing	resource management

	resource management (computing) (Nonpreferred)
	resource management (information) (Nonpreferred)
computer	*resource management (Nonpreferred)*
uniform	resource names
	resource sharing
access to	resources
human information	resources
information	resources
Internet information	resources
shared library	*resources (Nonpreferred)*
visual	*resources (Nonpreferred)*
human	resources management
information	resources management
	response time
	restoration
document	retention
answer passage	retrieval
associative	retrieval
audio	retrieval
cross lingual	*retrieval (Nonpreferred)*
document	retrieval
full text	*retrieval (Nonpreferred)*
image	retrieval
information	retrieval
multilingual	retrieval
online information	*retrieval (Nonpreferred)*
probabilistic	retrieval
question answering	*retrieval (Nonpreferred)*
statistical	*retrieval (Nonpreferred)*
text	*retrieval (Nonpreferred)*
information	*retrieval agents (Nonpreferred)*
	retrieval effectiveness
information	retricval indexes
	retrieval languages (Nonpreferred)
information	retrieval models
unified	retrieval models
information	retrieval noise
information	retrieval software
	retrieval software (Nonpreferred)
	retrieval speed (Nonpreferred)
bibliographic	*retrieval systems (Nonpreferred)*
fact	retrieval systems
fuzzy	retrieval system
information storage and	retrieval systems
online information	*retrieval systems (Nonpreferred)*
partial match	*retrieval systems (Nonpreferred)*
reference	retrieval systems
	retrospective cataloging
	retrospective conversion
information	reuse
software	reuse
peer	*review (Nonpreferred)*
	reviewing
	reviews
book	reviews

literary	*reviews (Nonpreferred)*
literature	reviews
	reviews of the literature (Nonpreferred)
	rewritable optical disks (Nonpreferred)
public lending	right
civil	rights
human	rights
digital	rights management
Electronic	*Rights Management Systems (Nonpreferred)*
Pacific	Rim
	RISC
	robotics
	robots
	role indicators
	rolling stacks (Nonpreferred)
	ROM (Nonpreferred)
	romanization
chat	rooms
word	roots
	rotated indexes (Nonpreferred)
	rotated term indexes (Nonpreferred)
	rough set theory
	royalties
	RT references (Nonpreferred)
	RT relationships (Nonpreferred)
80/20	*rule (Nonpreferred)*
	rule based systems (Nonpreferred)
Anglo American Cataloguing	Rules
cataloging	rules
	Russia
	sampling
	satellite communications
communications	*satellites (Nonpreferred)*
user	satisfaction
	satisfaction (Nonpreferred)
	scalability
large	scale grammars
large	*scale integration (Nonpreferred)*
very large	*scale integration (Nonpreferred)*
rating	scales
multidimensional	scaling
	Scandinavia
	scanners
optical	*scanners (Nonpreferred)*
	scanning
environmental	scanning
optical	*scanning (Nonpreferred)*
bibliometric	scatter
	scheduling
document	schemas
	schemata (Nonpreferred)
classification	schemes
	scholarly communication
	scholarly journals (Nonpreferred)
	scholarly literature (Nonpreferred)

	scholarly publishing
	scholars
	school libraries (Nonpreferred)
	school media centers (Nonpreferred)
home	*schooling (Nonpreferred)*
	schools
elementary	schools
high	schools
information science	schools
information studies	*schools (Nonpreferred)*
junior high	*schools (Nonpreferred)*
library	schools
middle	schools
	schools of information science (Nonpreferred)
archival	science
cognitive	science
computer	science
information	science
library	*science (Nonpreferred)*
library and information	*science (Nonpreferred)*
medical	science
political	science
schools of information	*science (Nonpreferred)*
information	science education
information	science history
information	science schools
behavioral	sciences
earth	sciences
environmental	sciences
health	*sciences (Nonpreferred)*
life	*sciences (Nonpreferred)*
natural	sciences
physical	sciences
social	sciences
	scientific and technical information
	scientific literature (Nonpreferred)
	scientific societies (Nonpreferred)
	scientists
information	scientists
	scientometrics
	scope notes
	Scotland
	screen design
touch	screen interfaces
cursive	script
nonroman	scripts
	scripts (writing systems) (Nonpreferred)
	SDI services
	SDQL
fuzzy	*search (Nonpreferred)*
	search agents (Nonpreferred)
	search behavior
	search engine optimization
	search engine persuasion (Nonpreferred)
	search engines

hybrid	search engines
meta	search engines
	search formulation (Nonpreferred)
	search hedges
	search histories
	search languages (Nonpreferred)
	search profiles (Nonpreferred)
	search services
	search statements (Nonpreferred)
	search strategies
Internet	search systems
	search systems (Nonpreferred)
	search term weighting (Nonpreferred)
	search terms
	search time
	searching
adjacency	*searching (Nonpreferred)*
assisted	searching
Boolean	searching
citation	searching
coordinate	*searching (Nonpreferred)*
end user	searching
federated	searching
free text	*searching (Nonpreferred)*
full text	searching
keyword	searching
known item	searching
natural language	*searching (Nonpreferred)*
numeric range	*searching (Nonpreferred)*
online	searching
proximity	searching
range	searching
spiders (automatic	*searching) (Nonpreferred)*
string	searching
subject	searching
	Sears Subject Headings
secondary information	*services (Nonpreferred)*
	secondary literature (Nonpreferred)
	secondary publishers
trade	secrets
information	sector
nonprofit	sector
private	sector
public	sector
economic	sectors
	security
computer	security
data	security
library	security
national	security
network	security
book	*security (Nonpreferred)*
	security classification
library	security systems
	see also references (Nonpreferred)

	see references (Nonpreferred)
information	seeking
information	*seeking behavior (Nonpreferred)*
data	segmentation
	selection
book	*selection (Nonpreferred)*
materials	selection
	selective dissemination of information (Nonpreferred)
	self citation
	self organizing maps
	self publishing
	semantic analysis
latent	semantic analysis
	semantic headers (Nonpreferred)
	semantic indexing (Nonpreferred)
	semantic nets (Nonpreferred)
	semantic networks
	semantic relationships
	semantic web
	semantics
document style	*semantics and specification language (Nonpreferred)*
	semiology (Nonpreferred)
	semiotics
common	sense knowledge
remote	sensing
	sensors
	sensory perception
	sensory processes
	sentence generation
	sentences
sort	sequences
	serendipity
	serial conversion
International Standard	*Serial Number (Nonpreferred)*
standard	*serial numbers (Nonpreferred)*
	serials
	seriation (Nonpreferred)
	series
time	series data
client	server software
client	server systems
e-mail list	servers
file	servers
image	servers
network	*servers (Nonpreferred)*
fees for	service
	service bureaus
abstracting and indexing	service bureaus
Internet	service providers
(product and	service providers)
A & I	*services (Nonpreferred)*
chat reference	*services (Nonpreferred)*
children's	services
community based library	*services (Nonpreferred)*
consulting	*services (Nonpreferred)*

community information	services
current awareness	services
digital reference	*services (Nonpreferred)*
electronic reference	services
expert	*services (Nonpreferred)*
home information	services
host	*services (Nonpreferred)*
I&R	*services (Nonpreferred)*
indexing	*services (Nonpreferred)*
information	services
information and referral	*services (Nonpreferred)*
legislative libraries and reference	services
library and archival	services
library outreach	services
library technical	services
library user	*services (Nonpreferred)*
live reference	*services (Nonpreferred)*
loose leaf	services
military	*services (Nonpreferred)*
news wire	*services (Nonpreferred)*
newswire	services
off campus library	services
reader	services
reference	services
referral	*services (Nonpreferred)*
SDI	services
secondary information	*services (Nonpreferred)*
search	services
virtual reference	*services (Nonpreferred)*
wire	*services (Nonpreferred)*
young adult	services
reduced instruction	*set computers (Nonpreferred)*
	set mapping
	set theory
rough	set theory
fuzzy	*set theory (Nonpreferred)*
character	sets
data	*sets (Nonpreferred)*
	sex (Nonpreferred)
	sex discrimination (Nonpreferred)
	SGML
	shape
	shared cataloging
	shared library resources (Nonpreferred)
	shareware
peer to peer file	sharing
resource	sharing
	shelving (Nonpreferred)
compact	*shelving (Nonpreferred)*
library	shelving
mobile	*shelving (Nonpreferred)*
movable	*shelving (Nonpreferred)*
	shelving, library (Nonpreferred)
	shopping, computer (Nonpreferred)
	short term memory

	sight (Nonpreferred)
	signal boundary detection
	signal detection (Nonpreferred)
	signal processing
	similarity
	simulation
computer	simulation
off	*site access (Nonpreferred)*
web	site traffic
mirror	sites
web	sites
	situated knowledge
	skewed distribution
	skills
communication	skills
information	*skills (Nonpreferred)*
information and reference	skills
professional	*skills (Nonpreferred)*
	skills databases (Nonpreferred)
photographic	slides
	small libraries
	small presses
	smart cards
	smart paper (Nonpreferred)
	SN (Nonpreferred)
	social aspects
	social discrimination
	social equity
	social filtering (Nonpreferred)
	social informatics
	social networking
	social psychology
	social sciences
	social systems (Nonpreferred)
	societies (Nonpreferred)
professional	*societies (Nonpreferred)*
scientific	*societies (Nonpreferred)*
information	society
learned	society publishers
	(sociocultural aspects)
	socioeconomic activities
	socioeconomic aspects
	socioeconomic status
	socioeconomics
	sociograms
	sociology
	sociometrics
authoring	software
bibliographic	software
client server	software
computer	software
e-mail	software
information retrieval	software
malicious	software
reference management	*software (Nonpreferred)*

retrieval	*software (Nonpreferred)*
utility	software
computer	software applications
	software development (Nonpreferred)
	software engineering
computer aided	software engineering
computer assisted	*software engineering (Nonpreferred)*
	software industry
	software programming (Nonpreferred)
	software publishers (Nonpreferred)
	software reuse
(hardware,	software, and equipment)
	software, computer (Nonpreferred)
	solo librarians (Nonpreferred)
problem	solving
nothing before	*something arrangement (Nonpreferred)*
	sort sequences
	sorting
	sound (Nonpreferred)
recordings,	*sound (Nonpreferred)*
	sound recorders (Nonpreferred)
	sound recordings (Nonpreferred)
open	source
	source materials
	South Africa
	South America
	Southeast Asia
cognitive	space
concept	*space (Nonpreferred)*
conceptual	*space (Nonpreferred)*
information	space
vector	space models
personality, matter, energy,	*space, and time (Nonpreferred)*
	Spain
keyword	spam
	spam (Nonpreferred)
	spamdexing (Nonpreferred)
boundary	spanners
	spatial information
	special collections
	special libraries
clearinghouses	*(special libraries) (Nonpreferred)*
information centers	*(special libraries) (Nonpreferred)*
media	specialists
information	*specialists (Nonpreferred)*
genus	species relationships
Open Archives Initiative Protocol for Metadata Harvesting	specification
document style semantics and	*specification language (Nonpreferred)*
indexing	specificity
index language	*specificity (Nonpreferred)*
figures of	*speech (Nonpreferred)*
freedom of	speech
human	speech
synthesis,	*speech (Nonpreferred)*

artificial	*speech production (Nonpreferred)*
	speech recognition
	speech synthesis
	speech understanding (Nonpreferred)
retrieval	*speed (Nonpreferred)*
transmission	speed
	spell checkers (Nonpreferred)
	spelling (Nonpreferred)
	spelling checkers
	spelling errors (Nonpreferred)
	spiders (automatic searching) (Nonpreferred)
	spoken communication
	spreading activation
	spreadsheets
	SQL
library	*stacks (Nonpreferred)*
rolling	*stacks (Nonpreferred)*
	stacks, library (Nonpreferred)
library	*staff (Nonpreferred)*
library support	*staff (Nonpreferred)*
	staff development
support	*staff, library (Nonpreferred)*
	stakeholders
International	Standard Bibliographic Description
International	*Standard Book Number (Nonpreferred)*
	standard book numbers (Nonpreferred)
	standard document query language (Nonpreferred)
International	*Standard Film Number (Nonpreferred)*
	standard film numbers (Nonpreferred)
	standard generalized markup language (Nonpreferred)
International	*Standard Music Number (Nonpreferred)*
	standard music numbers (Nonpreferred)
International	*Standard Record Code (Nonpreferred)*
	standard record codes (Nonpreferred)
International	*Standard Serial Number (Nonpreferred)*
	standard serial numbers (Nonpreferred)
	standardization
	standards
metadata	standards
	standards developing organizations
standing	orders
communications	*stars (Nonpreferred)*
	state agencies (Nonpreferred)
	state libraries (Nonpreferred)
	state library agencies
search	*statements (Nonpreferred)*
United	States
	statistical analysis (Nonpreferred)
	statistical data (Nonpreferred)
	statistical databases (Nonpreferred)
	statistical methods
	statistical retrieval (Nonpreferred)
	statistics
socioeconomic	status
	stemming

	STI (Nonpreferred)
	stochastic models
	stochastic processes
book	*stock (Nonpreferred)*
	stop lists (Nonpreferred)
	stop words (Nonpreferred)
	stoplists
archival	*storage (Nonpreferred)*
compact	storage
computer	*storage (Nonpreferred)*
data	*storage (Nonpreferred)*
document	*storage (Nonpreferred)*
high density data	storage
materials	storage
information	storage and retrieval systems
data	storage devices
	storytelling
	strategic planning
search	strategies
audio	*streaming (Nonpreferred)*
data	streaming
motion video	*streaming (Nonpreferred)*
video	*streaming (Nonpreferred)*
	streaming audio (Nonpreferred)
	streaming media (Nonpreferred)
	streaming video (Nonpreferred)
repetitive	stress injury
	string indexing
	string searching
chemical	structure models
	structured query language (Nonpreferred)
data	structures
file	structures
hierarchical file	structures
network	structures
syndetic	structures
tree	structures
	students
area	studies
case	studies
Delphi	studies
empirical	studies
information user	*studies (Nonpreferred)*
longitudinal	studies
replicative	studies
usage	studies
use	*studies (Nonpreferred)*
user	studies
web usage	studies
information	*studies schools (Nonpreferred)*
correspondence	study
document	*style semantics and specification language (Nonpreferred)*
cognitive	styles
personal	*styles (Nonpreferred)*
	subdivisions (indexing) (Nonpreferred)

243

	subheadings (Nonpreferred)
experts,	*subject (Nonpreferred)*
	subject access
	subject cataloging
	subject expertise (Nonpreferred)
	subject experts
	subject heading lists
	subject headings
Library of Congress	Subject Headings
Sears	Subject Headings
Medical	*Subject Headings (Nonpreferred)*
	subject index terms (Nonpreferred)
	subject indexes
	subject indexing
multilingual	subject indexing
	subject metadata (Nonpreferred)
	subject searching
	subject switching (Nonpreferred)
	sublanguages
	subscription agencies
	subscription cancellation
	subscriptions
	subsidies
	suffixes (Nonpreferred)
	summaries (Nonpreferred)
	summarization
	supercomputers
information	*superhighway (Nonpreferred)*
	superimposed coding
library	suppliers
	suppliers (Nonpreferred)
library	supplies
litigation	support
library	*support staff (Nonpreferred)*
	support staff, library (Nonpreferred)
decision	support systems
group decision	support systems
	Suriname
	surnames (Nonpreferred)
document	surrogates
	surveillance (Nonpreferred)
	surveys
library	surveys
packet	switching
subject	*switching (Nonpreferred)*
	switching languages
	symbols
	syndetic structures
	synonyms
	syntactic analysis
	syntactics
notation	synthesis
speech	synthesis
voice	*synthesis (Nonpreferred)*
	synthesis, notation (Nonpreferred)

	synthesis, speech (Nonpreferred)
	synthetic classification
distributed information management	*system (Nonpreferred)*
domain naming	system
user	*system interfaces (Nonpreferred)*
	system knowledge
	systematic arrangement
analog	systems
Bayesian	*systems (Nonpreferred)*
bibliographic retrieval	*systems (Nonpreferred)*
book detection	*systems (Nonpreferred)*
bulletin board	systems
charging	*systems (Nonpreferred)*
client server	systems
computer	systems
content management	*systems (Nonpreferred)*
control	systems
current awareness	*systems (Nonpreferred)*
database management	systems
decision	support systems
dedicated	systems
dynamic	systems
Electronic Copyright Management	*Systems (Nonpreferred)*
electronic document management	systems
electronic information	*systems (Nonpreferred)*
electronic meeting	*systems (Nonpreferred)*
Electronic Rights Management	*Systems (Nonpreferred)*
executive information	*systems (Nonpreferred)*
expert	systems
fact retrieval	systems
file	*systems (Nonpreferred)*
flexible manufacturing	systems
frame based	*systems (Nonpreferred)*
full text	*systems (Nonpreferred)*
full text information	*systems (Nonpreferred)*
fuzzy retrieval	systems
geographic information	systems
group decision support	systems
help	systems
hybrid	systems
image information	systems
information	*systems (Nonpreferred)*
information storage and retrieval	systems
integrated	systems
integrated library	systems
integrated online library	*systems (Nonpreferred)*
integration,	*systems (Nonpreferred)*
interactive	systems
Internet search	systems
knowledge based	*systems (Nonpreferred)*
knowledgebase management	*systems (Nonpreferred)*
knowledge organization	systems
library security	systems
library	*systems (Nonpreferred)*
linear	*systems (Nonpreferred)*

management information	systems
message	systems
messaging	*systems (Nonpreferred)*
online	*systems (Nonpreferred)*
online information retrieval	*systems (Nonpreferred)*
operating	systems
paper based information	systems
partial match retrieval	*systems (Nonpreferred)*
personal information	systems
pictorial information	*systems (Nonpreferred)*
question answering	*systems (Nonpreferred)*
reference retrieval	systems
rule based	*systems (Nonpreferred)*
search	*systems (Nonpreferred)*
social	*systems (Nonpreferred)*
theft detection	*systems (Nonpreferred)*
turnkey	systems
writing	systems
	systems analysis
(attributes of	systems and equipment)
	systems design
	systems development
	systems integration
access control (computer	*systems) (Nonpreferred)*
scripts (writing	*systems) (Nonpreferred)*
	table of contents lists (Nonpreferred)
chemical connection	tables
automatic	*tagging (Nonpreferred)*
content	*tagging (Nonpreferred)*
keyword	*tagging (Nonpreferred)*
	tagging, automatic (Nonpreferred)
	talking books
optical	tape
	tape leasing (Nonpreferred)
	tape recorders (Nonpreferred)
audio	*tapes (Nonpreferred)*
digital audio	tapes
magnetic	tapes
	task analysis
	task knowledge
	taxonomies
	taxonomy construction (Nonpreferred)
automatic	taxonomy generation
	teachers (Nonpreferred)
	teaching (Nonpreferred)
reports,	*technical (Nonpreferred)*
	technical and manufacturing operations
library	*technical assistants (Nonpreferred)*
scientific and	technical information
	technical information (Nonpreferred)
	technical processes (Nonpreferred)
	technical reports
library	technical services
	technical writing
library	*technicians (Nonpreferred)*

critical incident	*technique (Nonpreferred)*	
	technological gatekeepers (Nonpreferred)	
	technological innovation (Nonpreferred)	
adaptive	technologies	
direct read after write	*technology (Nonpreferred)*	
educational	technology	
information	technology	
instructional	*technology (Nonpreferred)*	
	technology impact	
	technology transfer	
	telecommunications	
	telecommunications equipment	
	telecommunications industry	
	telecommunications networks	
	telecommunications traffic	
	telecommuting	
	teleconferencing	
video	teleconferencing	
	telefacsimile (Nonpreferred)	
	telegraphy	
	telemarketing	
	telematics (Nonpreferred)	
	telemetry	
	telephones	
cellular	*telephones (Nonpreferred)*	
mobile	*telephones (Nonpreferred)*	
picture	*telephones (Nonpreferred)*	
	telephony	
Internet	telephony	
	telerobotics	
	teleshopping	
	teletext	
	television	
	teleworking (Nonpreferred)	
	telnet	
	temporal arrangement	
	temporal currency	
	temporal information	
	term co-occurrence analysis	*(Nonpreferred)*
	term frequency (Nonpreferred)	
rotated	*term indexes (Nonpreferred)*	
indexing	term links	
long	term memory	
short	term memory	
broader	*term references (Nonpreferred)*	
narrower	*term references (Nonpreferred)*	
nonpreferred	*term references (Nonpreferred)*	
preferred	*term references (Nonpreferred)*	
related	*term references (Nonpreferred)*	
broader	*term relationships (Nonpreferred)*	
narrower	*term relationships (Nonpreferred)*	
related	*term relationships (Nonpreferred)*	
	term weighting (Nonpreferred)	
index	*term weighting (Nonpreferred)*	
search	*term weighting (Nonpreferred)*	

cathode ray tube   *terminals (Nonpreferred)*
CRT   *terminals (Nonpreferred)*
graphics   *terminals (Nonpreferred)*
touch   *terminals (Nonpreferred)*
video display   terminals
visual display   *terminals (Nonpreferred)*
   terminals, video display (Nonpreferred)
   terminology
   terms
compound   terms
entry   *terms (Nonpreferred)*
guide   *terms (Nonpreferred)*
index   terms
indexing   *terms (Nonpreferred)*
nonpreferred   *terms (Nonpreferred)*
search   terms
subject index   *terms (Nonpreferred)*
used   *terms (Nonpreferred)*
top   terms
definitions (of   *terms) (Nonpreferred)*
   terms of use (Nonpreferred)
   terrorism
TREC   *test collection (Nonpreferred)*
   test data
   testing
   text analysis (Nonpreferred)
full   text databases
   text databases (Nonpreferred)
   text editors
free   *text indexing (Nonpreferred)*
full   *text information systems (Nonpreferred)*
   text messaging
   text mining
   text processing
   text retrieval (Nonpreferred)
full   *text retrieval (Nonpreferred)*
free   *text searching (Nonpreferred)*
full   text searching
full   *text systems (Nonpreferred)*
non   *text-based materials (Nonpreferred)*
   textbases (Nonpreferred)
   textbooks
   textual databases (Nonpreferred)
   texture
friends of   *the library organizations (Nonpreferred)*
reviews of   *the literature (Nonpreferred)*
   theft (Nonpreferred)
   theft detection systems (Nonpreferred)
   theoretical models (Nonpreferred)
Bayesian   *theory (Nonpreferred)*
chaos   theory
communications   *theory (Nonpreferred)*
decision   theory
fuzzy set   *theory (Nonpreferred)*
game   theory

graph	theory
information	theory
organization	theory
rough set	theory
set	theory
	thesauri
bilingual	*thesauri (Nonpreferred)*
graphical	thesauri
multilingual	thesauri
displays	*(thesauri) (Nonpreferred)*
	thesaurofacet
	thesaurus construction (Nonpreferred)
	thesaurus displays
automatic	*thesaurus generation (Nonpreferred)*
	thesaurus management
	thesaurus updating (Nonpreferred)
	theses (Nonpreferred)
	thinking (Nonpreferred)
topic	threads
	three dimensional imagery (Nonpreferred)
	thumbnail views
	till forbid orders (Nonpreferred)
response	time
search	time
personality, matter, energy, space, and	*time (Nonpreferred)*
	time data (Nonpreferred)
real	time processing
	time series data
	timeliness (Nonpreferred)
document	titles
fault	tolerance
database	tomography
	top terms
	topic maps
	topic threads
	topics
	topology (Nonpreferred)
	touch
	touch screen interfaces
	touch terminals (Nonpreferred)
	trackballs
book	*trade (Nonpreferred)*
	trade secrets
	trademark infringement
	trademarks
	telecommunications traffic
web site	traffic
crumb	*trails (Nonpreferred)*
	training
user	training
	transaction logs (Nonpreferred)
	transborder data flow
electronic funds	transfer
information	transfer
knowledge	*transfer (Nonpreferred)*

technology	transfer
	transfer of information (Nonpreferred)
file	*transfer protocol (Nonpreferred)*
hypertext	*transfer protocol (Nonpreferred)*
file	transfers
Fourier	*transforms (Nonpreferred)*
	translation
automatic	*translation (Nonpreferred)*
computer	*translation (Nonpreferred)*
computer aided	*translation (Nonpreferred)*
machine	translation
machine aided	*translation (Nonpreferred)*
	translators
	transliteration
broadband	transmission
data	transmission
facsimile	transmission
voice	transmission
	transmission speed
	transnational data flow (Nonpreferred)
	TREC test collection (Nonpreferred)
	tree structures
decision	trees
	trends
	Trojan horses
	tropes (Nonpreferred)
	truncation
	trust
	trustees (library) (Nonpreferred)
library	*trustees (Nonpreferred)*
	TT (Nonpreferred)
cathode ray	*tube terminals (Nonpreferred)*
	turnkey systems
	tutorials
Web	TV
document	*type descriptions (Nonpreferred)*
abstract data	types
language	types
(document	types)
	typesetting
computer	*typesetting (Nonpreferred)*
	typographical errors
	typography
	ubicomp (Nonpreferred)
	ubiquitous computing
	UDC (Nonpreferred)
	UF references (Nonpreferred)
	UF relationships (Nonpreferred)
	uncertainty
	uncontrolled indexing (Nonpreferred)
	underground presses (Nonpreferred)
	underground publications (Nonpreferred)
	understanding (comprehension) (Nonpreferred)
	understanding (natural language) (Nonpreferred)
language	*understanding (Nonpreferred)*

speech	*understanding (Nonpreferred)*
	unified retrieval models
	uniform resource characteristics
	uniform resource identifier (Nonpreferred)
	uniform resource locators (Nonpreferred)
	uniform resource names
European	Union
	union catalogs
labor	unions
	unions, labor (Nonpreferred)
	United Kingdom
	United States
	uniterm indexing (Nonpreferred)
computer processing	units
central processing	*units (Nonpreferred)*
	universal access
	Universal Decimal Classification
colleges and	universities
	universities (Nonpreferred)
	university libraries (Nonpreferred)
	university presses
	unsolicited bulk e-mail
	unsolicited commercial e-mail
	unsolicited e-mail
	up to dateness (Nonpreferred)
	updating
thesaurus	*updating (Nonpreferred)*
	uploading
	URC (Nonpreferred)
	URI
	URL
	URN (Nonpreferred)
	Uruguay
	usability
	usage agreements
	usage frequency (Nonpreferred)
	usage records
	usage studies
web	usage studies
document	*use (Nonpreferred)*
ease of	*use (Nonpreferred)*
fair	use
frequency of	use
information	use
library	*use (Nonpreferred)*
terms of	*use (Nonpreferred)*
use	*instruction (Nonpreferred)*
use of	*information (Nonpreferred)*
	use references (Nonpreferred)
	use relationships (Nonpreferred)
	use studies (Nonpreferred)
	used for references (Nonpreferred)
	used for relationships (Nonpreferred)
	used terms (Nonpreferred)
(indexing by method	used)

	Usenet newsgroups (Nonpreferred)
	user aids
	user attributes
	user behavior
end	user computing
	user education (Nonpreferred)
	user expectations
	user expertise
	user feedback (Nonpreferred)
	user friendliness (Nonpreferred)
	user guides (Nonpreferred)
	user information needs (Nonpreferred)
graphical	user interfaces
zoomable	user interfaces
	user manuals (Nonpreferred)
	user models
	user multitasking
	user needs (Nonpreferred)
	user preferences
	user profiles
library	user profiles
	user satisfaction
end	user searching
library	*user services (Nonpreferred)*
	user studies
information	*user studies (Nonpreferred)*
	user system interfaces (Nonpreferred)
	user training
	user warrant
	users
end	users
experienced	users
information	*users (Nonpreferred)*
library	users
novice	users
problem	*users (Nonpreferred)*
bibliographic	utilities
information	utilities
	utility
	utility software
data	*utilization (Nonpreferred)*
information	*utilization (Nonpreferred)*
	validation
	validity
	value added
	value of information (Nonpreferred)
default	values
	vandalism (Nonpreferred)
research	variables
analysis of	variance
	VDT (Nonpreferred)
	VDU (Nonpreferred)
	vector analysis
	vector space models
	vendors

book	vendors
database	*vendors (Nonpreferred)*
	Venezuela
	verbs
	verification
	vertical files
	very large databases
	very large scale integration (Nonpreferred)
full motion	*video (Nonpreferred)*
motion	video
recordings,	*video (Nonpreferred)*
streaming	*video (Nonpreferred)*
	video clips
	video communications
	video conferencing (Nonpreferred)
digital	*video disks (Nonpreferred)*
terminals,	*video display (Nonpreferred)*
	video display terminals
digital	video files
	video games
digital	video interactive
	video materials (Nonpreferred)
	video recorders
	video recordings
	video streaming (Nonpreferred)
motion	*video streaming (Nonpreferred)*
	video teleconferencing
	videocassettes
	videodisks
	videophones (Nonpreferred)
	videotelephones
	videotex
thumbnail	views
global	*village (Nonpreferred)*
	virtual communities
	virtual environment (Nonpreferred)
	virtual libraries
	virtual memory
	virtual reality
	virtual reference services (Nonpreferred)
computer	viruses
	vision
computer	vision
machine	*vision (Nonpreferred)*
	visual arts
	visual display terminals (Nonpreferred)
	visual information (Nonpreferred)
	visual materials
audio	*visual materials (Nonpreferred)*
	visual memory
	visual representation (Nonpreferred)
	visual resources (Nonpreferred)
electronic	visualization
information	*visualization (Nonpreferred)*
mental	visualization

visually impaired	persons
	VLSI
access	*vocabularies (Nonpreferred)*
controlled	vocabularies
entry	vocabularies
indexing	*vocabularies (Nonpreferred)*
	vocabulary control
	vocal interfaces (Nonpreferred)
	voice communications
	voice input (Nonpreferred)
	voice mail
	voice recognition (Nonpreferred)
	voice synthesis (Nonpreferred)
	voice transmission
	volunteers
	W3C (Nonpreferred)
	Wales
	WAN (Nonpreferred)
	wanderers (Nonpreferred)
light	*wands (Nonpreferred)*
data	*warehouses (Nonpreferred)*
data	warehousing
	warrant
literary	warrant
user	warrant
	Web (Nonpreferred)
deep	*web (Nonpreferred)*
hidden	*web (Nonpreferred)*
invisible	web
semantic	web
World Wide	Web
	web bibliometry (Nonpreferred)
	web browsers
	web conferencing
	web content management
	web designers
	web home pages
	web mining
	web pages
	web site traffic
	web sites
	Web TV
	web usage studies
	webbots (Nonpreferred)
	webliographies
	weblogs
	webometrics
	weeding (Nonpreferred)
library	weeks
	weighting
index term	*weighting (Nonpreferred)*
query	*weighting (Nonpreferred)*
search term	*weighting (Nonpreferred)*
term	*weighting (Nonpreferred)*
part	whole relationships

	wide area networks
World	Wide Web
	windows interfaces (Nonpreferred)
	winnowing (Nonpreferred)
	wire services (Nonpreferred)
news	*wire services (Nonpreferred)*
	wireless access
	Wireless Markup Language (Nonpreferred)
	WML
	women
	word by word arrangement
	word co-occurrence analysis (Nonpreferred)
	word frequency
	word processing
	word recognition
	word roots
	words
key	*words (Nonpreferred)*
stop	*words (Nonpreferred)*
collaborative	*work (Nonpreferred)*
cooperative	*work (Nonpreferred)*
group	*work (Nonpreferred)*
home	*work (Nonpreferred)*
	work flow analysis
information	workers
knowledge	*workers (Nonpreferred)*
	workflow (Nonpreferred)
	workgroup computing (Nonpreferred)
	working at home
	working memory (Nonpreferred)
	workshops
	workstations
	world knowledge (Nonpreferred)
	World Wide Web
	WORM disks
computer	worms
	write once read many (Nonpreferred)
direct read after	*write technology (Nonpreferred)*
	writers (Nonpreferred)
	writing (Nonpreferred)
technical	writing
	writing systems
scripts	*(writing systems) (Nonpreferred)*
	WWW (Nonpreferred)
	XML
	yearbooks
	young adult literature
	young adult services
	youth
New	Zealand
	Zipf's law
	Zipf-Mandelbrot law (Nonpreferred)
	zoomable user interfaces

More Titles of Interest from Information Today, Inc.

Theories of Information Behavior

Edited by Karen E. Fisher, Sanda Erdelez, and Lynne (E. F.) McKechnie

This unique book presents authoritative overviews of more than 70 conceptual frameworks for understanding how people seek, manage, share, and use information in different contexts. A practical and readable reference to both well established and newly proposed theories of information behavior, the book includes contributions from 85 scholars from 10 countries. Each theory description covers origins, propositions, methodological implications, usage, links to related conceptual frameworks, and listings of authoritative primary and secondary references. The introductory chapters explain key concepts, theory–method connections, and the process of theory development.

2005/456 pp/hardbound/ISBN 1-57387-230-X • ASIST Members $39.60 • Nonmembers $49.50

Covert and Overt

Recollecting and Connecting Intelligence Service and Information Science

Edited by Robert V. Williams and Ben-Ami Lipetz

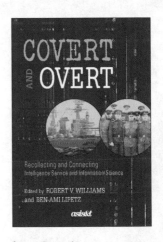

This volume explores the historical relationships between covert intelligence work and information/computer science. The book first examines the pivotal strides to utilize technology in the gathering and dissemination of government/military intelligence during World War II. Next, it traces the evolution of the relationship between spymasters, computers, and systems developers through the years of the Cold War.

2005/276 pp/hardbound/ISBN 1-57387-234-2 • ASIST Members $39.60 • Nonmembers $49.50

The History and Heritage of Scientific and Technological Information Systems

Edited by W. Boyd Rayward and Mary Ellen Bowden

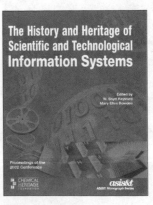

Emphasis for the second conference on the history of information science systems was on scientific and technical information systems in the period from World War II through the early 1990s. These proceedings present the papers of historians, information professionals, and scientists on a wide range of topics including informatics in chemistry, biology and medicine, and information developments in multinational, industrial, and military settings.

2004/440 pp/softbound/ISBN 1-57387-229-6 • ASIST Members $36.40 • Nonmembers $45.50

Understanding and Communicating Social Informatics
A Framework for Studying and Teaching the Human Contexts of Information and Communication Technologies

Rob Kling, Howard Rosenbaum, and Steve Sawyer

Here is a sustained investigation into the human contexts of information and communication technologies (ICTs), covering both research and theory. The authors demonstrate that the design, adoption, and use of ICTs are deeply connected to people's actions as well as to the environments in which ICTs are used. They offer a pragmatic overview of social informatics, articulating its fundamental ideas for specific audiences and presenting important research findings.

2005/240 pp/hardbound/ISBN 1-57387-228-8/$39.50

Information Representation and Retrieval in the Digital Age

Heting Chu

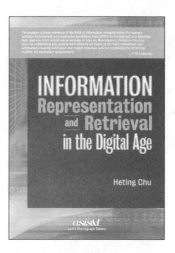

This is the first book to offer a clear, comprehensive view of Information Representation and Retrieval (IRR). With an emphasis on principles and fundamentals, the author first reviews key concepts and major developmental stages of the field, then systematically examines information representation methods, IRR languages, retrieval techniques and models, and Internet retrieval systems.

2003/250 pp/hardbound/ISBN 1-57387-172-9

ASIST Members $35.60 • Nonmembers $44.50

Statistical Methods for the Information Professional
Liwen Vaughan

Author and educator Liwen Vaughan clearly explains the statistical methods used in information science research, focusing on basic logic rather than mathematical intricacies. Her emphasis is on the meaning of statistics, when and how to apply them, and how to interpret the results of statistical analysis. Through the use of real-world examples, she shows how statistics can be used to improve services, make better decisions, and conduct more effective research.

2001/240 pp/hardbound/ISBN 1-57387-110-9

ASIST Members $31.60 • Nonmembers $39.50

To order or for a complete catalog, contact:
Information Today, Inc.
143 Old Marlton Pike, Medford, NJ 08055 • 609/654-6266
email: custserv@infotoday.com • Web site: www.infotoday.com